Bearing Witness,
Building Bridges

new society publishers
Philadelphia, Pennsylvania

Bearing Witness, Building Bridges:

Interviews with North Americans Living & Working in Nicaragua

Melissa Everett

Michael Kopec
Photographs

Congressman Bruce Morrison
Foreword

Sr. Marjorie Tuite, Church Women United
Afterword

Inquiries about requests to republish all or part of the materials
contained herein should be addressed to:
New Society Publishers
4722 Baltimore Avenue
Philadelphia, PA 19143

ISBN: Hardcover 0-86571-066-X
ISBN: Paperback 0-86571-065-1

Cover design by Sarah Mudd
Book design by Dion Lerman
Printed in the United States of America

New Society Publishers is a project of New Society Educational
Foundation and a collective of Movement for a New Society. New Society
Educational Foundation is a non-profit, tax-exempt, public foundation.
Movement for a New Society is a network of small groups and individuals
working for fundamental social change through nonviolent action. To
learn more about MNS write: Movement for a New Society, 4722
Baltimore Avenue, Philadelphia, PA 19143. Opinions expressed in this
book do not necessarily represent positions of either New Society
Educational Foundation or Movement for a New Society.

For Rosa and Lorena Zambrana
who introduced me to Nicaragua

Acknowledgments

During the gestation of this book, many people did more than their share to help, and most of them showed disgusting cheerfulness in the process.

Mike Kopec lugged forty pounds of camera equipment around in hundred-degree heat and never lost his enthusiasm for getting the perfect shot.

Steve Karian was a patient and good-humored tour guide during my first visit. Shelly Kellman, Chris Hager, and John Berman were marvelous traveling companions and sources of many ideas. Becky Leaf drove me all over the place.

A number of friends dug into their savings to help defray the cost of this project: Fenwick Smith, Susan Tallmadge, Bill Torcaso, Ira Benowitz, Sandy Diener, Eve Loren Wedeen, Denise Bourque, Mark Henrickson, Thad Bennett.

Glen Ring and Susan Lumenello transcribed hours and hours of interviews.

Ike Williams of Palmer & Dodge provided high quality legal advice at a low, low price.

Sam Crowe and the staff at Systemania in Melrose, Massachusetts, did a yeoman's job of trouble-shooting when the computer broke a week before our deadline.

My friends, family, and housemates put up with me while the book was in progress. Gladys and Will Everett have been a driving force behind this book, although they may not know it, because they make me want to make them proud of me.

Ellen Sawislak at NSP has been a supportive, no-nonsense editor.

Most of all, thanks go to the people who have so generously shared their stories, including many who do not appear in these pages because others covered similar ground and space was limited. It takes courage to reveal one's history so fully and thoughtfully, just as it takes courage to do the work these folks are doing.

Publishers' Note

This is a book about Nicaragua, a country in the midst of an ongoing revolutionary struggle. But it is also, and to my mind more importantly, about the North Americans who have chosen to live and work there.

From the pages of this book, it becomes clear that these are people we all know. They could be our neighbors, our friends, or our families. They contradict the dominant media image of North Americans as unconcerned about social justice and unwilling to take risks. From our own experience, we know that people like them are not just working in Nicaragua. We find them in the U.S., in Africa, in Asia, in fact all over the world. We also know that they are not few in number. And so we might ask why, within the dominant media and culture, do we hear so little about them?

The people interviewed in this book are a diverse group who have all found something within their own backgrounds as North Americans which empowers them to take responsibility for helping to build a better world for all of us. In the final analysis, their lives, their motivation, and their experiences help us learn about ourselves and about how we too can work to create the world within which we want to live. In that spirit, New Society Publishers is proud to publish *Bearing Witness, Building Bridges: Interviews with North Americans Living and Working in Nicaragua.*

Ellen Sawislak
for New Society Publishers

Foreword

Bearing Witness, Building Bridges presents a unique opportunity for Americans to learn from some of their fellow citizens about the current realities of Nicaragua. By allowing Americans living and working there to tell of their experiences, it presents a perspective not otherwise readily available to us regarding the events in that country. Dealing with a subject now very much on the front pages, this book does so in a way that offers firsthand experience and observation as a much-needed substitute for uninformed rhetorical excesses and for oversimplification of a complex issue.

Less than ten years ago, Nicaragua was a place virtually unknown to Americans. Now it often dominates the news and is never long out of the headlines. Yet, in fact, most Americans are hardly more aware now than they were then of where and what Nicaragua is.

The education we receive in this country rarely touches on Central America. What most of us have learned minimizes the distinct identities of Latin American countries; minimizes the destructive effects of past U.S. policies; and minimizes the history of popular resistance to these policies. Americans are more likely to see our role as opposition to right-wing military oppression in the region, when in fact, U.S. support of such regimes has far more often been the case. Unless this situation changes, we are likely to continue to pursue misguided policies in Nicaragua, indeed, throughout Latin America.

In February 1985, I spent eight days in Nicaragua. I travelled "unofficially" with a group dedicated to peace and to a sympathetic understanding of the struggle of Third World people. While I was there, President Reagan announced in a press conference that he would not be satisfied until the Sandinista government of Nicaragua said "uncle" to his demands for new leadership for that country.

These words would have shocked me at home. From my perspective in Managua, they evoked feelings of rage. I had spent a week talking with Nicaraguans of the potential for new, forward-looking approaches to the relationship between our two countries. Now, from home, came the same old voice of the past—the bully demanding his way and expecting abject submission that could not possible coexist with national pride, no matter what the ideology of the nation or its leaders. It is not that any of this was new. Rather, it was the making explicit of a policy that has been implicitly clear throughout the Reagan administration. A "covert" war, well known to all, justified by pretext, was about to become in name what it had always been in fact—a campaign to overthrow the revolutionary government of Nicaragua and to replace it with one more to the liking of the Reagan administration.

In the U.S. there was an outcry of protest, and the polls said the people of America opposed the President's objective by a substantial majority. But in Managua, the response was more matter-of-fact. History had taught Nicaraguans to expect U.S. intervention when events there were displeasing to leaders in Washington. The propagandists on both sides had drawn the lines. Take your pick to describe U.S. policy: Yankee imperialism or fighting communism. In such a contest of labels, truth and progress are the losers, death and despair are the only winners. Simple-minded factions may eventually persuade voters and their elected representatives, but they cannot make the reality simple.

What was so clear to the President that February evening in Washington was everything but clear that day in Managua. We had met with Sandinistas and their supporters, from Ortega and d'Escoto to military leaders and regional cadres, parish priests and campesinos. The revolution had broad support; the election held in November 1984, though less than perfect by U.S. standards, stacked up well against the much-heralded elections next door in El Salvador. The Sandinistas can certainly claim as great a mandate as Duarte.

Mistakes were admitted, as well, such as the forced relocation of the Miskito Indians and failures in central planning decisions in the economy. The militarization of the nation is an acknowledged fact; only the cause and effect are debated. Did the Sandinistas arm to repel the contra threat or is the U.S.-sponsored insurgency a response to a Soviet- or Cuban-sponsored build-up? Whoever has the initial order right—more likely it is a little of each—both the current need for the Sandinistas to fight for survival and the consequent tragedy of scarce human and material resources drained from an impoverished people are certainly beyond dispute.

We also met representatives of the full range of in-country opposition to the government, from the Catholic Archbishop, since made a Cardinal, to anti-government union and business leaders, to opposition politicians and the editor of *La Prenza*, the opposition newspaper. Once again it is the interpretation rather than the facts that raise the problems. The prerevolutionary well-to-do are decidedly less so, but could it be otherwise if revolutionary promises of land reform and economic distribution were to be kept? Certainly, all argue Somoza was a dictator whose demise was long overdue.

Press censorship and organized or unorganized harassment of former establishment figures and institutions were documented, but the degree seemed more like the same phenomena in the formative years of our own nation in the late eighteenth century and during our Civil War. The label "totalitarian" seems equally out of place in both contexts. That there is a vocal opposition represented in the press, labor, business, religions, and political sectors of Nicaragua itself belies the easy labelling of this regime as a traditional "Marxist-Leninist totalitarian regime."

There is much to be debated about what has happened and what is happening in Nicaragua. Some Americans will continue to choose to live in Nicaragua and be a part of the events there and cast their lot for now or forever with one or another vision of Nicaragua's future. For most of us, though, the issue is a more limited one—involving what role our country will play. In making the choice we should be mindful of some facts often overlooked, though seemingly self-evident:

> We are not Nicaraguans and it is not our place to impose on them our choice of government or economic system.
>
> Fiercely proud and independent Latin neighbors to Nicaragua like the Contadora nations (Mexico, Panama, Colombia, and Venezuela) have a more immediate stake in what happens in Nicaragua and in all of Central America than do we; thus a regional peace forged with their leadership is indispensable.
>
> "National Security" must not be profligately used to justify actions not truly demanded for our security lest the concept be debased and our nation unable to summon the consensus to defend itself when truly threatened.
>
> The developments during the four past years of escalating military and economic pressures on the Sandinistas have been contrary to our interests—more militarization, more Soviet-block influence, less economic progress in Nicaragua; thus, the burden is surely on the proponents of continuing this policy to make the case that these counterproductive results were not caused by that policy.
>
> The struggle of the Nicaraguan people against a history of oppression and poverty is not an isolated one, but is shared by millions throughout the third world; learning to play a positive role in support of that struggle is one of our greatest foreign policy challenges.

For me it is clear that what we have now as a policy toward Nicaragua is a failure. What is needed is not an economic and military offensive but a peace and development offensive in coordination with the Contadora nations and our European allies. Such a process can include the regional security guarantees and the exclusion of foreign bases we seek—the Contadora peace proposals accepted by the Sandinistas include these principles. That we may dislike the domestic policies of the Sandinistas is no more a bar to such an approach than is the lack of personal freedom in the People's Republic of China to our growing relationship with that country. Peace and security are not threatened by ideology and rhetoric, but by poverty and lack of reasonable control over one's destiny. If we confront the wrong enemies in Nicaragua, as I believe we have been doing, any victory we achieve will be hollow and short-lived.

By selective observation of Nicaragua you can certainly find facts to justify your preconceived label for that country, but in doing so you will of necessity be blind to the wealth of countervailing facts which would, standing alone, compel an opposite conclusion. The reality is far more complex and difficult. It is a reality strongly conveyed by this books and so necessary to be grasped by Americans otherwise led astray by the simple black and white labels which seem to be determining our current policies, as well as some of the opposition to them.

Congressman Bruce A. Morrison
U.S. House of Representatives
Connecticut
August, 1985

HONDURAS

Rio Coco

Waspam

Puerto Cabezas

Tasba Pri

Jalapa

Ocotal

Siuna

San Juan de Limay

Waslala

Esteli

Matagalpa

El Chaguitillo

ZELAYA

Chinandega

Paiwas

Corinto

Leon

Lake Managua

Masaya

Bluefields

CARIBBEAN SEA

Managua

Rama

Granada

Rio Escondido

Diriamba

Jinotepe

Lake Nicaragua

PACIFIC OCEAN

Solentiname

SanCarlos

COSTA RICA

Central America

= 50 miles

NICARAGUA

Orbis Books

Contents

Introduction

This is a book about seventeen extraordinary people. Each is talented, articulate, and thoroughly enjoyable. But they are more. They have in common a particular choice: to let go of the relative safety and comfort of life in the United States in order to live in a much more challenging environment: postrevolutionary Nicaragua. Their reasons for being there, and their interpretations of the situation, are unique and far from simple. But all of them are in Nicaragua to support, or at least open-mindedly to understand, the country's controversial Sandinista revolution—a position which puts them into strong conflict with the Reagan administration. *Bearing Witness, Building Bridges* is a collection of testimonies, in their own words, on the Nicaraguan reality and the personal evolution that led them to enter into it.

In Christian tradition, "bearing witness" to some hard time or injustice means more than observing, detached, from a safe distance. It means placing oneself in the midst of the situation, on equal footing with others, opening one's eyes, and standing firm. It means acting as a moral anchor in a sea of confusion.

The political debate over Central America currently raging in the United States is complicated by many kinds of distance and detachment. Although closer and more culturally similar to our country than was Vietnam, the region is still far enough away and alien enough in its language and customs to frustrate all but the most determined attempts at understanding. By their presence there, witnesses from the United States build a bridge between two political systems, two histories, two realities, and, most of all, between two peoples who have much to gain by greater contact. Many of these pilgrims bang out newsletters on rickety typewriters and make periodic visits to the U.S. to share their observations with networks of supporters. This book is an effort to bring their insights and experiences to the general public.

North Americans are sharing the Nicaraguan reality in many different ways. The professions represented in this book include education, psychology, music, science, engineering, research, and the ministry. But the variation doesn't stop there. Some, recognizing that they are there for the long haul, have bought comfortable homes and shipped their libraries down. Others live in working-class barrios under corrugated metal roofs, or rent rooms in the houses of Nicaraguan families. Some maintain an international circle of friends. Others go to great lengths to fraternize with Nicaraguans and avoid remnants of their own more affluent pasts. And, when talk inevitably turns to the threat of a full-scale invasion by our own troops, some say they would come home and try to educate the U.S. public about the impact of such a step, while others frankly state that they would stay in Nicaragua and continue their witness. A significant number of them, organized as the Committee of U.S. Citizens Living in Nicaragua, hold regular vigils in front of the U.S. embassy in Managua to protest our country's policies and emphasize that they want nothing to do with a Grenada-style rescue mission.

How many of us would want to live in such a troubled place, or consider ourselves up to the adventure, or just plain let the thought cross our minds? Moreover, when we do make such dramatic moves, how many of us can articulate our reasons for them or the factors in our background that made them possible? When this project first sparked my imagination, it appeared as a chance to learn about Nicaragua, but an equal attraction was the light it might shed on the process of human growth, the development of values, and the conditions or experiences that make people better able to live the beliefs they say they hold. Most of the travelers in this book are unusually open to change and able to embrace adventure. They put up with cold-water washes and crowded buses, and they knowingly step closer to the danger of war than most of us would care to. Indeed, many are so international in their outlook and so flexible in their lifestyles that one of the greatest challenges in bringing this book to fruition was getting them to verbalize their reasons for being that way: to them, it just seemed natural.

Still, several points were raised so often that they deserve mention here. For many white North Americans living in Nicaragua, the civil rights movement of the 1960s was a watershed, opening their eyes to the role of racial stereotypes in the development of public policy. Over and over, these observers raise a disturbing possibility: that our willingness to fund a war on Central American turf is enhanced by the fact that those who will be asked to fight and die do not look like us. Not surprisingly, then, a second key experience in the lives of many North Americans in Nicaragua was a growing sense of injustice during the Vietnam era: the belief that unconscionable violence was being committed for reasons more economic and geopolitical than moral. In addition to the consciousness raising effects of the civil rights and antiwar movements, two more personal types of experience were reported over and over: an awakening to the differences between rich and poor—and the ways in which social systems reinforce those differences—and a deep reassessment of the meaning of religious commitment.

The people in this book were chosen because they represent a wide spectrum of personal backgrounds and, at the same time, a particular range of viewpoints on Nicaragua. Most of them made the decision to go there after the 1979 revolution and because of it. They are all supportive of the stated goals of that revolution: redistribution of resources in favor of the poor; political pluralism; a mixed economy with a strong public sector; and nonalignment in foreign relations. But support for the goals does not mean uncritical endorsement of the revolution's every action. Ideally, supporters of a movement are its most rigorous critics. A primary purpose of these interviews was to determine how and to what extent the Nicaraguan revolution is living up to its own dreams. Each observer sees a particular piece of this process and compares it to a highly personal set of standards. But it is hoped that, taken together, these interviews will offer a coherent picture of a troubled young country.

Nicaragua has become the site of a bitter policy dispute. Should the U.S. support counterrevolutionary forces (contras), representing a potpourri of interests including the National Guard of the old Somoza dictatorship, a Nicaraguan business community that feels its power undermined, and disaffected elements from the country's Atlantic coast population? How will history judge actions like the CIA's mining of Nicaragua's ports, which crippled Civilian shipping, and its distribution of a comic book outlining methods by which Nicaraguans could disrupt their own government and economy? Ought we to continue hostile economic policies like the trade sanctions imposed in the spring of 1985 and our efforts to block loans to Nicaragua from the Inter-American Development Bank?

How can we grapple with these problems in both political and ethical terms? At what point does protection of our economic and political interests tread on the legitimate interests and rights of others? How shall we deal with a country like Nicaragua which has declared itself determined to steer a course quite independent of our direction? Does a socialist orientation always mean loyalty to the Soviet Union? Does it in Nicaragua's case? Can our country's behavior—the degree of its hostility or support—influence the course of revolutionary Nicaragua's dependence on the Eastern bloc? Fair or not, the U.S. government, and, by extension, the U.S. public, have become a major force in deciding Nicaragua's fate, either by our actions or by our indifference.

Unfortunately, the U.S. public seems pretty confused on the issue. A 1985 poll indicated that only twenty-six percent knows which side our government is on. But another poll, reported in April of 1985, bore out that, as a nation, we do not want another Vietnam. Sixty-three percent of the U.S. public told a Newsweek Gallup poll that we should never have gone into Vietnam at all, and seventy-five percent believed we had used excessive force while we were there.

Confusion, division, bitterness, and the shadow of Vietnam still largely define the debate on Central America, and they are an inadequate basis for this national dialogue. But the issue of Central America need not kindle only despair. Just as we face the risk of sinking into another Vietnam, we also have the opportunity to choose a different course and, by doing so, to heal ourselves and our political life of the injuries of the last generation's war. One of the prime requisites for doing this will be open-minded dialogue between the two sides here at home. As a contribution to that dialogue, *Bearing Witness, Building Bridges* seeks to represent the antiwar movement of the 1980s as fully and fairly as possible.

To turn the Central America dialogue into a healing experience, much effort will be needed. It is regrettable that, in many respects, the Reagan administration is pursuing policies which divide us even further and which impede rather than enrich the flow of information about Central America in the U.S. The administration has attempted to deny visas to a number of high Nicaraguan officials, blocking our chance to hear their stories firsthand until public pressure forced a reversal. The administration has thrown itself into public relations efforts for the contras in the form of a "White House Outreach Working Group" created to spread the message that Nicaragua is a communist beachhead threatening the security of the hemisphere. Former CIA analyst David MacMichael, who tried unsuccessfully for two years to document arms shipments through Nicaragua to El Salvador's rebels, accused the administration of "systematically misrepresenting Nicaraguan involvement in the supply of arms to Salvadoran guerrillas to justify its efforts to overthrow the Nicaraguan government." The administration has been sued by a group of legislators for violating the War Powers Act in Central America, and has drawn criticism from left and right for refusing to acknowledge the jurisdiction of the World Court on the CIA's mining of Nicaraguan harbors. In light of this pattern, it is not only Nicaragua's well-being that hangs in the balance; it is the integrity of the political process here at home.

No individual's observations can represent the multitextured reality of a nation and its position in the world, and no collection of interviews can do justice to the range of views possible on a subject. If the individuals represented in this book were gathered together in a room and asked to define the nature of Nicaragua, the United States, or anything else, chaos would be the result. Still, these statements deserve consideration as reflections of the experience of folks who have thrown themselves into the situation, and whose survival may depend on the clarity of their vision. *Bearing Witness, Building Bridges* is not an endorsement of every view represented here, for it will soon be obvious to the reader that these individuals' views collide as often as they mesh. What the book is meant to endorse is an approach to life and politics: going to the source, taking risks, opening oneself to change, and living in reality the values we hold in principle.

Justinian Liebl

Nicaragua Old and New

Mary Hartmann and a prisoner at an "open farm" prison

Nicaragua Old and New

Here in the United States, it is possible to live a long, fruitful, fulfilling life and not once think about Nicaragua. The news we receive about this and other foreign countries emphasizes the foreignness of the place, not the experiences there of people like us. Too often, that news comes to us in disconnected bursts rather than as continuously developing stories. And so, even as our government's activities and claims of national security interest in the region continue and build, it is easy for the ordinary citizen to leave such matters to the specialists. Easy and wrong. What we see on the tube is only a starting point for understanding this complex, long-suffering country, as one example will illustrate.

For many of us, the "modern era" in our awareness of Nicaragua began one day in June of 1979 when CBS news viewers were shocked to witness on camera the murder of correspondent Bill Stewart by security forces. Stewart, a popular reporter, had approached a police outpost in a poor barrio of Managua carrying a white flag and seeking information about the day's events in the uprising against dictator Anastasio Somoza Debayle. Many who witnessed Stewart's last moments—as he was forced to the ground, kicked, and then shot at point-blank range—might have turned away and dismissed such brutality as business as usual in a Latin American banana republic.

Frequently enough, they would be right. But, in Nicaragua, that increasingly naked institutionalized violence was being opposed by a popular movement whose base, by that time, had grown quite broad. The Frente Sandinista de la Liberacion Nacional (FSLN)—a coalition with Marxist, democratic populist, and strong Catholic participation—had gained the support of business and mainstream political leaders and was spearheading a military uprising that, on July 19, 1979, would send the dictator packing to Miami.

July 19, 1979 was a turning point for Nicaragua and for Central America's relationships with the superpowers of the globe. But there is enormous debate not only as to interpretation of the last six years' events in Nicaragua but as to the simple facts. Are the Sandinistas a cadre of externally inspired mischief makers who took power in the sheep's clothing of popular participation and pluralistic goals? Or are they, as they claim, *a revolutionary force groping for new ways to better people's lives, using some teachings of Marx, some of Christ, and many ideas of their own?*

A little textbook-style history may provide some basis for understanding the personal accounts which follow. For almost its entire history, Nicaragua has been a colony. More than two hundred years ago, the Spanish landed on the Pacific coast and intermarried with the native population to create the lineage of Spanish-speaking mestizos who remain the most common ethnic group. Soon after, the British took over the Atlantic side, establishing English as the official language and arming the Miskito Indians as their unwitting proxies to fight off the Spanish. The two sides of the country were not even unified until 1893. Industrial and economic development got off to a slow start and never did much for the majority of the population.

By the middle of the nineteenth century, native ruling elites were emerging, centered in Liberal and Conservative parties defined more by their home towns, Leon and Granada, than by any recognizable ideologies. But, at the same time, another major force had entered Nicaraguan politics with a clear intent to dominate: the United States. By 1850, Cornelius Vanderbilt was bankrolling thirty-five dollars a head for transporting thousands of potential prospectors to the California gold rush across Nicaragua's waterways. Not long afterward, the right to take permanent advantage of that resource by building a canal through Lake Nicaragua was divided between the U.S. and Britain without consulting Nicaragua.

In 1855, U.S. troops stepped into Nicaragua at the invitation of Granada Conservatives in a bid to depose the Liberals from power—and stayed. William Walker, a little-known adventurer at the head of the invading force, soon made a name for himself as Nicaragua's president by instituting slavery, declaring English to be the official language, and confiscating the property of political enemies. Although Walker was ejected a few years later, this was just the beginning of our country's military presence in Nicaragua. Invasions took place again in 1909, 1912-25, and 1927-33. During one of these periods, in 1914, Nicaraguan protest over the canal issue was quelled with the signing of the Bryan-Chamorro treaty, which was ratified by the Nicaraguan Congress while the National Palace was surrounded by U.S. Marines and after the terms of the treaty had been read to the legislators in English.

Many in U.S. policymaking circles and among the general public accepted the rationale of Theodore Roosevelt, who in 1904 established as a corollary to the Monroe Doctrine that "chronic wrongdoing, or an impotence which results in a general loosening of the ties of civilized society, may in America, as elsewhere, require intervention of some civilized nation, and in the western hemisphere the adherence of the United States to the Monroe Doctrine may force the U.S., however reluctantly, in flagrant cases of such wrongdoing or impotence, to the exercise of an international police power."

But a less favorable view of the interventions of the early twentieth century was powerfully stated by General Smedley Butler, one of a handful *of military men ever to receive two congressional medals of honor and the mastermind of a number of operations under the rubric of that police power. At a dinner in his honor in 1931, Butler condemned the military operations he had helped run in Nicaragua and elsewhere, and condemned them outspokenly:*

> *I spent 33 years being a high-class muscle man for big business, for Wall Street and the bankers. In short, I was a racketeer for capitalism. I helped purify Nicaragua for the international banking house of Brown Brothers in 1909-1912....I helped in the rape of half a dozen Central American republics for the benefit of Wall Street....I might have given Al Capone a few hints. The best he could do was to operate a racket in three cities. The Marines operated on three continents.[1]*

At any rate, when the United States military left Nicaragua in 1933, it did so after installing a cooperative interim president, Juan Sacasa, and creating a formidable police and military operation, the Guardia Nacional, headed by an unsuccessful car salesman named Anastasio Somoza. Somoza, and later his two sons, ruled Nicaragua for forty-five years, consolidating an enormous family fortune in the process and holding on to it by increasingly repressive means.

From the Reagan administration to the Sandinista directorate, there is acknowledgment that life under the Somoza dynasty was tough and unjust for the average (read: poor) Nicaraguan. Describing the period in the late 1960s when the Frente Sandinista was formed, Argentine journalist Eduardo Crawley writes:

> *Most of the land that was being exploited had been concentrated in a very few hands. Registered landholdings numbered only about 60,000, but even this figure disguises the fact that the bigger landowners—and Somoza was the biggest—had a large number of units to their names. The vast majority of the one million Nicaraguans who lived off the land were plantation hands or subsistence farmers, eking out a very precarious existence.*

> *Cold statistics showed that Nicaragua's per capita income was only slightly more than 350 U.S. dollars, an average that included the handful of millionaires who lived the good life commuting between Managua and Miami. Except in the cities, social security was real only on paper, as were the minimum legal wages of rural workers. Health care was nonexistent in many parts of the country, and the general state of sanitation is best illustrated by the fact that, after old age, the main causes of death in a country with an average life expectancy of about fifty years were gastritis, duodenitis, enteritis, colitis, and malaria.[2]*

A modern turning point as great as the insurrection, and as devastating, was the earthquake that turned three-quarters of Managua's buildings to rubble one December night in 1972. Twelve thousand died and half a million were made homeless from the quake and the fires that followed.

But the real transformation precipitated by the earthquake was ideological and political. Until then, Somoza had been widely tolerated by the middle classes for the order he maintained and the stable climate he provided for business. The earthquake signaled a sharp increase in the government's repressiveness and, on the part of the public, an enhanced awareness of, and opposition to, the corruption that had been going on all along. According to Crawley:

> *An impressive stream of relief supplies began to arrive at the airfield from all over the world. But huge quantities of these urgently needed wares were grabbed, as soon as they were unloaded, by greed-crazed Guardia officers who were already running a thriving black market in looted goods, food, medicine and blankets throughout the sprawling tent cities that had sprung up around Managua.*

By this time, the senior Somoza had been shot by a young poet, and his first son, Luis, had died of a heart attack at the helm of the country. Now Anastasio, the third Somoza in the series, used the crisis to restructure the government, vastly expanding his own powers. Citizens who protested, however sedately, even calling for the restoration of electricity and water to middle-class neighborhoods, were repressed with shocking efficiency. Starting in 1972, the gloves were off in the conflict between Somocismo and an increasingly broad segment of Nicaragua's population. Even moderates like newspaper publisher Pedro Joaquin Chamorro, who called for Somoza's replacement early in that period, found themselves isolated as Somoza solidified his command in the fraudulent 1974 election.

But soon a more powerful opposition to Somoza emerged—spectacularly. The Frente Sandinista amazed the dictator and anyone outside Nicaragua who happened to be paying attention to the tiny country when it stormed a 1974 Christmas party of high government officials and took seventeen hostages, including the president's brother-in-law. This action, billed by the FSLN as "Breaking the Silence," successfully forced the release of a number of Sandinista prisoners, including current Nicaraguan president Daniel Ortega, and brought into public awareness the fact that the small Sandinista movement had been organizing for nearly a decade to bring about the downfall of the dictator. It had actually been formed in 1966 by Carlos Fonseca, Silvio Mayorga, and Tomas Borge, and had published a program which harked back to the vision of the original Sandinista.

Augusto Cesar Sandino was an Indian from Masaya who spent part of his childhood with his mother in debtor's prison, and developed a particularly passionate vision of social justice. In the 1920s, after he had become a general in the Nicaraguan army, that vision led him to take up arms against a proposal that called for the continued presence of U.S. marines in the country. Nicaraguan history books until 1979 portray him as a bandit, but his troops at the time called him "the general of free men" for his particular nationalistic vision. Like his namesakes later, in areas under his control out in the countryside, Sandino organized farming and consumer cooperatives and taught peasants to read. Unlike the modern Sandinistas, he did not see the battle as winnable in his time, but only as the beginning of a historic tide. Many of his statements, kept alive by modern Sandinistas, are fervently nationalistic and focus on a vision in which smaller countries will not be dominated by larger, wealthier ones. He admonished the United States: "A great nation gains in honor and prestige by respecting the sovereignty of small, weak nations rather than by oppressing those who fight to secure their rights." Eerily paralleling the modern U.S. administration's rhetoric, the original Sandino was also accused of representing foreign subversion—Mexican bolshevism, according to President Calvin Coolidge.

Although he vowed to fight until the last foreign troops had left Nicaraguan soil, Sandino also made a commitment never to accept public office himself. And he kept his word, retiring after the departure of U.S. Marines in 1932 to one of the cooperatives he had organized in the northern mountains. But Sandino's coops were targets of continual harassment as Somoza's new National Guard cut its teeth. After several visits to Managua to protest these incursions, Sandino was invited to a banquet at the Presidential Palace in 1934 and, on his way home, was ambushed and killed by the Guard. The next day, three hundred of his followers were also murdered by the Guard.

This history was well-known by the Sandinistas who moved to take Nicaragua back from dictatorship—and to hold on to it this time. In pursuit of that goal, the new government declared that "Somocismo without Somoza" was not good enough. It dismantled the National Guard, imprisoned some of its members, and let others go into exile in Honduras. Nor was it willing to give the majority of high government positions to members of the business community, believing them to hold their own interests above those of the general public. A Council of State was formed (after months of wrangling) with representatives from the private sector but with a majority of seats held by the FSLN and popular organizations (such as women and agricultural workers) formed by the Frente and expected to support its general approach.

While maintaining a vision with room for many developmental strategies and with mechanisms for negotiation among competing groups, the Frente Sandinista made no bones about seizing the role of "vanguardia" in the "revolutionary process" that began July 19, 1979. The Government of National Reconstruction it set up was a hybrid of the political forces that had worked against Somoza, with a clear majority held by the FSLN. In a very real sense, what was set up by Nicaragua's revolutionary government was neither democracy nor dictatorship, but a structure which could be used to develop either one. It was an approach that clearly frustrated those who tried to understand it by comparison with U.S., British, Soviet, Cuban, and other models.

In Managua, Leon, Esteli, and other cities on the Pacific side of Nicaragua, the end of the insurrection was seen as a release from the violence that had terrified the population, stifled food production, crippled the economy, and killed over fifty thousand people in the previous two years. On the Atlantic side, where the war and national politics in general were remote from the common people's lives, July 19 marked the beginning of a painful new chapter in Nicaragua's history: a series of confrontations between the new government and the coastal population which the succeeding five years have only begun to clarify and heal.[3]

This textbook chronology comes alive through the eyes of two North Americans who have lived through it and, to their own surprise, become intimately involved and frankly partisan in the process. Mary Hartmann and Justinian Liebl have each lived in Nicaragua over twenty years. As religious workers who have covered a wide swath of country and city in their work, they have seen firsthand the living conditions under Somoza and heard the discussions of people hoping to change them. Both became supporters of the Frente Sandinista in the mid-1970s, and both remain critical yet enthusiastic. As their stories unfold, their reasons, and the issues facing Nicaragua, will become clearer.

Notes

1. Quoted in *The Shark and the Sardines,* by Juan Jose Arevalo.
2. Eduardo Crawley, *Nicaragua in Perspective* (N.Y.: St. Martin's, 1984).
3. As this book went to press, Nicaragua had begun letting the ten thousand Miskito Indians relocated to facilitate the war against the contras return to their lands. *The Boston Globe,* August 7, 1985, p. 16.

Mary Hartmann

Sister Mary Hartmann speaks with the authenticity of one who has spent half her life in Nicaragua. When I approached her to ask for an interview, her first response was, "I don't know if I can remember how to speak English well enough." But it soon became clear that she keeps up that skill by talking with the hundreds of international delegations that seek her out for information and perspective.

Mary is respected for her straight-shooting manner, her massive stores of information, and her bravery over the years in placing herself in the center of the misery, be it earthquake or revolution. She came to Nicaragua in 1962 as a teacher in an upper-class boys' school, but quickly branched out to work in leper colonies and to teach catechism in poor communities. When the earthquake devastated Managua in 1972, she was involved in the reconstruction. When the National Guard stepped up its repression in the mid-1970s, she helped to hide those who were threatened. Currently, she works for the Nicaraguan government's Commission for the Protection and Promotion of Human Rights.

I visited Mary Hartmann in the commission's office, a simple, one-story stucco building facing the Parque de las Palmas in Managua, a small green field with playground and monuments to various heroes and martyrs. The conference room where we spoke was bare of decoration except for two travel posters celebrating Nicaragua as "a country to discover" and a collection of obviously significant objects gathered on a woven straw mat: a statuette of Sandino, a trailing vine, a folk-crafted ashtray, and a placard. In keeping with the Central American custom of affirming that those killed in the war are still with us, the neat block lettering on this placard spelled out the name of one of the four nuns murdered by paramilitary forces in El Salvador: "Maura Clark—presente." There are heartfelt ties across national boundaries among the religious workers who are doing their best to help the poor in Central America. To hear Mary's observations, and the history that shaped them, is to understand a great deal about a larger movement.

I became a Sister of St. Agnes and then got my degree in Shakespeare from Marquette University. I thought I would be a schoolmarm all my life. Isn't it funny? I came to Nicaragua in 1962, at a time when the church was asking that ten percent of their personnel go to Latin America to work with the poor and evangelize the continent. They said you had to be finished with college and have a stable character. I wrote them a letter saying I felt a need for that stability in my life.

I never thought I'd be here so long. But there's always some crisis, something happening, that makes you reluctant to leave. At this point, I feel like English is my second language instead of Spanish.

Within the Latin American experience, I've understood as never before what it means to be a Christian, the reality of the gospel. In the early 1960s, you see, there was a revolution in the church that gave rise to the theology of liberation. In the Medellin document, which arose from the work of the Second Vatican Council, the bishops of Latin America called on Christians to incarnate ourselves into the lives of the poor and work not only for their spiritual liberation but for their well-being in anything that touches their lives, because people are made up of body as well as soul. This was something new. When I first came down here, the church's idea about poverty was that the poor always get to heaven but that we don't have a particular responsibility to them on earth. Just hold on and you'll get your reward, in other words. But the gospel says to give drink to the thirsty. That took on a concrete meaning down here.

When I first came down, I worked in Managua at a Christian boys' school. There were about sixty little six-year-olds, all from families wealthy enough to pay the tuition, and I taught them art and music. At the same time, to get a little bit more in touch with the reality of the people, I went to work in a leper colony on Sundays, and held some catechism classes out in the barrios. When the director of the school found out some of us sisters were going out to the leper colonies, he didn't forbid us, but he certainly wasn't in favor of it. That bothered me, but there didn't seem to be much to do about it.

I came from a rather well-to-do residential area, so I definitely was not prepared for the reality of a Third World country. Riding into Managua from the airport that first time in 1962 was unforgettable. Old Managua had very narrow streets, with beggar after beggar lined up. You just couldn't take care of them all. Saturday was beggars' day—they rapped on your door, and the law said you had to give them something. It was a country in a vacuum as far as social programs.

After a few years, I was sent to Puerto Cabezas, where I taught high school. Now that's up north on the Atlantic coast, almost to the Honduran border, and it's a port town, so there are a lot of international people passing in and out. There were also, in those years, a lot of U.S.-based companies working out of there, so people viewed the North Americans as people who brought in money. The school where I taught was practically free, thanks to subsidies by the church. But most children left school before sixth grade because of conditions at home. In visiting some of these homes, I discovered that eighty percent of the families had at least one member with tuberculosis simply because someone had worked in the mines owned by the U.S. companies. The disease spread to other family members because of the living conditions. And there was no medical care, no workers' compensation, or anything of the sort. When people got sick, they were simply let go. There was always someone to take their place.

From Puerto Cabezas, I went to Waspam, the largest town on the Rio Coco, and taught fifth grade for a few years. Then, back in Managua in 1969, I came to live and work in a poor neighborhood called Barrio Riguero, which is still my home today. That's where I really acquired consciousness of the economic and social conditions and their roots. People would work in the factories from seven in the morning until five, with maybe half an hour off, and they would earn the equivalent of thirty dollars a month. No health care, no retirement plans. They were exploited. Other people made do by selling vegetables from carts, or shining shoes or sharpening scissors. And many were unemployed or had very short-term labor. I got a job in the university, teaching English to earn my rice and beans.

The earthquake in 1972 was a turning point. Not only did the earth open, but a lot of people's minds opened when they saw that all the aid from around the world never reached them. Canned vegetables with labels from the relief agencies were sold on the shelves of Somoza's supermarkets. There were huge donations for rebuilding Managua, but the people had to scrounge their own cement and carry their own stones. There was absolutely no help.

Managua used to be a cosmopolitan city filled with skyscrapers. Now it's fields and shanties. Even basic services like water and electricity were not restored for years. Somoza just pocketed it all. So, working in a barrio where people were experiencing this hardship, I was faced with the question of how to help them organize to get what was theirs. And you can't do that without moving into the realm of politics. In carrying out the gospel, you become political. Now, what I'm telling you in a matter of seconds represents years of work, just trying to get the bare essentials of life.

At first, people went to talk to public officials and were told, "Yes, yes, we'll send somebody out to look at the situation." But nothing happened. One evening after mass, a group of people decided to hold a peaceful demonstration, just a march to give voice to their demands. This was met by repression from the National Guard. They came in throwing tear gas. It was frightening. Someone grabbed me and dragged me indoors and started throwing water all over me. That was the first experience of tear gas for a lot of people.

In the weeks that followed, people reflected and wondered what to do. There were meetings, retreats. Some people said we shouldn't make waves. Others said we've got to. In the Christian communities, they read a lot in the books of Exodus and Isaiah, where God led his people to the edge of the promised land but they had to cross the final desert themselves and it took them forty long years. The sentiment was: We believe in a God of light, and we believe that, even if we don't live to see a new Nicaragua, our children might, so let's unite and work for it. This began the participation of Christians in the revolution, with things like that happening all over the Pacific half of Nicaragua.

As people began to organize, there was repression and more repression. The jeeps would come in. You'd hear a jeep at midnight and everyone would hold their breath wondering, are they coming into my house? Who's going to be taken away now? Eventually, the Guardia Nacional got so bold that they didn't wait for darkness. A young fellow I knew was playing baseball at 7:30 in the morning. The Guardia came in and dragged him away. His mother saw it and ran after the jeeps, but she never could reach him. She went to every jail and got no response. In the afternoon, the Guardia came back and told her she could pick up her son in the morgue, if she had the money to get him out. They quickly took up a collection in the barrio. When she found him, his eyes were gouged out, he had no fingernails, he had been horribly tortured. Before the war even started, we lost forty-eight people in our barrio. They just disappeared, sometimes picked up on their way home from work. That's why it's so hard to get people in the U.S. to understand the reality. We've never had a war on our soil or experienced this kind of suffering.

When the war broke out, I was involved full-time running the refugee camp at the old seminary here. Actually, the whole neighborhood was turned into a refugee camp—almost twelve thousand people were made homeless by Somoza's bombing in this area. And at times I got pretty closely involved with the organizing. When people were threatened by the National Guard, sometimes they would stay in my home. I served as a chauffeur for people living underground and tried to find them locations to have meetings. If the kids were picked up and questioned about me, they would say, "Oh, yes. I go see her because I'm having trouble with my girlfriend." They were so brave. Everyone took a lot of risks. Sometimes there were demonstrations, and they would start out by having everyone bang their pots and pans together in protest, to get an idea of how many people were willing to take a risk. In the towns, the Guardia would usually shoot into the air or pick up a few young people. Sometimes, in the universities, they would fire into demonstrations. But in the countryside, they were savages because they thought no one would know. Whole villages disappeared. And the people haven't forgotten it.

This whole revolution was about the gospel message, giving life to those who didn't have it. The people wearing Sandinista uniforms now are people who risked their lives for their brothers way back and are still doing it. No one here is afraid of a man in uniform. They're very human. You can't fall in between on this question. You either choose the God of life, or the God on the penny where it says "In God We Trust."

Those who have benefited most in this revolution have been the poor. You can see that clearly out in the countryside and in the working class neighborhoods. And the poor are the vast majority of the population in a country like this. Here in the city, now, for example, there are relatively few unemployed. The old people also receive a small pension, and there are new homes where they can go and be taken care of if they have no relatives. There's the health service, with all its achievements. We have a long way to go but, unlike in the time of Somoza, you can look at a five-year-old and know it's likely that that child will live. In our barrio, probably ninety-five percent of the people know how to read and write now. They feel very confident in themselves because they can pick up a newspaper and find out what's going on, whereas they never could before. When you recognize that all this has happened in spite of the war the country is fighting, it's pretty impressive. And everywhere you can see signs of democratic institutions springing up. In our neighborhood, you see it in the meetings that take place to decide everything from trash collection to night watch to who goes into the militia. There's even a TV program, "Face the People," on which the comandantes go to different communities and answer the people's questions on anything at all. To call it totalitarian is just absurd.

My job since the revolution has been with the government's Commission for the Protection and Promotion of Human Rights, mostly running social programs. In 1979, when the United Nations issued a call for countries to form their own human rights commissions, Nicaragua was the first to respond. We act as a watchdog, investigating complaints and pressuring the government to take action when there are problems. The commission has even developed a curriculum on human rights for the schools. Now, as for the situation here, there have been international delegations streaming through one after another—Amnesty International, Americas Watch, groups from other countries. And their findings, consistently, have been that there are no political prisoners in the sense of people imprisoned for their beliefs. There are certainly people in prison for specific activities like treason or spying or sabotage. Some visitors ask why these are tried by special tribunals instead of in the regular court system, and the answer is in order not to clog up the process for regular criminal trials.

My major responsibility is in the prison system. We're developing a series of "open farms" with no guards, where there's a real commitment to rehabilitation. This is especially important when you realize that two thousand of these prisoners are former members of Somoza's National Guard, illiterate people who knew only how to use a gun. The first of the new programs in all the prisons was a literacy campaign. Prisoners grow and prepare their own food. They're learning all kinds of skills like photography, carpentry, furniture making, sewing, TV and radio repair. They get time off for good behavior. And in the whole system, there have been a total of four escapes out of eight hundred prisoners. Now, the maximum security prison is not such a lovely place. It was left over from the time of Somoza, and we've started enlarging it, but the construction has been held up because of the war. But there's that same commitment to rehabilitation even there.

Probably the greatest problem has been the slow pace of trying the accused in some remote areas. By law, after someone is arrested, the state has eight days to bring charges and present evidence against them. But we've had lots of cases where it's taken as long as a month or two. And there have been cases of physical abuse. In 1981, there was a battle near Puerto Cabezas called Red Christmas, in which the contra forces tried to take over a corner of Nicaragua to establish a provisional government. A number of Miskito Indians involved in Red Christmas were hit during their detention. Well, we presented our report to the Ministry of the Interior, and the people responsible for that were jailed themselves. All in all, more than three hundred Ministry of Interior employees—such as soldiers, prison officials, police—are serving time for human rights violations, and many of them are in jail for years.

The story of human rights in Nicaragua winds up terribly distorted in the U.S. press. For instance, there was an incident during Holy Week of 1983 when three soldiers on leave went on a spree in their jeep and drove through a crowd of a dozen people. That was reported at great length. What didn't make it into the newspapers was that the driver of that jeep is in jail for thirty years—the maximum sentence here, there is no death penalty—and the others are serving eight-year terms. The situation in Nicaragua is not paradise. There's room for improvement in everything. But what they're trying to do here is to build a new country, to build new human beings. That is not going to take place overnight.

I have to say, as a human rights worker and an American citizen, that the greatest violation of human rights suffered by Nicaraguans by far is the United States' actions toward this country, from the economic blockade to acts of sabotage to the funding of Somoza's old National Guard to do just what they did in the old days—torturing, mutilating, killing. Think about Nicaragua's so-called militarization from this country's point of view. The war is being fought here. People are dying here. What would we do in the U.S. if there were Soviet warships in our waters, Soviet troops by the thousands on the Canadian border, Soviet planes flying through our air space? Nicaragua is trying to defend its territory. This little country isn't a threat. Nicaragua has said since 1979 what Sandino said a generation ago, that they will deal with the United States on a basis of mutual respect, not from a second-rate status. When this little country decided to stand up for its dignity, the Reagan administration's response was to condemn it to death. You want to know where the United States is coming from? Read the Santa Fe Document, a position paper used by the Reagan transition team in 1980 which says that war, not peace, is the norm in foreign policy.

The real violators of human rights down here are the contras. Reed Brody, a former attorney general from New York, came down here and collected sworn affidavits from eyewitnesses and religious workers all over this country, and what he found was a consistent pattern of torture and mutilation and rape and murder. The people who are attacking Nicaragua as contras now are the same ones who terrorized it as National Guard before. They use the same tactics. And they've killed over eight thousand people.

I can only conclude that what Washington fears is precisely the hope of this revolution for the poor, here and all over Latin America. And the irony is that people here sensed from the first that this would happen. I think back to the first week after the triumph in 1979. I met Luis Carrion, who is now the vice minister of the interior. I had been with him back in 1972. He was doing pastoral work in our barrio as a university student. I hadn't seen him for all those years—he had been underground. I said to him, "Luis, you look so good." And he said, "Maybe, but inside we are all old men, and the worst is yet to come. They're going to blockade us. They're going to sabotage. It's going to be a contest of endurance in the end."

I just wish the war would end. These people have faced life-and-death decisions daily for years. The young people have never had a real childhood. That's bound to leave its mark. Look at the effects of Vietnam on our youth. Well, Nicaragua has lost more people proportionally during the counterrevolution than the U.S. did in all of Vietnam.

It's difficult. But a person gets courage from the Nicaraguans. I met a lady, Lupita, who lost both of her sons in the war within seven weeks. But she came up to me after the victory and said, "Maria, Maria, we won! I lost my sons, but it was worth it." Then there's Manuel Salvatieri, a comandante up in Esteli. He has three children, two, three, and four years old. But he said, "You know, I'm ready to die if I have to because I know that what has started here will never be stopped. Mr. Reagan can send all the weapons he wants, but the cry of the poor will never be silenced." Around people like that, you can't help but get strength and feel the presence of God. These aren't desperate people, for all they've been through. They're people of hope.

When I'm not working seven days a week, I guess my primary pastime is visiting with people. Oh, there are movies and TV and such, but I've learned a scale of values that puts people up at the top. Just sitting around and chatting is my favorite means of relaxation.

I still have close relationships with my family in the States, but other than that my closest contacts are with Nicaraguans and with the people who come down here on fact-finding trips. I feel very intimate with them, in the sense that I know they really want to know what's going on and it's an opportunity to share. I'm also involved with the Committee of U.S. Citizens Living in Nicaragua, a group of concerned people from the States who want to get the truth out because the U.S. embassy isn't telling it. I came down here very ignorant about what it meant to live in a dictatorship and how much our country was involved in propping up Somoza. And what upsets me now is how authoritarian the U.S. is becoming, how far it's drifting away from the democratic principles it says it stands for. I met a German who now lives in the U.S., and he made a startling comment: that the political climate in the United States is very similar to that in Germany in the 1930s. You don't have the summary executions, but you have a more subtle kind of fascism. Look at the arrests of church workers who are giving sanctuary to Salvadoran refugees, and the deportation of those refugees back to be killed. Look at the violation of international law in our campaign against Nicaragua—we've gone against the United Nations charter and the Organization of American States agreement, disregarded the World Court. . . And people haven't begun to wake up to it.

It's wonderful to live in Nicaragua because it's a country that's growing up, starting from scratch. The people are learning to speak out, to think for themselves, to make their own history, to be part of it all. As I see them gaining confidence and maturing, I think it must be the same kind of confidence there was in our own country two hundred years ago. You keep questioning yourself, asking what it all means. But I haven't had any fundamental doubts about what's going on here. I've read and observed and lived in it, and I believe it's honest and right. I'm very sure.

Justinian Liebl

"My wife says all I ever talk about is work and politics and religion. But what else is there?" asks Justinian Liebl half seriously. His point is not that he lacks a human, emotional side—Justinian, in fact, is a character. The point is that politics, religion, and his work as a teacher, which combines them, are interwoven in every facet of his life and provide a framework for understanding every experience. Justinian renounced material wealth to become a Franciscan and later a priest out of a vision that was both religious and political, and that vision led him to Nicaragua to help the poor. He spent years in rural parishes on the Atlantic coast, training illiterate peasants to take leadership roles in the church and in their communities, and this work made him a supporter of the Frente Sandinista in the late 1970s. In 1980, that same drive for a coherent relationship between work, religion, and politics led him to renounce the priesthood and marry a Nicaraguan woman who had worked with him as a nun. Justinian is now based in Managua as part of a small group which offers workshops on political participation and personal empowerment from a Christian point of view.

Nicaragua's Atlantic coast—really fifty-two percent of its land mass, but sparsely populated and poorly linked to the Pacific half of the country—is now the site of major controversy over the Sandinistas' record on human rights. The Reagan administration claims that the relocation of ten thousand Miskito Indians away from combat zones is tantamount to an extermination campaign. Americas Watch, a respected human rights agency, concludes in a March 1985 report that Sandinista abuses, including the murders of about twenty-one Miskitos and the disappearance of seventy more, all took place in a short period in 1981-82. They may well have been a response to the beginnings of covert operations by the United States rather than a systematic attempt at repression. Because Atlantic Nicaragua has different ethnic groups, language, and political concerns from the Pacific side, understanding the currently raging charges and countercharges requires a step back in history. Justinian Liebl, who arrived there in 1955 and was a priest in numerous parishes for twenty-five years, provides that context entertainingly. He is a delightful storyteller and refreshingly opinionated, enlivening even the hardest debates with his gift of laughter and irony.

By ideology, I'm a communist. Or maybe a commonist. Just like St. Francis. Just like Christ. In that spirit. I have nothing that I can call my own, or very little: my glasses, my Bible. I became a Capuchin Franciscan brother when I was seventeen. I followed St. Francis of Assisi in his idea of revolution. Franciscans are commonists—everything we earn goes into the kitty and everything we need comes out of it. The idea of socialist revolution is very close to my heart. But the temptation in thinking about a revolution is to think of the word coming down from the top. I believe that's backwards, that the crucial thing is to have the word come from the people. It can go up to the top and be organized and sent back, but it has to come from the people.

I'm fifty-eight, and I've spent more than half my life in Nicaragua, most of it on the Atlantic coast. How did I get here? Well, I joined the brotherhood in Wisconsin, where I grew up, in 1945. Then I spent four years in New York studying philosophy in school and Russian on my own, as a pastime. Then I came back to Wisconsin and did four more years of theology. In 1953, I became a priest. At first, they had me teaching social philosophy in the U.S., if you can imagine that. But I've always been interested in working with people from outside the United States, people to whom I might have something to offer. By the early 1950s, enthusiasm for the Soviet Union was dying down but my devotion to real popular revolutions wasn't. I got interested in the work the Franciscans were doing in Nicaragua, so I volunteered to come down. I wanted to get more basic, to get away from consumerism. I thought I could offer something here because there were so few priests.

So I came down here for about six months for training. Tried to pick up Spanish on my own. I had short assignments in Puerto Cabezas and in Siuna, a mining town. In July of 1956, I went to Rama, where I was one of three parish priests. I stayed there eleven years. Rama is a big parish of five thousand square miles, all bush, with about eight hundred people. From Rama, I moved to Puerto Cabezas for four years, then spent six in Bluefields. Then I went back to Siuna for a couple of years. And in 1980, I came to Managua, amid a whole lot of other changes I'll tell you about later.

Back in 1955, the Atlantic coast was just coming into the last section of a tremendous multinational blitz. United Fruit, down in the southern part, along the Rio Escondido, was just building up. The lumber companies up in the pine district were pulling out, moving into Honduras but still taking out the pine stumps here for turpentine. Precious lumber was being taken out, mahogany and rosewood. And there were the miners. A Canadian company had just opened up a big copper mine in 1950. The good fisheries were all worked by foreign companies, and by 1955 that harvest was just coming to an end.

The majority of people were never aware of the way the resources were being carried off and the economic consequences that would have years later. On the contrary, people felt very happy with the foreign companies. The dollar was on par with the cordoba for many years. People could send away to the United States with a catalog and order all kinds of things, which was a real big deal for them. There was very little realization of the rape of the Atlantic coast until there were holes left, and no more lumber. Until the fruit company left. Then people began to realize that the companies had left nothing at all except some mines in the north. People had some rude awakenings in terms of work. For example, the banana companies at one time used an enormous amount of labor in planting. But banana plants are perennials. You chop them down and the shoots come right up again. So those planters didn't have work for long. But, when people lost their jobs, they would just go back to farming.

You can hardly imagine how different and how hard life is out in the bush. I would ask the women, "How many children have you had?" and they would say, "Seventeen" or "Twelve." Then I would ask, "How many living?" And they'd answer, "Nine living and eight dead." You're talking about towns with not a single bathroom, never mind more modern conveniences. These people have a right to the basic things of life. We're talking about people who have never been to school, who had no hope ever to learn to read or write until now. For them, many things are happening today because of this revolution.

Besides the economics, another major factor to understand about the Atlantic coast is its isolation. It's an enormous, underpopulated area. The first road came across Nicaragua in July of 1967. It came into Rama the month after I left the parish there. The second, which goes over to Puerto Cabezas in the north, just opened in 1983. Building roads on the Atlantic coast is a nearly impossible situation because of the heavy rains. In a very lucky year, there might be six weeks or two months in which they can build. That first road, by the way, was a gift from Roosevelt to Somoza Senior. But it wasn't finished until 1967. Until then there was no land connection between the two coasts. And still, from Rama, it's four hours by boat to Bluefields, on the ocean.

Communication is really difficult over there. There is only one telegraph line going across from Managua to Bluefields, and that's nonfunctional when it rains. Until recently, there were no telephone lines. So the Atlantic coast is a completely different situation, culturally and politically, from the rest of the country.

In a very real sense, the whole Atlantic coast belonged to Somoza. His military power determined how things would be run. That, plus the isolation, made it impossible to have any political preparation for the Atlantic coast people when the revolution was in its formative stages. With a few exceptions, the Atlantic coast was oblivious to the insurrection and the revolution. There was very little political opposition through that whole period. There were some people who claimed to be conservatives against Somoza, but they were very quiet about it because any time anything happened they were the ones who got the crunch. When the old man Somoza was shot in September of '56, I was down river visiting some communities. I came up through the little dock at Rama, and there stood a guy with a twenty-two in his hand. So I said, "What's up?" and he said, "Old man Somoza was shot." So what they did was pick up all the people who were considered to be members of the opposition and throw them in jail. They were in jail for about two weeks, just because they were not of the Somoza party. And it was not a fancy jail, I assure you. They suffered. There were about sixteen people put into about a fifteen foot square room eight feet high, with a zinc roof and the sun beating on it. They lived in there naked for about two weeks, until things sort of blew over. Also, it was common, if you were in the opposition, that you had trouble getting a license to carry your rifle around. So it paid not to be part of the opposition.

And, of course, the voting was a little bit slanted, even though they called it "open elections," with the National Guard standing next to the voting booth where you very openly put down your "X." They would tell you what to put down. That's why I say the Atlantic coast belonged to Somoza. The big companies all kicked back to him. At the time of the triumph, they checked out the books at some of the mines, and the secretary to Somoza's party got a check every month from one for fifteen thousand cordobas, just as a little tribute. Right on the books. Part of expenses. This was common. In the mines, the military people got a salary from the mines. The labor judges were also paid by the mines.

My own interest in the Nicaraguan revolution was very heavily influenced by an earlier revolution, the one within the Catholic church that led to the second Vatican council in 1965. I was very much a part of those changes. We began emphasizing working much more with the people, getting them to work instead of having us priests go around playing the big cheese, going into the bush and giving masses to huge, adoring crowds. That's how it was in the old days. You were detached from the people and put yourself above them. Instead, we started working to form leaders in the local populations so that they could take care of their own churches. That trend began here in 1969 or 1970. We learned to keep quiet and let the people speak. What a difference! The last parish I was in was run by one Nicaragua black Indian and two North Americans. We decided we'd be out of there in about two years because of the way things were shaping up. And that's just about what happened. The Nicaraguans learned very quickly to do baptism, reconciliation, celebration of mass. Now the priests stop by once a year and say hello, and the local people run things.

When you work with people who are completely illiterate (and that was ninety-five percent of the Atlantic coast population), you have to work through dynamics and use all kinds of gimmicks because their attention span can be very short. What they don't learn by doing, they don't learn. But they can learn very well by seeing things and taking part. They come up with their own ideas.

For example, we would act out this dynamic about manipulation and power. We'd have a guy blindfolded, with ropes on his hands and feet. Another guy would come onstage and begin to pull on the ropes, and the "puppet" would dance. I would stand there playing the fiddle and letting people take this in for a while. Then we would stop and have people describe what they had seen—how the man on top feels, how the man who is dancing feels, and how everyone else feels about the whole deal.

After some discussion, we would start the music again and the puppet would be dancing. But this time another man would come up and try to set it free. But every time he touched the puppet's hands, the puppet would pull back and keep on dancing—because dancing is his life, you know? Finally, in exasperation, the man trying to free him steps back and takes out a Bible and reads a verse and says, "It's okay, you can suffer now because some day your life will be good in heaven."

Well, the skit goes on with more of the same rigamarole, with people trying all kinds of ways to free the puppet. One guy whacks the puppeteer with a machete, but then he tries manipulating the ropes himself and gets to like it. Eventually, someone takes the blindfold off the puppet's eyes and shows him the ropes and the puppeteer. And, together, they pull the ropes and the puppeteer comes tumbling down. The point is that one of the basic evils in the world is manipulation. That can be applied to everything: the marriage, home life, kids, community, and the nation.

So, the specifics would vary from workshop to workshop, but the idea was always to get people talking about things that mattered to them: poverty, housing, the banks, women. I'd diagram their ideas on the board, so they'd see a consensus evolving that included their own ideas plus many other people's. They'd realize they were the ones producing the knowledge. That's the really important thing.

In 1976, we Capuchins wrote up a letter to Somoza demanding the human rights of those people in the parish who were thought to have been "disappeared" by his National Guard. At that time, there was complete censorship in Nicaragua. We couldn't get the letter published here, so, the following year, I took it up to Detroit to our mission office and they put it on national news. That hit Somoza pretty hard. He said, "The American priests have a shotgun against my head." But since we were American priests, he never touched us. We were sort of immune.

The local politicians tried to throw me out of Bluefields around that time because I talked from a generally leftist perspective from the pulpit. Every week, I would be at the door after church saying goodnight as people left, and one week the local comandante of Somoza's forces made it a point to leave last. He commented on my sermon, and I commented to him about the problems in Nicaragua, and we talked for about ten minutes, clearly not seeing eye-to-eye.

Around that time, there was a lot of political vibration from the people in the bush. This period was when we got in contact with the Frente. Some local sisters were very strongly involved with it by 1977. That year, I decided to go back to Siuna, and I found that a lot of guerrilla fighters were active around there. Carlos Fonseca had just been killed there the previous fall. A lot of local people had become active in the guerrilla movement as defense against the National Guard.

For my part, I began having meetings with the Guards to try to fight with them because they were holding people in jail without due process who were suspected of being soft on the guerrillas. And those meetings at least had one benefit: by the time of the triumph, they knew and trusted me well enough that I could act as an intermediary between them and the Frente and maybe save some bloodshed. I had been in the battle of Rosita and stayed to bury a whole bunch of Guardsmen, and when that was done I said to their comandante, "I'm sick and tired of burying you people. You've got to stop this."

So, when Somoza finally fell, I went to see that same comandante and said, "The jig's up," and he said, "What should I do?"

I said, "Take your bedsheet and run it up the flagpole."

Then I went to the guerrilla fighters and set up the transfer of power. It took a bunch of trips back and forth to convince everybody to cooperate. I had to speak to about eighty ex-Guards and offer them sanctuary in the church before they would agree to lay down their arms. Finally, the head of the Guards and the head of the guerrilla fighters and I met at the edge of town and the fort was handed over.

The next day, a priest from Puerto Cabezas called me on the radio and said, "Hey, Justiniano. We've got about ninety ex-Guardia holed up in our church—first time they've been in church in our lives. What do we do?" So we spent a few days negotiating and at the same time protecting the Guardsmen from people who wanted to even the score right away. In fact, six or seven ex-Guardia did wake up dead on the trail in those first days. There wasn't any order. So I was in Siuna for about a year after the triumph, helping to set things up.

During those years, I became close to one of the sisters who had been actively involved in the revolution. Her name is Galilee—like the Sea of Galilee. Her father was born in Bethlehem; he's half Jewish and half Arab and came to Nicaragua in the 1920s. Her mother was a Nicaraguan Indian from the Pacific coast. Anyway, after the triumph the Frente asked her to set up the new social welfare ministry in the northern half of the Atlantic coast. She worked at that a few months. But then the other sisters told her, "Hey, you're moving around too much to be a sister. You have to make a choice." She said, "No problem," and stepped out of being a sister.

Then, in June of 1980, I stepped out of being a priest for similar reasons. Not out of the church—never—but I no longer function as a priest. In October of 1980 Galilee and I were married and we set up housekeeping in Managua. Now she's running a center for battered girls she set up with the Ministry of Social Welfare. And we have two little daughters: Rebecca Maria and Maria Jose. My brother, who has a huge family, thought I was crazy when he heard the news. But I've never been happier. I guess I got married because I realized I was living too much for my work. As a priest, you never have a day off. You take a vacation every two years. You go up to the States for a month or two. Other than that, you're on call seven days a week and twenty-four hours a day.

Our life now is really fine. We're living in Barrio Monsignor Lascano, a "popular barrio" or, as you'd call it, a working people's neighborhood. It's a good, comfortable place.

My work here is as administrator for a group of Christians organized to do what we call popular education, the same process I was working on in the bush over the years. We are a private group, not part of the government or the organized church. We work with rural people and their community leaders, church leaders, and members of government, conducting workshops and helping them prepare educational materials and so forth. We're busy. Our staff has just about doubled since the triumph.

Our purpose is not to teach a particular subject, but to teach people to think and to recognize basic truths about their own lives. We are very much a crusader group. We certainly aren't in it for the money. We don't even earn enough to pay income tax. We're doing this work in order to help people find their own truths and make a real revolution for themselves.

Now that I'm living in Managua, I need permission to travel back to the Atlantic coast because of the war situation and the fact that I'm a foreigner. But I've been back and talked to a lot of old friends. I would say that about thirty-five percent of the Miskito people are with the revolution enthusiastically, perhaps five percent are against it, and the rest are standing by to see what the revolution can do for them. The Atlantic coast has already seen a lot of positive change. Only since the triumph has there been Nicaraguan television in Bluefields. Before this, people there saw only Costa Rican television. Now we also have that second road across the country, and telephone lines. And the government is passing out land that wasn't in use before, giving titles to the people. Many people have been able to get government support for bank loans to buy farm equipment and so forth.

The whole deal has gained these people a new way of looking at their integration into the national situation. I've worked with the Miskito people. I speak their language. So I'm very interested in all this. The whole idea of emphasizing the role of the Atlantic coast in the nation as a whole is very new and important. The Atlantic coast is the soft underbelly of the revolution. That's why Reagan plotted back in 1981, with the "Red Christmas" attacks, to cut off the northeast corner of it to create a "free Nicaragua" and then move in and take over the rest of the country from that base. It's the same thing he tried to do with the southern part before. Still, the people are beginning to understand that game. For every year of risk we face ahead, we have these five years of existence to build on.

A lot of harm was done by the Sandinistas on the Atlantic coast due to their complete ignorance in the first two years after the triumph. We had no anthropologists in Nicaragua, no sociologists. The Frente Sandinista are children of the Pacific coast. The first year and a half of their activity on the Atlantic side of the country was rooted in ignorance, childishness, and overbearingness. Still, by the time of the relocations in 1981, they had learned and developed a lot of sensitivity.

The Frente Sandinista is unique. It's got a Marxist/Leninist line in terms of opposing the capitalist system for its tendency toward imperialist domination, but they are for making a really new system. Their approach has many similarities to Allende's "third way" in Chile and the "new way" tried in Guatemala in the 1950s—both of which were undermined by the CIA. But the idea, once again, is a new socialism, with the people involved. Look at the involvement of the church and Christian people before, during, and after the triumph. This is something new.

The Nicaraguan revolution is pragmatic, not dogmatic. Have you ever heard of Antonio Gramsci? His line is probably pretty close to ours: we feel free to pick and choose, to adopt what's good in Marxism but to see how we can integrate some of those ideas with the needs of the people here who are, for example, very religious, at least eighty-five percent Roman Catholic. The Latin American culture simply demands that, whatever system you try to implement, you take religion into account. And this one does. Everybody goes to mass. We shut down the entire country for ten days at Christmas and ten days at Holy Week.

What has been portrayed as repression against the church has been actions specifically against church people who see a different vision, the bishops who have allied ideologically with the bourgeoisie. It's not religion that the government has challenged; it's the political activity of some priests against the government. For example, ten foreign priests were denied visas in 1984 because of their counterrevolutionary political activity, and they made a big deal of being thrown out. Then the archbishop led a big march of support for this priest who is openly against the government, who has been caught on videotape with plans to blow up different parks and bridges here in Managua. It's that kind of thing.

What I consider the biggest infringement on religious freedom, in fact, is the archbishop's tendency to throw out priests and sisters who have been working in the communities. He has taken them out of their parishes and out of the country.

That same polarization in the church reached a peak when the Pope visited here on March 4, 1983. He openly backed the bishops and again called for the priests to get out of government here, and he said not a single word in favor of the revolution. Frankly, we felt that he was very nasty to us. Instead of speaking to us, he spoke to the ones governing us. He didn't listen to anything the people were trying to say. The day before his visit, we had buried seventeen youths who were ambushed by the contras. Their parents were there with pictures of the kids, asking the Pope to say a prayer for these dead, and he never even recognized them. "Then say a prayer for peace," we called out. But he kept on ignoring us.

The church in Nicaragua took a quantum step that day, because the people's attitudes toward the Pope changed so much. On March 3, he was still a mystical figure, half deified. On March 5, he was understood as another person, a man with faith but also with a strong ideology shaping his actions. He's been demystified. People see him as a man in authority.

We've had two big ideological jumps since the triumph. The first one was the literacy campaign. Twenty-five thousand scholars and students went into the bush to teach the campesinos, to live with them and to work with them.

But an equally substantial ideological boost was Reagan's rise to power. He has become the grindstone on which we sharpen ourselves. The first year after the triumph, the Nicaraguan government couldn't really get the thing off the ground, in my opinion. But in January of 1981, when Ronald Reagan stepped in, the whole country organized in a flash in the popular militia. It is a pity that we have lost so many thousands of lives, so many civilians, because of his activity. But ideologically he's been very helpful. When he began killing our people, when we all began to see the continuous aggression along so many lines—economic, political, and military—many people here were forced to look at themselves and to ask where they stood. And they were willing to take a stand.

When Grenada was invaded, I spoke with friends who were strongly antirevolutionary, strongly bourgeois professional people, and they said, "If anybody invades us, we will fight on the side of the revolution." I myself, who am an American citizen, would take up a rifle now if there were an invasion. I know that my two little girls would be at risk. We've built bomb shelters on our block, so they already are being exposed to the potential, and the oldest one is only four. I still have family ties in the U.S., and it's good to visit and to see so many people involved in solidarity work with us. But down here is where our lives are as we know and love them.

As we work with people, we think about the long-range effects of the changes taking place now. Nicaragua is not just Nicaragua. It is the peak of an iceberg. The iceberg is the Third World. It is not going to stay submerged much longer.

I think that some day the United States will become converted by Nicaragua's example. People are already getting a new consciousness because of what they see and hear about Nicaragua. And that's always the way change takes place. The rider never has dialogue with the horse, but one day the horse begins to buck, and eventually the rider had better pay attention.

Linda Roth (right) and a student

The Dream of Bread and Roses

Fred Royce

Edgar Romero with Melissa Everett

Marco Romero

Frances Romero and a student

The Dream of Bread and Roses

Months after the Sandinista triumph, Managua was flooded with supporters and seekers from the U.S., Europe, and Latin America, drawn both by what this new government promised to do for its people and by the way it promised to do it. The new Nicaragua announced itself to the world not as a rigid socialism but as a flexible new system attempting to incorporate the best of many models. "We identify with socialism while retaining a critical attitude to the socialist experiences," FSLN cofounder Carlos Fonseca had written. In keeping with that vision, Nicaragua pledged to keep a significant percentage of the economy in private hands (fifty-five percent as of 1985). It declared a policy of "walking on all four legs" or diversifying its trade by relying equally on dealings with four regions: Latin America, Western Europe, the socialist bloc, and Arab oil suppliers.

In many respects, the programs launched by Nicaragua's leadership reflect not only ideology but also the personal experiences of the country's new leaders. When Tomas Borge, who was held in an underground cell and tortured during the struggle against Somoza, came to head the criminal justice system as minister of the interior, his early acts included abolition of the death penalty. The story of his first meeting with his torturer—and Borge's words, "My revenge will be to make you shake my hand"—have taken a position in Nicaraguan revolutionary history similar to that of the legend of George Washington and his cherry tree in our own.

Similarly, Ernesto Cardenal has used his position as minister of culture to implement on a national scale the vision he had worked so hard to shape in the primitive Christian community of Solentiname, "the democratization of culture." The murals that enliven the cities and the Centers for Popular Culture in the countryside are testimony to that vision.

The government has also put itself to work rebuilding and extending the country's infrastructure, bringing roads, electricity, drinking water, telephone and TV hookups, and public transportation to regions that had never enjoyed these things before. Following "the logic of the majority," the priority of government programs and social reforms was to give the most to those who had had the least. Some of the difficulty in communication between Nicaragua and its critics in the U.S. may even stem from the low priority given to ideological purity or consistency in *the revolutionary scheme. As Borge, the only surviving founder of the FSLN, explained in the* Washington Post *in 1983, goals like political pluralism and a mixed economy are important to the new government, but not as important as feeding and housing the people.*

By all appearances, decisions about who gets what and who sacrifices what in order to balance those goals have to a very great extent been made pragmatically rather than ideologically. In 1980, scarce foreign exchange capacity was even used to import a modest amount of Mother's Day gift items in deference to the middle classes. A more substantial and far-reaching example of that thinking is the land reform program which—unlike the stalled attempts in El Salvador—has really turned over plots of farmland to over forty thousand families. By law, the only land taken from its owners was the holdings of Somoza and his closest supporters and any other privately held land that was not being fully utilized. What's more, this law was administered at the local level so that neighbors could work out problems among themselves. In fact, exceptions were made to reallocate additional land in areas where rural poverty was greatest; but here, ironically, it was the peasants themselves—taught by the new government how to organize in their own behalf—who mounted the campaign for more radical redistribution.

A common thread in the reforms launched by postrevolutionary Nicaragua has been an emphasis on building long-term self-sufficiency. The literacy campaign, which won the UNESCO prize in 1981, used volunteer high school and college students from the cities who got their first taste of rural life as they helped on farms by day and taught reading by night. Thanks to that campaign, Nicaragua became the third most literate country in Latin America, after Cuba and Argentina, having cut its illiteracy rate from fifty percent to thirteen percent.

Using the same "each one reach one" approach, the new government set up a vaccination drive coordinated by the network of block organizations or Comites de Defensa Sandinista (CDS). Volunteers were trained to administer vaccines, which in rural areas meant trekking for days or weeks. But the campaign paid off in the elimination of polio and dramatic decreases in malaria, tuberculosis, measles, and other childhood diseases. Health continues to be the country's number two budget priority, second only to defense. In the view of Nicaragua's social architects, these accomplishments, which have cut infant mortality in half in five years, constitute a profoundly positive human rights policy.

But supporters of the Sandinista regime too often celebrate these advances without tackling the hard questions about aspects of human rights for which Nicaragua has been criticized: press freedom, religious liberty, economic and political pluralism. In 1982, on the heels of news that the U.S. government had authorized nineteen million dollars for covert operations inside and against Nicaragua, a state of emergency was declared. The Sandinistas maintain that the two are intimately connected, and that any restrictive policies they have adopted are in response to the Reagan administration's stated intent to "destabilize" Nicaragua through *manipulation of churches, labor, the press, and native populations. The Reagan administration insists that its policies are the Sandinistas' excuse but not their reason.*

One example will illustrate the variety of issues to be dealt with in coming up with a position on Nicaragua's emergency measures. By its new "press law," the government assumed review power over published material dealing with strategic military information or sensitive economic data that could encourage speculation or hoarding. In fact, observers on the left and the right concur that censorship of the main opposition paper, La Prensa, has sometimes been broader. But a few days' reading of what is published in that paper makes it clear that sharp criticism of the government and its policies is still daily fare. On this writer's first visit to Nicaragua, when former junta member Arturo Cruz had just announced his boycott of the 1984 national election and our own government was claiming that high-ranking Sandinista officials were involved in cocaine smuggling, La Prensa offered front-page coverage of both stories and an editorial cartoon portraying the people's choice as "Cruz or communism."

In understanding the role of press censorship in Nicaragua's political life, it is important to remember that a majority of Nicaraguans, in spite of the literacy campaign, still function at below fourth-grade reading level. Radio and television are primary sources of political news and debate, and most Nicaraguans live within earshot of Honduran or Costa Rican radio stations, including those operated by the same Chamorro family that publishes La Prensa.

Still, it is clear that a power struggle is going on, and the cornucopia of promises made in the revolution's honeymoon years has yet to become reality. An overriding question in assessing the new Nicaragua is whether a socialist revolution of any sort will tend to starve the spirit as it tries to nourish the body and to keep itself alive. Nicaragua is unique for even trying to avoid that course, for its dual emphasis on material well-being and cultural vibrancy, as illustrated by its adult education programs, murals everywhere, and community cultural centers—bread and roses.

The individuals in this next section examine this vision in light of five years' unglamorous reality, discussing what they see in terms of personal and political liberty and how they determine for themselves whether the glass is half empty or half full—or empty, or overflowing, or not a glass at all. They also share with us their reasons for deciding that the dream was sincerely held by the Sandinistas and realistically possible for Nicaragua today. Here is a look at a powerful dream and what happens when flawed, conflicted human beings try to implement it. Here, too, are stories of the changes experienced by people born in the very different reality of the United States—changes which convinced them to make the Nicaraguan dream their cause.

Fred Royce

Fred Royce greets you with the businesslike friendliness of a man whose life really is his work. And, during the weekend we spent at the school of agricultural mechanics where he is an administrator, this seemed pretty close to the truth. From the time we followed his pickup truck on the dusty road from El Choguitillo, the nearest town, until we left the next afternoon, I did not see Fred without a small group of people waiting to ask him a question, impart information, or just pass some time.

Fred stepped out of an intellectual path back at Stanford University during the Vietnam era and spent years in search of a more satisfying life. He says he's found it, teaching rural Nicaraguans how to operate and repair farm machinery and using his school as a focal point to educate people in the U.S. about Nicaragua. In the process, he's learned how to bridge many gulfs. Although he left Stanford to become a full-time antiwar activist, he embodies very few qualities of the stereotypical protester. His manner is concrete, clear, and calm. In addition, he is a political progressive who hails from the rather conservative state of Florida. Yet his fondness for, and close connections to, his home are evident. During our visit, a volunteer brigade from the southern U.S. was bunked out at the school, building a kitchen and dining area. It is clear that, beyond the protest politics of the antiwar or any other "anti" movement, Fred has learned what it means to work to realize a heartfelt dream. Sitting on the second-floor balcony of the school, which was once the summer home of a Somocista senator, Fred shared some details of the positive vision he has found—and is building on—in Nicaragua.

I was born in Jacksonville, Florida in 1952 and went to a variety of different public and private grammar and high schools throughout the years, both in Jacksonville and later in Miami. My upbringing was in a very agnostic, liberal family. I eventually went off to college in California in 1970, at Stanford.

I had always wanted to be a marine biologist. I liked math and science a lot. I went to Stanford because they had a good biology program. But in the last years of high school, I guess the ambience of the United States in the late sixties had even sent ripples to Jacksonville, Florida a little bit. I was becoming increasingly aware of the problems that affected people, and those problems were becoming increasingly disturbing to me. Maybe even interesting, but mostly just disturbing. By the time I actually got to Stanford, I was reconsidering what I would do with my life. So I very quickly became involved with the antiwar movement and actually dropped out to work with students for a couple of years.

It's hard to say exactly what particular images or experiences caused my values to develop that way. Certainly my parents were always very adamant in pointing out injustice, particularly discrimination, and I suppose it affected me as it did my sisters. What I remember is gradually becoming aware of hunger and suffering in general, and of the massive scale on which they exist in the world. I don't know why, but it gradually began to seem untenable to me, somehow improper, incorrect, that that situation should be allowed to continue. The more I thought about it, the more incorrect or wrong it seemed, and eventually I became convinced that I ought to do what I could to contribute to a solution.

Well, by '72 the student scene and antiwar movement were winding down even though the war wasn't, so I decided to do other things for a while. I moved to South Carolina and worked in a foundry. I got a job spinning cotton. I worked in a manufacturing company. I attended a merchant marine training center for a while, but that relationship went badly, because of my antiwar and generally left-wing views, I suppose.

Eventually I saved up some money and went down to Mexico to learn Spanish, in the early seventies. I actually ended up traveling all the way down to Costa Rica, and spent several weeks in Nicaragua in the fall of '74. I suppose that's the beginning of the story of how I got to be where I am now.

Nicaragua was absolutely horrible then. Somoza in '74 was probably near the height of his power. This was before the Frente did their first big, very public action, the taking of the house of a high government official around Christmas of '74. They call that action "Breaking the Silence," and it really did.

Being here, it was evident that very few people liked Somoza and most people hated him. People were very much afraid of the National Guard. They would warn me, even as a foreign visitor, to stay away from them and be careful. The Guards would saunter around and people wouldn't even look at them. No one even wanted to have eye contact, because something might be triggered and the Guard might say, "Come here."

It was the most oppressive situation I'd ever seen traveling around Central America, Mexico, and the Caribbean. It was also evident to me from being here that something was going to change. I didn't see any other outcome, given such an intense hatred for the government and such a clear conception of where the people's problems were coming from: they were coming from Somoza and the National Guard. I didn't hear about the Sandinistas while I was in the country, or even know there was any organized activity against Somoza. I learned that later. But it was still obvious that something was going to happen. I was sufficiently impressed with the situation to keep up with it when I came back to the United States. I read some books about Sandino and Nicaragua and paid attention to the news.

Finally in about '77, things really heated up in Nicaragua. I became active in the solidarity movement that was trying to prevent the U.S. from trying to save Somoza. I was studying diesel mechanics at San Jose City College in California at the time. Many of my friends were Chicanos, so I ended up working with the Chicano student organization. I would coordinate film showings and meetings about Central America in general and just try to educate our members.

After taking my technical course, studying days and working nights, I graduated and started working days and studying nights. Eventually, I bought tools and worked on heavy road equipment, heavy trucks, then later on Caterpillar equipment. In becoming a mechanic, my goal was to have some way of earning a living which I could use in almost any situation, in any country, so that I could earn a decent living, but at the same time a job which wouldn't take all my energy, either emotional or intellectual. It would leave time—I'm not sure I knew for what—for political or cultural activities or writing or just living life. I had no idea that I would be teaching a skill like that in an undeveloped country.

In 1980 I finally decided it was time to get down to Nicaragua and see what was going on for myself. I had been thinking about that pretty much nonstop since 1974, although not always thinking of moving here. Obviously there were a number of years when no sane person would have thought of moving here from the United States unless you had pretty good connections on one side or another. But, after the triumph, I was sure that I'd be living here at some point.

What motivated me wasn't a real rejection of the United States; it was just a fascination with these other countries. Politically, the situation in Nicaragua was the most interesting in Latin America in the early eighties.

I had become engaged to a woman I met at Stanford, and we decided to move to Nicaragua together. In 1980 I went to Mexico where she was working in a rural education project, and in early 1981 we began to make concrete plans in Mexico to come here, writing letters, looking into job possibilities. We finally got it together to get down here in October of '81.

Carmen quickly found work with the agrarian reform, helping the peasants who were organizing cooperatives, and I began working with people who were going to form a school—which turned out to be this one. For a while, I was also involved in a project to use alternative fuels to run internal combustion engines. I basically worked with both until I could figure out which one was getting off the ground faster, and the school seemed to be developing more solidly.

In some respects, the job to be done here has been obvious at every stage. As you travel this region, you notice huge valleys of totally flat land

and not very many people around to farm them, so obviously what you need is equipment to make the job manageable. But there hasn't been much machinery around, and, to compound the problem, educational levels in this region are very, very low. So there's a need to train people who have worked with machetes—that's the only tool they know—to work with a tractor. The task is obvious, but how to go about it is what we've been discovering for going on four years.

Besides teaching, I was a kind of bridge between some staff people who had a very good practical knowledge but little or no formal education, and those who had lots of formal education but no hands-on experience. It's very difficult to find competent workers who also have the theoretical knowledge of what they're doing.

During the first year of this school's existence, there were hardly any tools. I tell you, the things I brought from the Jacksonville Flea Market and a few junk tractors were about it. We didn't have nearly as nice a fleet as we do now, and it's still pretty funky. We had one old tractor and pieces of a few more that we could take apart and put back together to show people what a tractor was about. At first, we just did courses for tractor operators. It was only later that we expanded to train mechanics, maintenance people, welders, machinists, and so on.

Initially, they called me the technical advisor, but I was one of three who more or less ran the place. Pretty soon, we decided we really had to think more ambitiously to create a training center that was adequate to the needs of the region, which are tremendous. Even now, the machinery that gets wasted here for lack of maintenance or proper repair or even oil costs Nicaragua an awful lot of money. We realized we needed a lot more tools and equipment to do this thing right.

So, late in 1982, about a year after I'd come here, I left for the United States to ask the American people to give us a hand. I had a slide show. I traveled around from Florida to D.C. and across the South to California, doing dozens upon hundreds of slide shows, radio and newspaper interviews, visiting foundations, passing the hat in living rooms, everything. I learned a tremendous amount. I met with a group of millionaires in California, a bunch of illegal farmworkers in Phoenix, and a lot of different folks in between.

You know, that's a kind of work, if you can call it work, that really brings out the best in people in the United States. When I came back, I had the first of several container loads of tools for Nicaragua. It's really been the support of the hundreds of people in the U.S., writing five dollar checks and ten dollar checks and fifteen dollar checks, and a handful of foundations, that have kept us going.

One of the benefits for me of traveling around the U.S. is getting to find out the misconceptions people have about Nicaragua. Most people think that the situation in general is one of unfreedom. They might ask about the Miskito Indians or they might ask about the Jews, or about freedom of the press, or about the military, but the premise very often seems to be that people are very restricted in Nicaragua.

The eye-opener for people who hear me speak or come here to visit is the discovery that that's completely off-base. It's quite a free country. It's not perfectly free, I suppose, but I don't know what country is. For Central America in 1985, this is an extraordinarily free country. Above all, there is the freedom from terror.

In Nicaragua today, I have heard of isolated cases of people being locked up for a very short period of time on something that looked to me like it was mostly political. I have heard of political persecution of a fairly innocuous sort, such as one person who made a complaint against some politician or something and later got thrown in jail for a while, ostensibly for something else. But the scale of things like that is simply not in the same league with what happens in the rest of the countries in Central America on a daily basis. Here, people do not get murdered for speaking out against the government or trying to create a better society. The only terror that's here comes from the contras in Honduras and Costa Rica and from Washington. Everyone who lives in the northern countryside is a little bit aware of that terror, as we are here too.

We're about sixty miles from the Honduran border, so we're not a border area. But we are in a region where some of the most concentrated fighting is going on between the contras and the Nicaraguan army. Occasionally counterrevolutionary forces make it pretty close to our door. They've attacked out toward San Isidro, about four or five miles as the crow flies. They burned up a bunch of trucks and burned a state college. Two or three miles up the road from here, they ambushed and killed two members of the local cooperative.

About every three or four months, the state security alerts us that a significant force—fifty to five hundred contras—are within striking distance from here and a lot of us stay up all night with weapons waiting for them. And it's no fun. It's kind of scary, and it certainly takes a chunk out of your work day.

I've come within a few feet of being hit by some loose shots that somebody here fired while they were doing guard duty—it just kind of went off, you know. If that guy had killed me, it would have been just like the contras killing me, 'cause we wouldn't be playing with guns here if we didn't have those idiotic mercenaries all around. But, you see, that's the point of the contras. The best they can do is keep people off balance and force a tremendous amount of the resources to be diverted away from health centers and schools and all the other things that the Sandinistas and the Nicaraguans would much rather spend their money on. As long as that dirty little war continues, they have to spend their money on military preparedness because if they don't, they'll be obliterated. It's that simple.

One night, a bunch of us were sitting around this house, which used to be the vacation home of a Somocista senator from the Atlantic coast named Pablo Renner. Somebody said, "Can you imagine what would happen if old Pablo's son came marching up that road with a hundred or so cronies to take his house back?'' Well, the crowd just laughed, and it was a confident laugh, because they were all determined that this house wasn't going to be given back to anybody. That's the way people feel here.

The people who fear the contras are people who live closer to the border and who are connected with the programs of the revolution—cooperative members, agricultural technicians, tractor mechanics, adult education teachers, literacy teachers. The people who aren't particularly afraid of the contras are the Sandinista army because the contras go out of their way not to have a fight with the army. The Sandinistas overthrew the contras when they were in power, for heaven's sake, and now the contras are wandering around the woods in and out of Honduras, trying to find some cooperative to attack, some Ministry of Agriculture technicians to chop up into little pieces, looking for some way to terrorize the productive population without risking their own mercenary necks.

Unfortunately, terror works. A lot of people are leaving the northern areas, and that land is very rich. Bean production is down because a lot of beans are grown up there. But the march of the contra army back into the centers of population in Nicaragua could only be done on the coattails of hundreds of thousands of U.S. troops with air support and everything. That's the only way they'll get back in here.

I guess this would all be a lot harder emotionally if the environment here weren't so overwhelmingly positive. The negative stuff is all coming from Washington. There are hard decisions like whether or not to stay here, or perhaps in the worst of cases whether to be killed or have to kill somebody else defending the school. Those are heavy decisions, I suppose. But within the context of Nicaragua, and the tremendous sacrifices people are making here for something that's unquestionably worthwhile, those decisions don't seem particularly weighty or important. It's just part of living. I haven't thought that much about it.

The thing that really brings me tremendous sadness is the thought that this is where the resources of my own country are going, into such horrible destruction and terror. It's taken me over two years now to raise forty thousand dollars to buy equipment and essentially create what we see here at the school. I don't know how many hours of contra operation forty thousand dollars represents, but they get many millions every year from the U.S. government. When I think of how much good we could do with that kind of money, plus freeing up the Nicaraguan resources now expended on defense, this country could reach a whole different level of development. There would be much less suffering. But, unfortunately, I've come to believe that suffering is irrelevant to the people who make decisions in Washington. The only thing that's relevant is their own definition of our country's economic and perhaps national security interests.

There's hardly an end to the effects of the war and the economic crisis which it aggravates. The class for tractor drivers which just ended three weeks ago had as its principal instructor one of our first graduates from three years ago, and he was a very good instructor. But that same class was named after one of his classmates who had been killed by the contras in the mountains of the north, as a number of other graduates and workers have been. Then, of course, there are the shortages—we'd run out of paper if we tried to list them: gasoline, diesel fuel, spare parts, tools, tires, food. I've learned a lot in terms of how to deal with mechanical problems when you just don't have everything you need at hand.

But the satisfactions outweigh the hardships immeasurably. It's hard to say whether the biggest rewards are working in Nicaragua or working in the United States around this project. Here, of course, every graduation is a really fine event, with lots of people from the community here. I know the students from the time they come in, and I can imagine how they're going to be when they leave but there's always a few surprises.

Nicaraguans are extraordinarily appreciative, particularly with people from the United States who come here to help them out. Since the revolution, the idea of doing something because that's the way you've always done it does not have much validity in Nicaragua, at least not among rural and working-class people. They are very receptive to new ideas. On the other hand, the material conditions here are still such that people can be aware of problems with the old ways but simply have no alternative. You may see a peasant using a can that had pesticides in it to hold water, and they might know perfectly well that that's wrong, but there might not be anything else to put water in. It's the conditions of scarcity that make people, for example, sew a split, blown-out tire together with copper wire and keep riding on it—which is extremely dangerous.

I do regret that I've become a full-time administrator and I have very little time for teaching. When I can get down to being a mechanic, I really like working with the students in small groups on an engine or some component, and training people in how to use tools properly. People may be a little bit defensive at first. But they quickly see that the environment at the school is not one of competition, but rather one of sharing. If there's any competition here, it's to see who can do the most to help each other.

One element in the positive spirit here is a realization that self-sacrifice is worthwhile. The insurrection, which was begun perhaps twenty years ago by a small handful of people and eventually culminated in an uprising of the whole country, taught people that a relatively small group of dedicated, selfless people—who for many years had seemed a little crazy—could actually win. They weren't crackpots, they weren't idealistic dreamers, they were practical people who knew what they had to do and how to do it. Their sacrifices paid off because they won, and it's hard to argue with that.

That was a tremendously transcendental experience. Going from one reality to a completely different reality, through the purgatory of revolution, brought that lesson home concretely to a lot of people. Of course that doesn't mean that all people here are totally altruistic. On the contrary, almost everyone is a bundle of contradictory feelings about how much they're willing to sacrifice.

But, all in all, there's a tremendously positive outlook on what's happened in the last few years and where we're going now. In many ways, things are much better than they have been in people's lives. The situation is difficult, but it's one of those classic times when people say, "We ain't got much but we got each other." These times will be remembered as hard, but also as very important in the formation of a new Nicaraguan national personality.

As for my life here, there's not a lot of leisure time. Both the director and I would be considered fairly hyper by rural Nicaraguan standards, although he is a rural Nicaraguan. We set a fairly demanding pace here. We try to seek out people who are serious about building an institution which is an integral part of the development of the future of this region of Nicaragua, who have that consciousness and realize the importance of what we're doing, however limited it may be, to the economic progress of this region.

I live here at the school, and we have enough space that visitors are welcome and pass through all the time. The meals are simple but wonderful—rice, beans, maybe some salad and a tortilla. Every now and then there's a little cheese and some goodies from the garden. Actually, the vegetable garden we've started here is coming along more and more every week.

It's been a long time since I had any kind of a routine. Monday morning, for example, the first thing I have to do is go pick up two lathes, both of which we're going to repair and one of which we get to keep for fixing them both. That's typical of my work—finding equipment and resources, picking up shipments people have sent down, supervising instructors. Whatever it is, it begins at about 5:30 and the formal part of it ends around five in the afternoon, with the informal work often taking up the remainder of the waking hours. Sometimes, of course, we sit around and enjoy each other's company—particularly now, because one of my best friends from the U.S. is here, and so is my father. They're both part of a group from the southeastern U.S. who are helping to build a dining room and kitchen for the school. So I take time to chat with them. The work will get done—it's not going anywhere.

There are frustrations here. We're way underfunded. But we remember how far we've come in four years. Back then, we were in a little house in the middle of a dusty field with not a tree in sight, hauling our water in a fifty-five-gallon drum on a tractor. The mosquitos were so thick you could just cut them with a knife. Then we got this place and built the shop out back. Tools began to come in and more and more people started helping us. Now hardly a month or even a week goes by without a donation either small or large—it may be tools or money. What keeps us going is the knowledge that we're doing what we can and so are people all over Nicaragua. If it weren't for that, I wouldn't do this work because it wouldn't make sense.

Linda Roth

I first saw Linda Roth at a crowded vigil in front of the U.S. embassy in Managua. She was playing guitar and singing for the group of over five hundred international visitors, many of whom had come to celebrate the fifth anniversary of the revolution which faces so much hostility from their own country. This particular blazing hot morning, crowds and television cameras gave extra urgency to the gathering, but there has been such a vigil in front of the embassy every week since the U.S. invasion of Grenada in the fall of 1983. Who gathers? Members and friends of the Committee of U.S. Citizens Living in Nicaragua, an ad hoc group of missionaries and other religious, teachers, brigadistas, health workers, researchers—anyone from our country who is uncomfortable with our government's military and economic policies toward Nicaragua. The committee formed with a haste bordering on panic when the U.S. invaded Grenada, kept the press out, and still maintained broad domestic support for its action. It was born of the chilling recognition that, if a few hundred medical students on Grenada could provide the pretext for a military rescue mission, so could the estimated three thousand North Americans who have chosen to make Nicaragua their home. The committee has maintained an activist presence even while all its members hold down full-time jobs and worry about their own day-to-day survival. They are trying to reach the international press and U.S. embassy staff with the plea Linda sang that morning, an original folk song aptly called, "Don't Rescue Us."

Songwriting is one of the things Linda has taught herself to do well, but it isn't her profession, I discovered when we were introduced later. Educated in Latin America studies and later in ecology, she has been a journalist, teacher, and community organizer. Now she is teaching forestry and ecology at the University of Central America, the smaller of two higher educational facilities in Nicaragua. Through her changing careers and despite an undeniable wanderlust, several things have remained constant in her life: a desire both to live well and to choose work that benefits her community; a sense that her individual life can have profound political meaning; and a sense of justice that she remembers learning at her mother's side.

I guess I've traveled a pretty complicated path. My father was in the navy, so I grew up all over the States. I've moved around for so long that it would seem strange to me to stay in the same place for more than a few years. So when I came to Nicaragua in late 1981, knowing virtually no one, it wasn't my first time as a transplant.

Moving around had another effect. When my family moved from Washington, D.C., to San Francisco, we crossed the country by car and camped from the Midwest on out. That gave me a strong feeling for the importance of natural areas, and that feeling has lasted.

My parents have always shown a strong sense of justice, and their values took root by example. My mother read a good deal and shared with us the inspiring writings of Martin Luther King and others during the civil rights struggles of the sixties. On the navy base in San Francisco, our neighbors all warned my folks against sending their kids to the public school, citing its eighty percent enrollment of blacks and calling it "tough" and so on. We'd always attended public schools, so they visited Pelton, liked it, and ignored our neighbors. I'll always thank them for that, and feel sad for the kids who grow up learning to fear and to hate.

I can remember one particular incident, back in high school, that really opened me up to thinking critically about our country's international role. I grew up believing what I'd been taught—that the United States always won its wars and always defended democracy. But, in eleventh grade, I had one of these super teachers—the kind whose influence can last your whole lifetime. He gave us ten times the usual amount to read and to think about. One day, just once, he got us into a sociodrama. We were studying the Mexican War. We walked into the classroom and he drew a line down the middle. He said, "OK, you people on this side represent the U.S., and you others are the Mexicans. Now debate the war." So we got together and tried to plan out what to say. I landed on the U.S. side, and I simply could not find a way to justify what our country had done when I had to face up to the other side in such a direct way. Looking back, we could say we had won that war and expanded our territory. But that wasn't enough. I think that taught me to listen hard to the people of other countries to avoid the dangerous conception that "democracy" means "what the U.S. chooses to do."

In college, at Harvard-Radcliffe, I majored in the history and literature of Hispanic America, essentially a Latin American studies rogram. I took a number of ecology and other science courses too, but I didn't see a way to apply them at the time.

My college years coincided with the times of most heated student protest against the Vietnam war. In the context of the Harvard strike, I was confronted with some harsh realities about U.S. involvement in other parts of the world, including Latin America. I wound up learning about the number of battles that had been fought there against outside invaders, with the U.S. prominent among them, and the number of times the U.S. marines had been called into various countries on pretty flimsy excuses.

The U.S. would invade someplace and say that it was to rescue somebody or that it was for democracy. But when you see Nixon's warnings from the fifties about losing the Southeast Asian rubber and tin resources, and then read Eisenhower's explanation that we had to block the Vietnamese elections planned under the Geneva accords because intelligence reports were saying Ho Chi Minh was sure to win a free election, you begin to wonder about the altruism of the motivations. There was almost always some reason connected with access to resources in those past invasions. In Nicaragua, earlier North American involvements sought an alternative canal route using Lake Nicaragua and protection of lumber and mining interests.

After graduation, I went into bilingual teaching and eventually lived in Puerto Rico for a while. It was there that my interest in the environment was reawakened. There was a heated controversy over plans to build a port for supertankers. At the same time, agriculture had disintegrated to practically nothing because of irresponsible development of suburbs and factories, which too often wound up on the best farmland. Hotels were eating into the mangrove areas. Industries were polluting both coasts. And there were copper mining ventures planned in spite of threatened environmental and economic consequences. I felt strongly about these issues, but lacked a technical understanding, and that finally led me back to school. I wound up getting an M.S. at the Yale School of Forestry and Environmental Studies in 1979.

I returned to Boston and soon began working for the Suffolk County Cooperative Extension Service, running a program to test urban growers' soil for lead contamination. I loved that job; it combined public education, lab work, writing, research, and constructing compost piles with folks all over the city.

Then a classmate from forestry school sent me information about a position in my field at a university in Nicaragua. I wasn't anxious to leave the work I was doing, but I had to admit I was interested. I'd been following news of the literacy campaign and learned some historical background to the recent changes there from Nicaraguans who were living in Boston.

Nicaragua was appealing because its new government was putting an explicit priority on serving the poor majority. To teach at a university in a country working to obliterate poverty was a really intriguing idea. I think a lot of people who come here feel a similar pull: they've learned a skill, but many of the situations in which they could apply it are more harmful than constructive. Here, you can not only enjoy your work but enjoy what it's for.

My job here has included teaching forestry, ecology, and a course in basic map and aerial photo interpretation for field use in natural resource work.

I also work with a program training student teachers. Like much of the education here ever since the literacy campaign, it's modeled on the concept "each one teach one." As soon as you know something, there are a million opportunities to teach it to someone else, and to use it as well. University students learn to teach subjects they have excelled in under the guidance of a faculty member like me. There are some very dedicated, hardworking students in the program, and working with them is a joy.

Another aspect of my work here has been to prepare teaching materials. Books are scarce and expensive, despite increased national stress on education, so students count on their teachers to provide many of their texts. Aside from several shorter things, I wrote and illustrated a text for the map interpretation course which the university should be publishing soon.

Perhaps the most exciting aspect of my work is getting kids out into the field. Education here was traditionally pure theory, in preparation to be a "professional," which meant vegetating at a desk. Students weren't encouraged to investigate anything on their own or even to trust their own observations, much less scuff their shoes or dirty their hands. So here they were, third- or fourth-year ecology students, and many of them had never been on a field trip in any class. The new education here stresses field practice, which suits me just fine—so I quickly got a reputation....I'll never forget one young woman staring anxiously down a path into a rain forest and whispering to her companions, "Look where Lin is taking us *now....*" As students do field work and research projects, you can see their self-confidence growing and their studies coming to life.

I've been free here to pack my students into a bus and take them anywhere I choose and go poking around in the woods. And as far as my own experience here, I can't think of a single situation where I haven't felt as free as people are in the U.S. There are combat areas where I'm sure I wouldn't be allowed to go. But I've had no problems in anything I've tried to do.

I feel safer in Managua than in my old neighborhood in Boston: I'll walk around alone after dark, hitchhike or give rides to strangers much more readily here, it's sad to admit. This sense of a foreigner's safety doesn't stem from having a poor majority subjected to a repressive police state, as it might in some other countries. Nicaragua is in a state of emergency, and that's a phrase that inspires images of curfews, limits on mobility, fear. But that's not what it's like here. Political parties of all stripes operate freely, as they can't in Guatemala. There is no curfew, as there is in Chile. There are no death squads, as there are in El Salvador.

I've been asked for identification a number of times by immigration authorities, as have most foreigners. But I've never been harassed or frightened in any way. I bet everyone's told you this—the police are nice! The army and the police force are explicitly schooled not to be repressive bodies like Somoza's hated National Guard was; they're not here to push people around.

The one "confrontation" I've had with the police here was actually pretty amusing. I got stopped for crossing a solid line in a merge lane. The policeman was extremely courteous and told me at great length that I had to be more careful. That same week, it seemed that every driver

I knew had a similar experience. Then I found out why: the traffic police were having these in-service trainings to brush up on the laws, emphasizing a particular statute each week. That week, it was solid lines.

This is not to say that individual abuses never occur, but that the system works to discourage them. A European woman told a friend of mine this story: She was walking through what's left of "downtown" Managua when a young soldier made a lewd comment at her. She shouted in Spanish, "Have a little respect." At that, the guy took his rifle—I've never seen behavior like this here—and cocked it. The woman kept walking, and of course nothing happened, but when she reported the incident to a passing police patrol, they went back and gave the soldier a citation and some strong words. That ending would have been inconceivable six years ago!

Bribery's another traditional abuse that's pretty well eradicated now. When I was getting ready to come here, I met with a mixed group of North American and Nicaraguan educators. One person asked a question about getting through customs coming into the country, and someone from the U.S. who hadn't been here said, "Don't worry, just slip them a few cordobas"—at which all the Nicaraguans stepped back and stared, wide-eyed, completely shocked. Their response was, "Don't even think about it. You would be arrested and so would the person accepting the bribe." That's a fairly major change in a few years.

A lot of things have been turned around that dramatically. The literacy campaign alone was an incredible feat and an obvious prerequisite for democratic participation. The agrarian reform has given thousands of campesino families access to land and credit. The vaccination programs have eradicated polio and controlled malaria. The achievements of this revolution are somewhere between impressive and miraculous: housing, adult education, preschool, health care, and extension of services such as running water, electricity, communications, roads. These things have really been felt by the majority of Nicaraguans, and I see wide support for the FSLN because people see how consistently it is fulfilling the program it set out for itself twenty years ago.

Still, things are not easy here. Denials of foreign credit and attacks on cash-crop harvests have meant that foreign exchange is scarce. So there are scarcities of material goods, particularly imported ones. Hoarding and speculation aggravate matters. One month, it will be hard to find toilet paper or soap; another month, light bulbs are nowhere to be found. Some people complain, but the biggest complainers have left. In general, the dependability of the distribution system keeps people's confidence up. Also, most folks are keenly aware of the roots of the problem. Daily, they see photos of burned-down grain silos, boats mining their harbors, mortared shells of trucks on the roadside. They also hear the market vendor say there's no soap, and they see her pull out a bar to sell for three times the legal price. It doesn't take an economist to see what's going on.

Of course, there are also people who very much feel a threat to their interests in this revolution, people who made a good living off their ties with Somoza or his businesses or his army or the whole system of favoritism and corruption. There are people who want their old system back. Corruption was shot through this society for generations; it isn't going to disappear overnight.

Here's an example I see every day: copying in school. I don't know if I'm a total innocent, but I never saw or heard of or imagined copying the whole time I was a university student in the States. Here, it's rife. You turn your back for a minute while exams are going on and everybody's copying from each other. Now, there may be a generous motivation behind sharing one's work sometimes. But this is sad, because it reflects a total lack of confidence in one's own work, one's own mind. The tradition here is that you get ahead by being somebody's friend. And interestingly, people's sense of academic ethics and their reluctance to copy seems in direct proportion to their "Sandinismo."

The school system here during the Somoza era reinforced people's sense of hopelessness and inferiority. People used to buy diplomas all the time. The teaching often consisted of a teacher rattling stuff off and the students copying it down verbatim, partly because there were hardly any books to be had. Somoza brought a lot of Cadillacs and Mercedes to Nicaragua, but he wasn't much for books. A customs worker from those days told me that printed matter being brought in had to be examined page by page in case it contained anything "Marxist"; evidently not many people bothered to import books.

Unfortunately, many people here have been through an educational system that has dulled them, made them stop asking questions, undermined their trust in themselves. Now, with kids starting school earlier and being exposed to much broader educational influences, there is more encouragement for them to be open-minded. People growing up now are going to be really different.

One exciting project going on in our department now is a seminar created to give the student teachers a better understanding of scientific thinking: What's research? What do we mean by scientific method? At first, I thought the students might think the whole thing was too theoretical or just boring, but, boy, was I wrong! They were fascinated and have really taken part.

Now, a course like that—to teach people about thinking for themselves—is not something a really repressive government would greet with enthusiasm. The image in the States seems to be that Nicaraguans are being propagandized into not thinking. But my experience is quite the opposite, and I think it reflects how little the Sandinistas have to fear.

One of the biggest changes in the academic climate is the emphasis that's being put on practical education: labs, field trips, student gardening endeavors, even science research fairs emphasizing useful projects. My initial reaction to the utilitarian thrust was cautious. We're taught a lot about science being "objective" and often interpret this to mean "useless." At the universities I attended in the States, people tended to devise elegant experiments and to conduct them in the most pleasant tropical islands they could find, even if the experiment was figuring out the number of angels that can dance on the head of a pin. But I've realized here the need for basic, objective science to be oriented toward solving real problems. When you teach in a place like this, you gain a feeling of responsibility for what you're teaching. You're serving people whose first priority is getting their country off the ground, getting people fed.

There are a lot of cooperative projects going on between government agencies and the universities. In the School of Ecology and Natural Resources, we have coordinated volunteer student projects with the Institute for Natural Resources and the Environment in areas like reforestation and wildlife management. Students are helping in the creation of national parks. They are doing forest inventories. There are projects in protection of endangered species, like the turtles on the coast. There are windbreak and other erosion-control projects. The way it often works is that the institute will provide transportation and materials and maybe pay for meals, and we provide student labor. The students get hands-on experience in their field and enjoy the outing, and everybody benefits.

Like many foreigners here, I made it a point to observe the Nicaraguan elections in November of 1984. I don't think it's necessary to belabor the point that they were valid—journalists, church people, jurists, legislators from all over have concurred that the process was impeccable. Watching them would have been pretty humdrum if I hadn't asked people a lot about previous elections for comparison. Just to illustrate the change from the prerevolutionary "elections," when Somoza's gang would ply voters with rum and drive them in truckloads from poll to poll to cast transparent ballots, here's a story that typifies the 1984 election. At one polling station I visited, a middle-aged woman was properly instructed to "Go into the voting booth and put your X under the flag of the party of your choice." She either misunderstood or thought she was still in the old days, because she slapped her finger down on the FSLN flag on the sample ballot and said loudly, "This one." Well, I was the only one at the registration table who saw where her finger was pointed. Everyone else covered his eyes and wheeled around in the opposite direction shouting, "NO, no, no—go into the booth."

What Reagan is saying about Nicaragua being a totalitarian country is simply not grounded in fact. Every time I read the news weeklies or the speeches by administration spokespeople, I worry for the future of democracy in *our* country, if an informed populace has anything to do with that. The line they're putting out provides a journalistic textbook example of what not to do in critical analysis. The different forms of misinformation are mind-boggling. There are the plain and simple lies. There are the more subtle cases of insinuation. And there are projections like crazy. Reagan says Nicaragua is militaristic while he's got his battleships surrounding this country and supersonic spy planes flying overhead, he's ordered endless maneuvers on its borders, he's built airstrips all over Honduras, he's mined Nicaraguan harbors, and he's paid terrorist bands that have already killed thousands of people. There's no comparison between those offensive actions and Nicaragua's legitimate self-defense.

The reporting of Nicaraguan attitudes toward our country in the U.S. press increases ignorance. One ad for a TV documentary in the States showed an image of a young girl behind a cyclone fence, which I guess is supposed to be charged with some kind of symbolism, with the heading, "Why does this girl hate you?" Perhaps they were referring to the passage in the Sandinista hymn about the Yankee oppressor. But that passage must be seen in context. Nicaraguans have lived through a history of U.S. intervention. During the time of Sandino, their country was actually occupied by our marines. Right now, "Yankee" money is killing their brothers and sisters. And still, there is a wide ability to differentiate between a given administration and our people, and an almost unfair reluctance to hold us responsible for our government's actions. No one here has ever called me or anyone I know a Yankee, and in fact, I think you'd be hard put to find another Latin American country whose people were as generally warm toward North Americans: people who rule themselves don't seem to bottle up resentments.

To understand the debate about whether there is freedom and democracy in Nicaragua, you have to look at specifics and not just argue on an abstract level. Take the issue of censorship. There is a certain amount, though nothing approaching the situation in Somoza's time. The government has the legal right to censor strategic military information and unverified claims about shortages. You can't publish things that clearly have dangerous consequences, like claiming falsely that there's going to be a shortage of some commodity so that people will panic and hoard, which the opposition press was doing for a while. It's analogous to yelling "fire" in a crowded theatre, which is not even protected speech in the U.S. because it can cause a lot of harm. There are scarcities of food here. If some people hoard or speculate, others go hungry. But in spite of those restrictions, the opposition paper is still pretty radical and at times inflammatory.

Let me give you an example of the extent to which people can and do speak up. The biggest mouth in our department for a long time was a woman who was totally against the revolution. She's now left the country. But the things she could say in public came awfully close to treason in wartime, in my opinion. I remember her saying, in front of a parent who came in to discuss a student's progress, "Some day the contras will come in and clean this place up." That mother just stared in awe, then said, "Don't you remember the war? Can you really be saying you want to go back to that?" Her answer was, "We're already living in a war of hunger." Now, this was a woman who had probably five times the income of the average Nicaraguan, who at least once a week took herself out to a fancy lunch and came back saying she was so stuffed she couldn't work. Yet she was much louder—and was able to be—than most of the people who support the revolution and who just quietly keep going.

In deciding what to believe with all these conflicting claims being made, I try to listen to all sides as much as possible. I don't write anybody off. But when there seems to be a conflict of interest going on, my bias is in favor of the rural poor who are the majority in Nicaragua. I try to ask myself, "If I were a campesino reading this claim, how would it sound?" When gas was rationed, for example, a lot of city folk screamed, even though the ration was pretty ample and there are buses and taxis available in the cities. Then a friend of mine in agriculture told me, "In the countryside where I work people couldn't care *less* about gasoline rations. They *walk* their ten miles every day, and they've been in a car maybe twice in their lives. The rationing may mean some day they'll have the use of a tractor—that's fine with them."

In all this hardship, I have great admiration for the Nicaraguan people, and especially for how hard they're willing to work. Students come to seminars during vacations; they volunteer for work brigades; they work eight hours and then come to school at night and do projects on weekends. I also admire the physical resourcefulness and the care with which people use resources here. Nothing seems to be wasted.

A third thing I notice is the political maturity of the people. People in the States have asked me if Bolivia was in South or Central America. I don't think you'll find too many Nicaraguans—even people who have just learned to read—who don't know where the countries are and something of their history and their relations with other countries.

But I've also been brought close to the tragedy here. The war has wrought unspeakable losses. And, next semester I'll have fewer students because many of the guys will be going off to the army. It's hard, knowing the possibilities. A few months ago, a wonderful student of mine lost her brother, a sweet, studious kid who'd done really well at work and school.... When the word would get out that someone was being mobilized, my first thought used to be "Aren't you going to try to get out of it?"—the way people I knew in college reacted to the draft. But this isn't an intervention in a distant conflict like our country's involvement in Vietnam; these kids are literally going to defend themselves, their families, their country, and the alternative is fresh in their minds. So most go, I wouldn't say enthusiastically, but willingly, bravely.

A lot of the wooded areas where I'd like to study and work are now too dangerous: most of the pine areas, rain forest, and a beautiful mangrove area near the northern border where we began a project, but now there's no way. I took a field trip in 1984 to an area that was supposedly free of contra activity. During the trip, I got into a long conversation with a campesino hired to work on a reforestation project. He was enormously knowledgeable, as most campesinos are, and very articulate. People like that make me feel embarrassed to call myself an ecologist, because they have such detailed knowledge of this and that plant, when it flowers and what it's doing and what eats it. Anyway, we had a wonderful talk as we rode together in the back of this truck. Two days later, the same truck was attacked by contras and he was kidnapped. Fortunately, he was able to escape during a later skirmish and make it back home. But that's how it is.

A few months later, a close associate of his was murdered, a guy who had been real nice to me and the students. None of us will forget that.

Right now, in Managua, it is almost totally safe. Perhaps deceptively safe. But it feels somewhat self-indulgent sitting around thinking about the danger, when people in other areas are suffering daily losses. What would I do if the invasion escalated somehow? It's hard to tell in advance what one should do. But after all this time, my first impulse wouldn't be to seek "escape" or "rescue" and leave dear friends here to face it alone. There wouldn't be any consolation in that.

Judy Butler

One of the enduring adages contributed to our culture by the activists of the 1960s is: "The personal is the political." Our daily lives—what we consume, the values our work supports, our alliances, the issues on which we speak out—these are as significant as the vote we cast in determining the nature of the world around us. Of all the North Americans I spoke with in Nicaragua, Judy Butler is one of the clearest illustrations of that principle. She remembers having a social conscience even as a child, but spent years as an adult discovering ways to bring her work into closer harmony with her beliefs. From a background in design and advertising and a high-powered career in New York, Judy moved into political journalism and scholarship on Latin America. As a writer and editor for NACLA Report on the Americas, a journal published by the North American Congress on Latin America, she studied the Nicaraguan insurrection and made her first of many trips there. When NACLA began offering tours of the new Nicaragua, Judy led them. In 1983, she accepted an invitation to edit a magazine for the Center for Investigation and Documentation of the Atlantic Coast, a research institution funded by the Nicaraguan educational system and numerous international agencies. This has turned out to be one of the many projects that keep her moving around the country.

Judy Butler is an admitted workaholic who tends to see even the most personal questions in political terms; her career path has been in pursuit of effectiveness in social change, not money or glory or comfort. Even to relax, she favors conversation and cultural events with political overtones. While such a person may seem like an anomaly to those of us, this writer included, who are sitting fat and happy in the United States, my overwhelming impression of Judy was of a woman who lives her politics because doing so brings her deep fulfillment.

When she is in Managua, Judy resides in a bright, comfortable cooperative house with a number of other academics from the U.S. I met her there, in a living room filled with greenery, for what was intended to be a quick, early-morning interview. We sat down with mugs of coffee at 7:30. For every question, she had an abundance of historical detail, analysis, and examples—and, with prodding, she would return to the personal side of her stories as well. Around ten o'clock, having scratched the surface of half the topics my heart was set on discussing, she stopped to offer me a snack of tortillas and peanut butter. Finally, pushing two in the afternoon, Judy ran out the door with apologies for not having more time. The following offering is a doomed but well-meant attempt to do justice to the complexity of the Nicaraguan situation and the equal complexity of Judy Butler.

I was born in 1940, in a working-class district of downtown Los Angeles. We moved to Lake Arrowhead, a mountain resort town, when I was ten, and that place had a very strong effect on how I saw the world. It revolved around the very wealthy movie stars and retired people who lived there or came up on vacation, and the rest of the people, who lived off the tourism. Growing up there, I got my first sense of class difference.

I think in some respects I became politicized then. I'm fascinated by how that happens—in my case, with no role models, no teachers or mentors. Why would a child of the fifties, and a woman particularly, growing up in a conservative community end up being involved in progressive politics, and in Latin America?

My high-school years in Arrowhead were during the McCarthy period, and I'm sure much of my perspective developed as a reaction to that atmosphere. The prevailing attitude seemed to be that communists eat babies for breakfast.

I was an interior design major in college. My interest had been in designing furniture and fabrics, but what they had us doing was decorating people's homes. In my senior year, I began gravitating toward philosophy and politics, and was having more and more trouble reconciling my values with my studies. One morning, I woke up and said, "Judy, you are about to go out into the world and spend twenty thousand dollars of somebody else's money to design their house. They have to live in it, and you can walk away. What kind of crazy notion is that?" I never went back.

I got married and came to New York about twenty years ago. I worked as an advertising director, with a pretty high-powered lifestyle. My husband and I were both involved in the civil rights movement and in active opposition to the war in Vietnam.

Most of the time during those years in New York, there was a big gulf between my workday life and my political life. But then one particular experience led me to rethink that schizophrenic existence. By 1973, my husband and I had separated, and an Argentine friend invited me to visit his country. It was a very interesting period for Argentina, when Juan Peron was about to return after almost twenty years of exile. I did some research before my trip and was struck by the dearth of useful journalistic information on the country. Some called Peron a communist, others a fascist, but no one really explained the incredible popularity of peronismo after all those years.

After my visit, I read a passable article by a journalist who had spent two months down there. I remember putting the magazine down and thinking, "Judy, I bet if you'd gone there for two months you could have written something just as good." I promptly went back to school at Boston University in Latin American studies and journalism. In September of that same year, a coup deposed the progressive government of Salvador Allende in Chile, and I became active in a solidarity committee in Boston.

I remember having a very clear vision of what I would do after school, and I remember it well because it was so wrong. My idea was that what the world really needed was a good Latin American journalist, so I was going to get a job on a newspaper. The thing that didn't occur to me until a little later was that what we read about Latin America is inadequate for a number of deeper reasons than just a shortage of good journalists.

First, most people in the United States don't think Latin America has any relation to them. As a child in Los Angeles, I experienced Latin America as a second culture. The streets are named for Hispanic heroes; the architecture is colonial; and you can't find anything to eat that isn't made with tortillas and jalapeño peppers. I didn't realize how unique that was until I came to New York and saw that everyone looked to Europe as their second culture, even though New York has a huge Hispanic population.

A second problem in mainstream journalism covering Latin America is that the region is in the shape it's in largely due to the role the United States has played. Most newspapers—and most readers—don't want to hear much about that.

Fortunately, in 1976, I found *NACLA Report on the Americas*, a bimonthly journal put out by the North American Congress on Latin America, which is committed to just the kind of in-depth work I wanted to do. I joined their staff, and a couple of years later became editor. Finally, I had the luck to have my breadwinning, political life, and social life part of the same fabric.

In September 1978, NACLA did a special issue on Nicaragua. Just as it was about to come out, after months and months of research, there was an insurrection in Nicaragua which threw us into a last-minute frenzy. This wasn't the final uprising, but it did mobilize a lot of Nicaraguans, and it brought international attention to the situation of that country.

The previous month, the Sandinistas had taken over the National Palace, which forced Somoza to release a number of prisoners. Until then, he had been busy saying that the Sandinistas had no following, but, despite the threat of retaliation, people lined the highway to the Managua airport to cheer and wave at the release of these prisoners, who were then flown to Panama.

This event sparked the creation of a new solidarity movement in the United States, this time to pressure the Carter administration to end support to Somoza. Naturally I got involved. For one thing, continued support for the Somoza regime was just indefensible. For another, the Sandinistas had a certain romance, a certain audacity. They had articulate spokespeople. They had symbols like red and black kerchiefs. And they had what looked like a coherent program in favor of the poor, in a country that throughout its history has been organized around the interests of the wealthy. It's really in the best tradition of what the U.S. says it's about. So, not surprisingly, a strong solidarity movement sprang up in the months leading up to the overthrow of Somoza on July 19, 1979.

I finally visited Nicaragua in July of 1980, on a press tour, for the celebration of the revolution's first anniversary. There were half a million people standing out in the tropical sun to hear Daniel Ortega and Tomas Borge speak. It was absolutely amazing, the enthusiasm, and the sense of liberation.

Soon after that, NACLA decided to organize tours for its readers, and I took on the job of coordinating and leading them. It was a wonderful opportunity to travel around Nicaragua every six months or so to get a broad sense of what was happening and to keep track of change.

On my first tour, I got very interested in the Atlantic coast and its problems. My interest was sparked by a musicologist friend who told me about the Caribbean musical styles there, but I soon learned that the differences are far greater than that. The region, which is actually a province called Zelaya that takes up half the country, has six different ethnic groups and a history that sets it apart from the rest of Nicaragua.

That interest continued and, in 1983, I was invited to work for CIDCA, the Center for Research and Documentation of the Atlantic Coast, an autonomous Nicaraguan institute. They wanted help in creating a magazine, called *Wani*, about the coast, and developing other communications projects. NACLA granted me a leave of absence, so here I am.

I am every bit as much a workaholic as I seem, and I love it: the learning process, the participation, the work with other people. Thinking through problems that have to do with improving people's lives is as rich a thing as I can think of doing.

Here in Nicaragua, my lifestyle has fallen into place pretty simply. I live in a group household with other North American academics and scientists. For relaxation, I go to the beach or for a long walk or to the theatre. But I don't seem to have a lot of needs that aren't satisfied by what I do all day long.

It's been exciting to watch this revolutionary process evolve. It's not a completely clean slate, but it is a sharp break with the past. A revolution isn't just a change of top leaders; by definition, it's the overthrow of an entire power system. This leaves a temporary vacuum and tremendous power struggles, as happened in Mexico for decades. It's impossible to understand what's going on in Nicaragua today without recognizing that. It would have been suicidal for the movement that overthrew the Somoza dictatorship not to fight to quickly consolidate its power and its vision of the future.

I think you have to take this into account in judging events here, such as the controls on *La Prensa*. If anything, what's unique about the Sandinista revolution is that there are fewer restrictions than in any other similar situation, including right after the American revolution, or the

French. General Lafayette, a French constitutionalist, wrote to Thomas Jefferson that he was very concerned about what was happening in France after their revolution, and Jefferson wrote back, "We are not to expect to be translated from despotism to liberty in a feather bed."

There have been real, concrete changes here, and they have been in favor of the poor. In 1980, I visited a former Somocista country club that had been converted into a recreation center for the war orphans. That symbolizes the change as well as anything.

One of the greatest changes I've witnessed here is a tremendous uncorking of the people. There's no other word for it. You had, in 1979, a society that was largely peasant, illiterate, and living on the edge of survival. Among many of these people, there was an incredibly reduced sense of self. They would say outright, "We are just animals. Our opinion doesn't matter." Their oppression ran so deep that it had become a self-definition.

You can imagine, then, how difficult it was when the Sandinistas found they had a whole country in their lap. Apart from all the government positions that had to be filled, they also inherited the twenty-five percent of the country's economy that had been owned by Somoza and friends. On top of that, mass organizations were springing up in towns all over the country and needing leadership. I remember talking to farm workers in 1980 who were trying to organize unions, and they weren't quite clear on what a union was supposed to do. People had to start taking responsibility for the life of their country.

One thing that exploded their old bottled-in existence was the literacy crusade. I wasn't living here during that period, but I helped write a book on it afterward. [*And Also Teach Them to Read*, by Sheryl Hirschon with Judy Butler] A month after the triumph, when this place was nothing but rubble, the new government decided to teach everyone to read and write. They sent out volunteers, even to the remotest areas, to find out who could not read and who wanted to learn. Then sixty thousand high school and college kids from the cities spent five months in the countryside, living with the peasants, helping them work their land by day, and then, when everyone was exhausted at night, teaching them to read by kerosene lanterns. Not only did they reduce illiteracy from fifty percent to twelve percent in those five months, they also began teaching people to think, and teaching them to believe that their thoughts were valuable.

That outpouring of spirit was evident everywhere in Nicaragua for the first couple of years after 1979. The Centers for Popular Culture, created by the government, were flourishing. There were musicians and theatre troupes all over the place. Now, many of these artists are off fighting the war, and those who are still active in their communities are prime targets for the contras. As are health workers. As are teachers. So much positive effort has simply been trashed by this counterrevolution.

The contra strategy, it seems, is not to win hearts and minds, but to make things so awful that the population will decide the revolution offers nothing, and will therefore topple it, the way they toppled Somoza.

It's not a war between two armies, and it's for sure not some genuine liberation struggle by legitimate "freedom fighters." It's a grinding, horrible, ugly war in which the main contra targets are simply the people who bring the possibility of participation, of benefits, to the population. In addition to being sick and twisted, that's a stupid strategy. People here will never go back to being under the thumb of the Somocistas and the U.S.

Close friends of mine have been killed in this war. If I were living in the United States and so many people I knew were killed, I'd be devastated. It's still terrible, but here you're surrounded by so many people who have gone through that tragedy, and they've learned how to socialize their loss. I'll always remember this taxi driver, an old, gnarl-handed peasant. As I got out of the cab, he handed me a modest little leaflet commemorating the loss of his son, who had been killed in the insurrection a year earlier. Here was this father, too old to really understand the revolution and too fatalistic to let himself believe in it, but linked to it and to the future by his son. He was so proud of him. This spreading of the grief and turning it into something positive, this is how they keep going.

What is clear to all of us living here is that the administration is determined to defeat this revolution not only in a military sense, but also to defeat it as a model. And why? Well, if a poor country like Nicaragua can make real strides toward a new kind of democracy, can succeed in improving the lives of its poor majority, can really give arms to its people without the fear that they will turn them on the government itself, then how could the U.S. go on justifying its support for Pinochet in Chile, or for Guatemala or El Salvador? If Nicaragua can insist on its right to forge new relations with the U.S. that are based on respect, not subjugation to U.S. dictates, then what happens to U.S. traditional domination of the hemisphere, which has been going on since long before the Russian Revolution?

I won't dispute the fact that Nicaragua has a close relationship with Cuba. It's perfectly natural that Cuba and Nicaragua would be close. I also won't argue that the Soviet Union endorses social revolutions and has helped Nicaragua. But actually Mexico has been one of Nicaragua's biggest trading partners; does that make it a Mexican satellite? Nicaragua has no intention of being another Cuba; it only wants to be another Nicaragua from the one it's been for so long. To do that, it has learned lessons from Cuba, from Chile, from Africa, from the United States, and from its own history.

That's been true in Nicaragua's literacy campaign, in its electoral law, and in the autonomy project for the peoples of the Atlantic coast, a process which could end up ranking among the most seminal projects of this revolution. Since the coast is what I came down here to study and to write about, let me give you some background on it from my perspective.

Many people in the U.S. think the entire population of the Atlantic coast is Miskito Indian. In fact, a 1981 census showed 180,000 mestizos (mixed Spanish and Indian), 67,000 Miskitos, 5000-6000 Sumu Indians,

700 Rama, about 1500 Garifonos, who are black Carib Indians, and 27,000 English-speaking Creoles (Afro-European mixtures).

The problems aren't just between the Miskitos and the Sandinistas, but between the two halves of Nicaragua, and they began with conflicts between the two colonial powers more than three centuries ago. The British, who dominated the Caribbean region, gave the Miskitos arms to fight the Spanish, who colonized the Pacific side of Nicaragua. The goal of the Miskitos was to keep from getting exterminated. The goal of the British was to let the Indians and the Spanish fight it out while they kept control of a profitable Caribbean trade.

With U.S. help, the British were finally displaced in 1893, more than seventy years after Nicaraguan independence from Spain. American companies had already begun to move into the Atlantic coast in large numbers. Over the years, they mined the gold and silver, created banana plantations, ravaged the forests of hardwoods, and cleaned the waters of shrimp and lobsters. It was all for export. Nothing, nothing was reinvested in the region. When the resources ran out, the companies would tear up their railroad ties and leave.

Somoza never paid much attention to the Atlantic coast, so the people's traditional hatred of the "Spanish," as they still call those on the Pacific side, didn't change much one way or the other as a result of the dictatorship. All the schools and health centers had been built by missionary churches, especially the Moravian Church based in the U.S. Because of the missionaries and other paternalistic programs like the Alliance for Progress, the Americans appeared as benefactors, a fact which obscured the long-term damage the U.S. companies were doing.

The insurrection that overthrew Somoza took place almost exclusively in the Pacific, so the Sandinistas knew very little about the coastal peoples, although their 1969 program had pledged to end the discrimination and margination that had plagued this impoverished region. After the triumph, they came to the coast, full of ambitious plans to incorporate the population into the changes they were making, assuming that everybody would love the revolution. Well, it didn't happen that way.

It would take volumes to give fair treatment to the conflicts that began to grow in the first couple of years. On the Sandinista side was a lack of analysis of the indigenous question, racist attitudes on the part of some young FSLN cadre who went to the coast to work, and the genuine fear of a separatist movement which could be easily manipulated by the U.S. On the indigenous side, it had to do with the immaturity and impatience of some leaders and the pure opportunism of others such as Steadman Fagoth, who later became a really vicious contra leader. There was also a generalized skepticism that this was just "one more 'Spanish' government," and every flaw in Sandinista practice was seen as proof of this.

Into that volatile mix must be added some other important factors. There were the conservative Protestant churches, which preached the U.S. line that the Sandinistas were "communist-atheists." Then there were language problems which meant the Sandinistas couldn't communicate directly with most people and had to rely on Spanish-speaking Indians who sometimes represented only their own interests. In particular, this was true of Fagoth, a very charismatic Miskito leader who, it turned out, had been an informer for Somoza during the 1970s. And finally, as tensions were reaching a peak, there was Reagan, who came into power vowing to "roll back" the Sandinista revolution.

With some nervousness, the government gave its support to MISURASATA, an organization of Miskito, Sumu, and Rama that was formed in 1979. It soon exploded into a very militant mass organization dominated by the largest and most sophisticated group, the Miskitos. While the government and MISURASATA worked together on a number of projects, such as the literacy crusade in native languages, the organization soon became the focal point for tensions between the indigenous people and the Sandinistas.

By September 1981, the government had withdrawn recognition of MISURASATA, convinced that it was organizing against the revolution itself. Fagoth and a number of other leaders had been arrested months earlier on suspicion of planning a separatist attempt. When he was released in May, Fagoth had promptly gone to Honduras and joined the contras. Several months later, another leader, Brooklyn Rivera, followed him.

That following year was the lowest point in relations between the Sandinistas and the coast peoples, particularly the Miskitos. Still believing in Fagoth, they were furious and frightened by the Sandinistas, and he helped that by broadcasting malicious lies back across the border over the contra radio transmitter. By December 1981, an armed band put together by Fagoth had killed sixty Sandinista soldiers and Miskito civilians along the river border with Honduras. That was what led to the well-known decision to evacuate all the communities from the Coco River.

In order to get to the bottom of all the conflicting reports about human rights violations on the coast, CIDCA did its own detailed study in 1984. What emerged was a picture that, yes, there have been human rights abuses, but nothing that remotely justifies Reagan's accusations of genocide.

Most of the abuses we documented happened in early- to mid-1982, when the contras were trying to set up internal bases. Nicaraguans were really tense at this point, because it had just come out that Reagan had given the contras nineteen million dollars, and a state of emergency had been put into effect. Soldiers were being sent to the Atlantic coast who were green recruits, many with stereotypical racial baggage, including a new one which was that all Miskitos supported the counterrevolution. With all these frightened soldiers fighting in swamps up to their shoulders, among a people they didn't understand and couldn't communicate with, it's amazing that there weren't more abuses.

What was clear was that the abuses that took place did not reflect policy. Any time an abuse was discovered and it was known who was responsible, that soldier was punished. Everyone we interviewed said that mistreatment had virtually stopped by the end of 1982, which in fact coincides with the setting up of regional government structures on the coast and stricter military accountability.

Americas Watch, which monitors human rights in Latin America, came out with a report about the coast in April 1984, the same time as ours. The parallels between the two were a relief to me, because there are real problems with language and cultural barriers—people telling you what they think you want to hear, that sort of thing. Also, we had heard a number of stories that had come in over contra radio and had somehow gotten incorporated into people's vision of reality, but when we tried to follow them up they led nowhere.

The wounds of the coast are slowly healing. In 1983, the government gave amnesty to almost all the Miskito prisoners charged with counterrevolutionary activity. Miskitos have formed a new organization, MISATAN, which, among other things, is helping to repatriate Miskitos who have fled or were kidnapped to Honduras or Costa Rica. Amid enormous confusion about whom to trust, increasing numbers of Miskitos are figuring out that the Sandinistas are not the devil incarnate, that they do care about the people.

One encouraging sign is the emergence of native leaders on the coast who, whether or not they're members of the Frente, are trusted by their constituents and are working with the revolutionary process. The most famous example is Ray Hooker, the Creole educator and guidance counselor from Bluefields who accepted the Frente's invitation to run as their candidate for National Assembly. Ray made the news because he was kidnapped by Brooklyn Rivera's group, MISURASATA, and held for most of the campaign period. The widespread respect for him and his family is probably what kept him alive. And he won the election—quite handily, in fact—three days after his release.

Finally, despite the war, there's an agreement in principle on autonomy for the region. A special statute will be written into the new constitution, based on extensive dialogue in the communities as to what issues people consider important, both politically and culturally. The Sandinistas seem to have realized that the real Nicaragua is multiethnic and multilingual, and that those on the coast who have traditionally been second-class citizens will only begin to feel truly Nicaraguan when they have the opportunity and encouragement to develop according to their own cultural systems.

There are a lot of thorny questions remaining. How will regional power be shared among the various ethnic groups to assure equal representation and equal rights for all? The Sumus are very sensitive to this, because their history includes domination by the Miskitos who sold them as slaves during the colonial period.

The encouraging sign is that all these issues and more are now being discussed, and the people are being directly involved. The central government will continue to conduct foreign policy and national defense, as well as overall economic planning, but everything else is up for discussion. Autonomy is not a panacea, but it is a means by which, over time, historic problems can be resolved. It could also have a real impact on the rest of Latin America, which has not dealt with these issues very well.

You know, one of the many things I've learned down here is a healthy respect for the complexity of the issues, not only on the coast, which is incredibly complicated, but in the whole country. I just wish people back home could get a fair picture in the media of this experiment, but reporters all get to know what their editors want to hear. I know journalists who have even taken to saving copies of their telexes to show that what they wrote is not what got printed.

But it's not only the editors. Journalists, like all of us, come down here with a full set of baggage from their own life experiences. They bend over backwards to be skeptical of the revolution, but they're far less skeptical of our own government, and even less so of their own preconceptions. Journalistic skepticism is very valuable, but it can get unhealthy in this context because we already have such an ethnocentric view of Latin America.

Too many reporters and fact-finding delegations come down here and take what I call the reverse Potemkin Village tour. They visit the Democratic Coordinadora, the coalition of opposition parties that boycotted the elections; they talk to the Catholic hierarchy; they talk to *La Prensa*. Those people represent the sectors of society journalists are used to relating to, and they're highly visible opponents of the revolution. Journalists and congressional delegations seldom go out into the countryside, where the majority of the people live, to see what they think. That results in a portrait of Nicaragua that is about as broad as the one you would get of the United States by spending two days in New York. I think people up there have to start asking themselves why we, and all the thousands upon thousands of church groups, solidarity tours, and individuals who have come down here, go back with an entirely different impression. Can we really all be dupes of a communist conspiracy?

Life can be hard down here sometimes for someone from the States. Particularly with Reagan's economic and military war, there are lots of shortages, and none of the amenities we're used to. But so what if there's no chocolate? My treat now is the people. There is something about their openness and warmth, their gentleness combined with combativeness, that's very special.

The Sandinistas especially are a remarkably intelligent group of people, quite creative and dedicated. Within the limited options available, they're really trying to do the best they can. It's a young government, run by young people, none of whom were ever trained for it. They fumble a lot, and sometimes their decisions turn out to be wrong. But all they ask is the right to make their mistakes and to be given the space to correct them in peace.

The Romero Family

The intertwined stories of Frances, Marco, and Edgar Romero show us a family that stays strongly united across many miles and enormous changes. Frances and Marco brought up their two children in a politically active household, working hard with the civil rights movement and the United Farmworkers in Seattle during their childhood. And their son, Edgar, in turn has inspired them, sparking their interest in Nicaragua with his first visit. As we spoke on the patio of their spacious house on the outskirts of Managua, the closeness of this family was easy to see; their individual accounts of their lives turned repeatedly into warm, collective reminiscences.

The Romeros typify a new kind of antiwar activist who is becoming visible in the movement against U.S. policy in Central America. They are middle-class people who were prominent members of their community until they decided, as a family, to transplant themselves to Nicaragua. They are successful and well-educated. Marco was an engineer with Boeing for twenty-two years before taking an early retirement and signing on with Aeronica, the Nicaraguan airline. Frances, who began as a baby-boom mother with neither outside work nor interest in politics, now has a master's degree and a fulfilling career as an educational consultant. And Edgar, with an advanced degree in mathematics from MIT, could command a high salary in industry, but he is finding greater rewards teaching very basic math at Nicaragua's national university. Theirs is the economic and social level from which folk wisdom maintains that no progressive activists will emerge. "Before we came to Nicaragua, we were living quite well," Frances says with an air of understatement. But their affluent life did not blind them to the injustices experienced by those around them, and they have been willing to sacrifice some measure of comfort and leisure to do what they can for others.

Even in Managua, a visit to the Romero home evokes a bit of suburban Seattle. The bookshelves are well-stocked, the appliances are modern, the yard is big. Marco and Frances dress impeccably, and Edgar favors jeans and T-shirts. But this sense of being back in the States with staid Middle Americans evaporated when an unidentifiable, rodentlike creature about a foot long scuttled across the patio where we sat. I drew back. And Frances, without missing a beat, said drily, "It isn't ours."

Of all those who speak out in these pages, the Romeros are among the firmest in their commitment to remain in Nicaragua no matter how much hostilities—and dangers—may escalate. Yet they are also among the most conscientious in maintaining their connections with the United States. They collaborate on a newsletter which is mailed regularly to supporters in Seattle and to others who have met them on visits to Nicaragua. They frequently return to the States for speaking tours and to visit Edgar's brother who lives with his wife and children in Albuquerque. Despite their sharp criticism of their country's foreign policy, they have remained constructively engaged rather than alienated.

Marco Romero

I was born and raised in Puerto Rico, in a rather modest, middle-class family that didn't have much education. I studied business administration in Puerto Rico, but I never worked in that field. I was in the Second World War and the Korean War too. Then I went to school in the States on the G.I. Bill. I graduated in 1950 in engineering, and worked ten years for Texaco.

Early in my career, I got the idea that I wanted to help the poor in Latin America, so I went to work for an oil company in Venezuela. I guess my desire was rather delicately framed. We thought that, by going down there, we would be living in the country with the people. But, as it turned out, we lived in oil production camps. It turned out to be a very challenging, interesting professional life, but with very little contact with the local environment. It was like living in a small town in Texas.

In those days, we didn't have the benefit of the orientation of the younger generation today. Younger people are always thinking about what they want to do with their lives. Back then, we were very scared. We were taught: go to school, learn something, go to work, do it right, and that's the game.

Growing up, I really didn't understand much about politics. I did know about revolutions in Latin America because my parents were Colombian and my grandfather had died as part of the army in that country's civil war.

I also understood the reality of colonialism in Puerto Rico, of course. In those days, the island was essentially a sugar cane farm for the U.S.

It operated five to seven months every year. The other months, there was no work anywhere. That was the basic economic dynamic of the country. I understood that, and I understood the relationship between that and the fact that only one in four school-age children in Puerto Rico went to school in those days. But in many respects I stayed naive for quite a few years.

My wife and I really had our political awakening in the 1960s, when there was such widespread concern about social problems and the Vietnam War. We had come back from Venezuela and were living in Seattle. One of the things that deepened our understanding was working with the United Farm Workers, doing fundraising and a little bit of everything to help them with their boycott. I was thirty-three or thirty-four at the time. What I came to realize is that the problem of migrant workers is basically a problem of racial discrimination in the service of economic exploitation. I know that's a fact because people become so offended when it's mentioned.

My politics in general have become very progressive, very liberal. Through my years at Boeing, my values kept changing, my position shifted, but at the same time I had obligations to my family, so I stayed with the company. Of course, I felt some conflict. But, to be fair to Boeing, it's a businesslike company where there is not much pressure on employees for what they do on the outside, like in politics. The vast majority of people working there are conservative because it's in their self-interest to be and because they don't know enough about the world. But there are also a number of progressives there, and they participate quite openly in politics.

A few years ago, I found out that I had intestinal cancer, and I had some fairly major surgery. They took out a big section of my intestine. At that point, I took an early retirement from Boeing and began asking some serious questions about what I wanted to do with the rest of my life. At that point, our son had been talking about living and working in Nicaragua, and he convinced us to come down and check the place out. As you can see, we were favorably impressed.

When I came here, it was to teach engineering at the University of Central America. But, when I arrived, my papers were screened and the immigration people said, "Oh, you've been an airplane man for twenty-two years. You really ought to come and work at Aeronica, the national airline." I said, "But I have this commitment to teach." But they convinced me that I should do that half-time. So I'm juggling the two jobs. I've worked harder here than ever before in my life, and I've lost quite a few ounces as a result. But the pressure isn't too hard to handle. It's like any organization: they keep the pressure up, and you do what you can.

About a year and a half ago, I was asked to become the head of a small technical group at the airline, and I made the mistake of accepting it. Mainly we work on improving the systems for planning and controlling the maintenance of the airplanes, and on studies of particular maintenance problems, some of which are very hairy. We have airplanes up to forty years old, mostly from the U.S. Our main commercial planes are two Boeing jets, each of which has flown over fifty thousand hours.

We also have a nice collection of small airplanes, some modern and some older, including three C-46s, which are really old planes. I found out something very interesting about these airplanes. We couldn't find any records for them because, back when the airline was not only controlled but mostly owned by General Somoza himself, he had sold these airplanes to I don't know whom from the States. Later, they fell into the hands of the U.S. drug control administration because they had been involved in the drug business. They were impounded. The way we got them back is that someone told Aeronica, "Look, those airplanes are sitting in Arizona in the desert someplace, rusting. Why don't you ask for them back?" Well, they did, during the final days of the Carter Administration, and someone in the administration said, "Just get them out of here fast and we won't look." That's how Aeronica got its planes back.

Anyway, this has just been another experience of learning something new, which I've done all along in my career. It's the same thing with the course I'm teaching at nights: I had to learn it myself, and now I can teach it. That's what an engineering education is about. In the thirty-five years I've been an engineer, I've never worked on anything that I had learned in school.

Of course, it isn't easy to run an airline under these economic conditions. The only way an airline can function is by really biting the bullet and facing up to the fact that we have to spend huge sums of money. And that money is getting scarcer and scarcer. The government makes it available when it's really needed to keep going. The things that are necessary for safety are done, of course. But many things that aren't absolutely indispensible are postponed until after the next coffee crop—or longer.

At the university, too, we feel the effects. In the engineering department, we're really rushing to develop a few thousand engineers. But there are serious problems in terms of the facilities. For the most part, there are no textbooks at the college level, so you write your own on the blackboard.

Then there are the mysterious events some of us have experienced down here. It's a well-known phenomenon that mail to the U.S. takes a very long time to reach its destination if it's mailed from Nicaragua, and almost as long if you give it to a returning traveler to mail at the Miami airport. I sent a letter to the Institute for Policy Studies, a think tank rather well known for its liberal views, around Christmas time, 1983. It was one of those "guaranteed delivery" overnight express letters, mailed by a friend from the Miami airport. And exactly half of it reached its destination.

Even before the administration's economic sanctions barred Aeronica from landing in the U.S., the airline had its share of unexplained problems. There have been seasons when travelers returning to the U.S. have reported harassment such as searching of their political literature, and Aeronica has had an awful problem with luggage being damaged in foreign airports.

Then, of course, there have been bigger problems like the contra incursions over Nicaragua with small planes. One, apparently trying to bomb the airport, was hit by some air defense; as it came crashing down, it really caught on fire big. One guy was seriously burned, and the airport building had to be completely redone inside because of smoke damage.

Although I work in Managua, I've managed to have a few adventures in the countryside. At one point, Edgar and I drove up to a gold mine a little northeast of Leon to help the mine managers put in a generator and lights. I did that because the young man who was in charge of the mine is a member of a family that has been extremely nice and good to us in every way, and when he asked for some help I realized I could save them a significant amount of money and a lot of trouble in coming up with the money to pay a consultant. The work itself was pretty straightforward, but the drive back down the mountain is one I'll never forget. For one thing, we went through a couple of tires. For another, we got a taste of Nicaraguan driving at its hairiest.

One interesting thing we learned was that the mine, which is a cooperative with twenty-eight members, pays its miners very nicely. The miners earn more than the manager, who is a nice young guy furnished by the mining ministry. But, even though they're doing well for themselves, they don't seem to have too much of a revolutionary consciousness yet. It's a very isolated part of the country, and the revolution hasn't touched them except for giving them a little help in organizing and financing the operation. And, in spite of those benefits, their attitude is anything but cooperative. They steal every eating utensil from the mess hall. It's amazing.

When it comes to small-time theft and things that are scarce I know many, many minor horror stories. At Leon University, in the lunchroom, you get your meal on a plastic plate with a glass but no utensils. You have to bring your own. Very rarely will you find toilet paper in the restrooms, even in fancy hotels. At the university, the professor brings in the chalk with his own personal eraser to every class because otherwise they would just walk off. At Aeronica there are five hundred employees, and there are days when no one can make any copies because there isn't any paper. I brought my own scissors from the states along with the stuff from my middle desk drawer, and no one has really stolen anything except everything that cuts: those scissors and two other pairs I bought locally.

Coming here from an organization like Boeing, I'm certainly aware of the difference. But you make up your mind that it has to be done. I didn't come all the way down here to be comfortable. I was really comfortable where we were.

On one hand, the Nicaraguans cope with all this really well. But we know there's a tremendous amount of psychosomatic trouble among the population. Everybody has headaches all the time. We even wrote an article for them about the minor drugs such as tranquilizers and even caffeine, because there's such reliance on them and so little awareness.

I've had many positive experiences, working with very fine young people who are really trying to pick themselves up by their bootstraps and take advantage of the opportunities given by the revolution. But I also find a lot of people like our secretary, who is an awful hypochondriac and she's going to have to figure out how to get over it on her own. I've given up trying to help her by holding her hand. But I know it's all the strains she's under: the strains of living in a poor country plus the strains of a machismo society plus the strains of the war situation. And still everybody is trying to advance, so now she's enrolling at the university.

Emotionally, all this difficulty has one major effect on me, as I think it does on a lot of Nicaraguans: it makes you more determined to stick it out.

But also, in order to cope with all this, I've had to cut down—or try to cut down—on my activities. I even like to take a nap after work these days. Back in Seattle, we were always up until after eleven, but now with all the heat and turmoil we find that ten o'clock or even nine is more like normal bedtime. When we first came here, we were very active with the Committee of U.S. Citizens, but we found that a meeting every week and the vigil on Thursday mornings was just too much, so we're leaving that to other folks.

Since I've been here in Nicaragua, one thing I've come to terms with is how much more serious the mood is than we first thought. I think we recognized the degree of poverty, but not what is behind it, part of which is lack of education, lack of exposure to ideas. It's not something that can be solved overnight. They talk about developing a new human being. Well, that's going to take a generation, at least. There's so much to be undone, so many centuries of exposure to bad examples.

Even without the U.S. making things more difficult, this little country has a tough task in building itself up. There's nothing here to build on. Sixty percent of the country still doesn't have running water at home. Sixty-seven percent doesn't have electricity. There is potential wealth, but in some areas it's never been developed and in other areas it's been overdeveloped until there's nothing left. Lake Managua has been so badly polluted that it's virtually dead. The forests have been depleted by clearcutting, much of it by U.S. corporations. On the Atlantic coast, there are no really significant towns or cities. They have to rebuild the land and pay some attention to the infrastructure before the country can be wealthy.

But it's possible. It's even possible for business to function quite well in this climate, as some people are proving by staying here and cooperating with the government. For instance, everyone around here knows the Nicaraguan businessman who runs the Toyota dealership and owns the rum and beer manufacturing and the sugar mill and runs banks in other countries. He's happy to work here. Business people are pragmatic enough that they're generally willing to work where they're allowed to make profits, which is the case here.

Another thing you learn living here is the number of countries that have reached out to help Nicaragua, and it's not just socialist countries. There are innumerable missions in Nicaragua. I just came back from talking to some Dutch people who are going to sell Nicaragua some used airplanes. Most of the Western European nations have been tremendously helpful— except England and, recently, West Germany, which have adopted the U.S. line. The Prime Minister of Sweden came here personally, and many of the nonaligned countries are supportive because Nicaragua is really trying to remain nonaligned.

Contrast this with what the U.S. has done. Long before the economic sanctions were declared, the Commerce Department had declared Nicaragua a high risk area, with the result that many insurance companies that cover marine shipments were no longer dealing with Nicaragua. And the Reagan administration has done its best to limit the availability of dollars here, like by applying pressure on international lending agencies not to make loans. See, a lot of countries that were helping Nicaragua, like Brazil and Venezuela, are in trouble with the U.S. over their own loans. So all the U.S. has to do is put a little squeeze on them and they come around.

Economically, of course, the war against the contras is absorbing a tremendous amount of the country's resources. The war waged by the contras is guided by U.S. intelligence. They go after economic targets. For example, they've destroyed the two largest sawmills in Nicaragua, so production of lumber has been down, and there's a critical housing shortage. So they're creating a real crunch.

In spite of all those problems, though, Nicaragua as recently as 1983 was the only country in Latin America that was a net importer of dollars. Based on what they've been able to keep together here, the leadership of this country is either a pretty bright bunch of young men or they have some awfully wise advisors. Even their foreign policy shows that. They have become a leader among the nonaligned countries, of which there are 110. They've been elected to the Security Council at the U.N. All things considered, we feel that we're in very good hands under this government.

Frances Romero

My father was a civil engineer and he worked on highways and railroads. So I was born in Oregon, but I lived in California, Oregon, Washington, Montana and Utah—all over the West, in small and big towns.

After the children were grown, I decided it was time to go back to school. To give you an idea how long it took me to get myself moving, when I finally graduated from the University of Washington, one of my friends congratulated me for condensing four years of knowledge into twenty years. Anyway, then I went on and got a master's degree from Antioch and began working in the mental health field.

I started out quite non-political. When Marco was in the Korean War, I felt very badly that he was gone, but I had no political consciousness about it. To me, it was just a rather tragic personal experience to have my husband taken away from me while I had a small baby. Even at the beginning of the Vietnam War, I didn't have much of an overall political analysis. But as it went on and on and on, I became more aware that the United States had gotten itself into something it couldn't get out of. Later, I saw that the U.S. never had any moral justification for being there in the first place. It was a matter of protecting economic interests—not really the interests of the American people—and it was manipulating the fear of communism in order to justify this.

The development of my politics has really been a rather slow process. When we returned to Seattle from Venezuela about twenty-five years ago, I was active with the League of Women Voters, and I became interested in the political process through that. Then Marco and I began working with the civil rights movement and with the United Farm Workers, and I became aware, again rather gradually, that a lot of people aren't able to really make it well within the system, either because of direct discrimination or because for one reason or another they're blocked from having the opportunities. Little by little, I have become aware of things I would not have believed if I had been exposed to them all at one time. When we've gone out with the United Farm Workers, I've seen the police acting toward some of the minorities in a way that they would never act toward me, absolutely bullying them.

Since my husband is from Puerto Rico and since we had lived in Venezuela, we had a lot of non-white friends when we settled in Seattle, and we were aware that they had as much to contribute as anyone else. Even before the civil rights movement started, we made the decision that, when we had a group of people over to our house, we wanted that group to be integrated. Many of the whites would remark that this was their first contact with a non-white person, and they were generally appreciative.

When the civil rights movement did come along in the sixties, we were very active. Then the United Farm Workers movement came along, and we were also active with that. Eventually, we became concerned with the situation in Central America. By that time, our son, Edgar, who was out of college, was beginning to talk about moving here to Nicaragua, and he came down here for a visit. Well, Marco was ready for an early retirement, so Edgar suggested that we come too and look the place over. We were very impressed with what we saw, so we chose to move here ourselves.

I suppose all the moving I did as a child made it easy to think about moving out of the United States as an adult. However, this move to Nicaragua was a lot easier than the move to Venezuela, partly because we've gotten to know the Latin American culture since then. But the other reason it's been easy is that I see so many positive things going on. When the country is so alive and active in improving itself, it's exciting to be here.

We've felt very welcome from the start. We have many Nicaraguan friends. In fact, we've been virtually adopted by some of the younger people.

When we arrived, I had some serious reservations about communist influence and wondered what restrictions there would be. I was impressed to find that, at least in practical terms, there were none at all. For a country that's just gone through a revolution, that's remarkable. And, as far as the question of Soviet or Cuban influence, it looks to me like the Nicaraguans are running the country on their own much more than I expected. They have advisers from all over, but they're determined that this is going to be their revolution.

Another thing that impressed me was the political awareness all the people had, regardless of their income or education. I had worked with lots of welfare clients in the U.S., and I had felt that many of them lacked education and knowledge. Here, I was amazed to see the vibrancy of the people. Even those who couldn't read or write very well could talk politics.

Another pleasant surprise for me was that there can be so many people in the Sandinista government who are really and truly dedicated people, who live on minimal salaries and work extremely long hours.

I work for the Ministry of Education at the School of Special Education in Managua—it's one big, rather disorganized facility for all the blind, deaf, and handicapped children.

My primary job is working with the teachers to show them basic techniques of behavior modification and a little about various ways of teaching small children. It has been real exciting to figure out simplified ways to get these concepts across; people are quite enthusiastic, and the ideas seem completely new to the country.

The teachers essentially have eleventh-grade training. Some now are going on and working toward their college degrees at night while they teach in the daytime. But the school itself is one of the nicer facilities in the country. They try to give the most needy people some of the better things. On the other hand, there are fourteen children per teacher, which is probably about twice what it should be when the kids have these special needs. There are quite a few behavioral problems, and the children are not very well sorted out in terms of their ability, so there is quite a load put on the teachers. I really admire what they're able to do.

It's disorganized enough that sometimes it's even a little bit difficult for me to pin down precisely all I'm doing there, but another thing I've started doing is being available to talk to parents about problems that they have with their children. This is wonderful work because these are ordinary Nicaraguans who don't have too much education or anything. I can give them a lot of support and information, as well as learning a whole lot from them. For example, I was chatting with the mother of a deaf little girl and she mentioned that she had taken her daughter to a doctor to see about a bump on her forehead. Well, the doctor made the mother feel the bump to see if it was hard or soft, if it moved, and so on. He wouldn't touch it. "Foreign doctors aren't like that," said the mother, "but Nicaraguan doctors think handicapped people are dirty."

When I started at the school, it took the other faculty members a while to get used to me, but the reason turned out to have nothing to do with me. There had been some problems between the faculty and the administration, so when I first started observing some of the classes, the teachers felt that I was coming from the higher ups, and they felt that they had to act "the proper way." But after a while they relaxed.

At this point, though, I really feel accepted. For instance, I went to a series of workshops in one of the poorer neighborhoods. I thought I'd get something to eat in a local restaurant, but one of my coworkers insisted that I come along with her to some friends' house for dinner, and they ended up feeding us lunch the next three days!

The teachers are lovely people. It was even their prodding that got me to take my first Nicaraguan bus ride, which I did today after two and a half years of living here. We went to a river outside of town with a bunch of the children, and the kids were much better than I was at pushing through the crowds the way you have to in order to get off at your stop. It was crowded, I will leave it at that. My arms and shoulders are going to be sore.

The whole school system here is lacking in textbooks and materials. Yesterday, at my school, the blind children ran out of paper to write on in braille. They do have some braille books, but even when there's writing paper around they have to write on both sides to economize, which makes it much harder to read. You wouldn't think they could run a school with so little.

A lot of the ideas I've had have ended up on the back burner because it's so hectic. I had been thinking of starting a shelter for battered children, but it will have to wait. However, I have managed to write a series of articles that I'll probably present to the teachers' union. They're on—well, not exactly women's liberation, but the equality of the sexes. I've observed, being around the teachers, who are mostly women, that a lot of them have serious problems with the machismo male down here.

What got me thinking was a book of Philip Slater's. He suggests that machismo develops because a mother has been deprived of the companionship of her husband and therefore she sees in her little boy the satisfaction her husband hasn't been able to give her. So there develops a very, very strong attachment between the mother and the son. That is passed on to the next generation; the son maintains his attachment to the mother and doesn't wind up having an attachment to his wife.

But in Nicaragua today, women's hopes here have already been raised, partly because they played such a strong role in the revolution and because this government is giving them opportunities. But it's still a struggle that they have to fight for themselves. With the rights of women, as with a lot of social issues in this country, the way I see it is that the revolution has opened the door for the people to fight for certain rights without fear of being shot or some other dire consequence, but all of these things still have to be worked out.

As a matter of fact, we've managed to set quite an example with our Nicaraguan friends. We find that the women are so used to serving the men that a lot of them don't realize it can be done any other way. Then they come here and see Marco go into the kitchen and get whatever he wants.

If we have a group over for dinner, the women don't serve the men. A few months back, some people from the office came over—four couples, I think—and each wife had a baby in her arms. When it came time to eat, I said to the men, "OK, the women are busy so you go in and fill up their plates and bring them out." Well, they walked into the kitchen and one man took a look and came right back out and he took the baby from his wife so she could dish up the food. She was starting to fill the plates, but I couldn't let it go so easily, so I looked at them and said, "You know, if you're not smart enough to dish up your own plate, you're not smart enough to eat." They laughed and eventually the men served the plates. Since I started this kind of thing, the wives have told me their husbands are helping them a little at home.

I may be a catalyst, but the women in Nicaragua are definitely ready for a change. Almost daily, I get into a conversation with some woman about that fact. It may be a woman in a marriage that is not going too well, but she'll say her mother is telling her to stick it out because of the children. So she'll want to have a long talk with me and get my feelings about that. Usually I say that you don't necessarily take the advice of your mother. Generally the mother stuck it out, so I ask, "Well, do you think your mother did the right thing? Do you want to live through the same life your mother did?" Most of them say no.

We've always felt safe in Managua, but the war still has an impact. Life is more hectic with all the shortages. Our food has become much more routine. There's less availability of everything except rice and beans. As I said, there is a tremendous shortage of things for the school. Last year it had five school buses; this year there are only three. This is a real hardship because these are children that are unable to get to school on their own. And there are never enough supplies. They desperately need clay, crayons, scissors, paper, just everything for the children. Even teachers are sometimes in short supply because they may have to be mobilized to help with the coffee harvest or to fight.

So far, we haven't been too worried about our own safety. We know that Americans in other parts of the country are taking greater risks, to say nothing of what the Nicaraguans have to put up with. Some of our friends up in Ocotal have been under attack. We do have our trench dug in case of an air-raid attack. But, in our daily lives, I think we're busy enough that we're not preoccupied with the danger.

We expect to stay here indefinitely. We sure hope that the U.S. government doesn't interfere with our plans by dropping a few bombs or something. But even if they did—we've discussed this, of course, and we feel we'd still stay in the event of an invasion. We would see it as our responsibility to keep people informed about what's going on. It's not only that we're concerned for Nicaragua. We also believe that what the U.S. is doing is harmful to the American people. We can't be doing something like this to a foreign country without it having detrimental effects on our own people: the cost of the arms, the impact on morale, and even the risk that a war could be ignited that would eventually reach the U.S. borders.

I come from the mainstream of America. I have never wanted for anything. I have sympathy for the groups that haven't made it in the U.S., but I personally identify with the mainstream. I feel that many people in the upper and middle classes in the U.S. need a lot of education in order to recognize what is being done in their names, and providing some of that education is part of my purpose in being here.

Edgar Romero

I have never been overly idealistic about the United States. I had an excellent U.S. history course from a guy who had an easygoing cynicism, and he never presented U.S. history as the march of great ideas or anything.

I'm sure my perspective was broadened by the fact that, in high school, I played on a baseball team in the black part of town. I can remember seeing referees make judgments that were pretty racist. And, more generally, I was growing up in a climate of social awareness. By my junior year in high school, I was going after school to meetings of the Black Power movement.

I majored in math at Amherst College in Massachusetts, a very isolated place. There was a lot of antiwar sentiment and agitation when I came there, during the Vietnam years. There was also a lot of frustration among students as to what could be done about it, there in the dead center of Massachusetts, as we used to call it. I was never really involved in politics there. I went to a few SDS meetings and decided there wasn't anything going on there that would make a difference.

Amherst has this field study program, so I took a year away from campus. I was interested in teaching, so I went back to the school I had attended in Washington and taught some courses there, and I also took courses myself at the University of Washington. That was quite a different experience because it's a big-city university, much more like a factory and without the niceties of Amherst. Most of the people are not intellectually motivated, but instead are motivated to find their part in the machine and get ahead. Add to that the fact that the political situation was drawing people out of the schools to demonstrations all the time. And the teaching was horrendous. If I had gone there instead of to Amherst, I probably would never have graduated because I would have rebelled against the whole system and become a real hot-headed radical. But, back at Amherst, I was able to pour my energy into doing something I felt would make a difference. This was in 1972, so the logical thing was the McGovern campaign, and I put a lot of energy into that. I loved it because I really felt I was seeing concrete results for my efforts.

I went immediately into a graduate program in mathematical logic at MIT. But I dropped out after a year and a half to find some work that was more in harmony with my values. A lot of Amherst graduates drop out of graduate school because they've gotten too rosy a picture of what academics is like. At Amherst, students are always being invited to lunch at the faculty club and sitting around being intellectual. Graduate schools are very different, more like factories. And at MIT, it hit me right away that, even if all I wanted to do was teach pure mathematics, I would still be training other people to go off and build better bombs. I couldn't do it.

I spent two years working for the United Farm Workers. I worked as an organizer for the Washington Public Interest Research Group. I worked at a big food coop in Seattle. I taught in a special physics program at the University of Washington for minority students. That was a lot of fun. But that program ended when Reagan eliminated its funding. And my friends were urging me to go back and finish the work on my degree, which I had left behind.

So, the next year, I went to the University of Washington to get my master's in math. But before doing that I visited Nicaragua. The reason I was still interested in getting a technical degree was to do something a little more socially worthwhile than most people do with their education, particularly now that Reagan has eliminated funding for so many of the better things you can do. So I visited here because I knew Nicaragua was in need of people with technical capabilities. I had spent all those years developing myself as a pure mathematician, all those years. In pure math, you don't feel like you really know how to do anything. It's a lot like the humanities.

I was, at that time, pretty well hooked into the progressive political scene in Seattle. It was impossible not to be aware of what was happening in Nicaragua. A lot of Nicaraguan speakers came through the campus. And I would read the *New York Times* every day and the *Christian Science Monitor* almost as often, so I was on top of the developments and strongly supportive of what was going on down here.

When I first came in 1981, it was to look the place over and to hunt for a job with the idea that I'd go back, finish my master's degree, and then come down to stay. Well, my studies got delayed again because I got heavily involved in political activity, this time as coordinator of an initiative campaign on Central America in the city of Seattle. So I finally came for good—with my wife, Virginia—in the summer of 1984.

One of the first things I noticed—even on that brief visit in 1981—was a strong sense of national pride and identity. I remember going into the literacy campaign office to get some information and talking with a woman who worked there. I looked at a few pages of description and said, "This seems to be following the program of Paolo Freire, the Brazilian sociologist." She corrected me real quickly: "No, no. This is our own Nicaraguan program. We looked at Paolo Freire's idea, but we changed it. This is ours." Nicaraguans have emerged from a history of being ashamed of being Nicaraguan to being very assertive about it. When I was first here, I made some comments comparing their culture with Mexico, and I noticed that this was a sore point because Mexico is bigger and richer. Whenever I made comparisons with Mexico, people would really react.

When I came here in September of 1981, a lot of North Americans were coming down. It still wasn't terribly difficult to come here and find work, but the government was beginning to discourage it. I had nothing lined up. I didn't know anybody here. I made hotel reservations by phone. I just showed up.

My first day in Managua was a total disaster. I came in at night on a plane from Mexico. Not knowing anything about the intricacies of exchanging foreign money, I had exchanged all my dollars for Mexican pesos the minute I got to Mexico. When I arrived at the airport here, the exchange window was closed, so I couldn't get any Nicaraguan money. I talked a taxi driver into taking me to my hotel and working out an arrangement to put the fare on my hotel bill.

The next morning, I asked at the hotel where I could change some money. The proprietor, not very helpfully, said: "Ciudad Jardin." Where that was—or what that was—I had no idea. I got a taxi driver to take me there with a promise of pay afterward, and he obviously knew exactly where to go. It turned out that this place was the black market in dollars—highly illegal, not good for the Nicaraguan economy, and not what I would have done if I'd had much choice. But the cab driver said, "Wait here" and brought back a friend who was ready to change my dollars. Boy, was he annoyed when he found out all I had was Mexican pesos!

My next major project was finding a map—which, in itself, was difficult—and learning to get around Managua. Well, I found a few points of interest, like the ruins of the old cathedral near Carlos Fonseca's tomb, but I realized pretty quickly that you don't learn Managua the way you do any other town because of the earthquake damage and the crazy transportation.

I had been told by Nicaraguans that I ought to go to the Ministry of Planning. From my experience with bureaucracies, the first thing I did was try to figure out how to avoid that because I didn't want to put all my eggs in one basket.

Thinking it might be a little more direct, I trekked out to the Ministry of Education to start my job search. They sent me to the Ministry of Planning. I went there and explained to a secretary that I was here for about three weeks and wanted to talk to somebody about lining up work. She said, "No, no. You're doing it wrong. You're supposed to send us your resume from back in the States and then, if we're interested in having you come, we'll correspond with you and then invite you for an interview."

Now, I knew very well that if I had tried to do this thing by correspondence, my letter would have sat on somebody's desk unread forever. So I calmed her down and said, "Think of it this way. Instead of mailing a letter, I'm delivering it in person. You can respond when you're ready to, just as if this were a letter. I'll be here three weeks. OK?"

"OK," she said. "That's different." She conferred with somebody and told me to report back there at 8:30 the next morning. I was happy that I'd made that much progress, but worried that all my eggs were in that one basket. I didn't know what would happen, if anything would.

To wrap up that first day, I got my first taste of rain in the rainy season, and I learned from additional rude experience about the taxi system here. I stopped several taxis and tried giving them the name of my hotel, but they wouldn't even discuss taking me anywhere because I didn't have a landmark for the place. That's how people navigate in Managua. So I ended up getting drenched and walking forever to get back to the hotel.

The next morning, I went back to the Ministry of Education and was introduced to a guy named Cairo who has since become a close friend. I had written out a long resume, detailing all my teaching experience and my political activities as well. I wanted to emphasize all the things I had done and could do for the revolution. I was interviewed together with a Colombian woman who was also interested in working. So Cairo just took my resume and read it all out loud, line by line, right in front of her. At the same time, I was talking as fast as I could to convince him of all the ways I could be useful. So he stopped and said, "OK, we want you to come teach mathematics at the university." Just like that. So I had a job the second day. When I went to the university to meet the people there, I discovered that they had just sent two of the faculty to the United States to look for a mathematician.

I'm basically satisfied with life here. My wife and I have a tiny little house across town from my parents'. I'm active with the U.S. Citizens Committee, and I spend a lot of time with journalists and other visitors. I get real enjoyment out of showing people the culture, showing them around, giving them a taste of the foods. One of my favorite things is going to the little comedors, the cheap little corner food stands where you always get a better meal than in the restaurants. They'll have a grill going and you can get plantains, fried chicken, rice, beans, and these delicious fruit drinks called refrescoes.

Where I teach is the National Autonomous University of Nicaragua, the larger of the two universities, and they say it has thirty-five thousand students. I teach daytime classes, so I don't see the place at its liveliest, because the university really comes alive at night when all the working people come.

I'm working on teaching younger students who are supposed to study full-time, and I'm happy to do that because I know Nicaragua is going to need a technical elite, and that it's not going to be able to achieve that with people who are only studying at night. There are enough obstacles anyway.

The most obvious of those obstacles, of course, is the displacement caused by the war. People are constantly being mobilized to pick coffee or to fight or even for rallies and various things. Other than the draft, that stuff isn't compulsory, but a lot of people are into volunteering as much as they can. The Sandinista youth group kind of organizes it. If the national leadership is stressing that people are needed to work on the harvests, then a call goes out. It's not much different from the antiwar movement on U.S. campuses during the Vietnam era, except that this organization is on the same side as the government.

Anyway, there are problems even deeper than the ones caused by the war. Even people who are getting the most education are not getting educated to be leaders, to be innovators. The social and economic elite in Nicaragua in the past did not produce many good scientists and engineers. They were stuck with the receptacle concept of education: drop the truth into the mind of the student, don't concentrate on developing the student's independent capacities. To a great degree, I think this may be a problem common to Hispanic cultures. Spain never went through a major scientific revolution. So, on a very deep level, people aren't prepared to go after real scientific knowledge, to become more than technicians.

In the university math department, most of the faculty is very young. A few have studied in the United States and have a good idea of the capacities a mathematician should have. Most of them don't seem to. I've had a lot of frustration in teaching because there's some pretty strict educational bureaucracy and you have to follow course outlines and lesson plans pretty rigidly. I plan to try some changes on a small scale and see what kind of feedback I get from my students, then work for some deeper changes.

But it's not too bad. It's very relaxed at the university, particularly for the foreigners, of which there are a lot.

A lot of my experiences and observations are similar to my parents . So let me take it from there and give you a little analysis of what I think the U.S. is really up to and why. First, to put it all in context, the prevailing attitude within the U.S. government toward Latin America in general is very negative. I'm sure my awareness of this stems from my early sensitivity to racial issues. There's an assumption that the Latin Americans are not capable of many things that people in the developed world are. For example, there was a famous encounter between Henry Kissinger and an official in Allende's government, which I remember reading in a book by Seymour Hirsh. The Chilean listened to Kissinger for a while and then told him, "You're ignorant. You don't know what you're talking about. Here you're making policies for the United States and you're acting in gross ignorance of the situation in South America." Well, Kissinger didn't deny that. But what he said was that he wasn't interested in knowing anything about South America, that it didn't matter because nothing important had ever happened in the South—the whole southern half of the world! That's the mentality that comes into play when U.S. officials say it's a sign of Soviet influence when the people of Central America say something intelligent.

When it comes to the economic issues, I think both sides of the debate are guilty of oversimplification. In the mainstream press, the suggestion seems to be that the shortages are created by communism or by incompetence. Those are the themes. From the left, on the other hand, what you hear is that there's a blockade. That's a simplification. It may also be an analogy with Cuba. There's a tendency in this movement to use analogies that may not be valid. I get a little uneasy when people compare the conflict down here with Vietnam, even though it's politically useful to do that. It's a good way to awaken mainstream people to the risks we're running. But when it comes to seriously analyzing the situation in Latin America, you've got to recognize that it's different. We have thousands of people from the United States down here, and it's closer, and the U.S. has a history of involvement in the affairs of these countries. Besides that, we share with the countries of Central America some cultural similarities and a common religion, so there's a lot more basis for understanding. Not only that, but we have Vietnam behind us now, and that changes the picture too.

When you look at all the effort that has been made to destroy the economy here, you have to wonder if this isn't a replay of Southeast Asia in another respect. According to William Shawcross in *Sideshow*, this book about Laos, Nixon had conceded to himself that the Vietnam War would be lost a long time before he pulled the troops out. But his geopolitical analysis was that the U.S. had to maintain its credibility. So, to do that, he put in some time just to do as much damage as possible, to leave the other side with a victory that wouldn't be worth anything because the country would be impossible to govern. It looks to me that the same thing is being done now to Nicaragua.

Maybe because it's traveled this route before, the U.S. government is able to do a lot of damage to Nicaragua without the people back home being aware of it. A lot of really horrible things it might like to do are impossible politically. But it doesn't have to do much to really strangle Nicaragua.

Since I've been down here, I've been putting together a newsletter every two or three months to send back home. I have a list of personal friends, political contacts in Seattle, people who come through here from the States, and so on—activists and opinion makers. It goes to about eight hundred people. So that helps get information out about what's really happening down here. Of course, not everyone believes everything we have to say. But I like to think in pragmatic terms, to figure that I'm making some difference. People who might have backed Reagan completely might begin to doubt, and the people who are with us emotionally get more information, which makes them more effective in talking to others. And we meet a steady stream of people who are down here to see the situation for themselves. That's one of the most encouraging things of all.

Gayle McGarrity

Gayle McGarrity is refreshingly hard to stereotype. She is attractive and dresses impeccably, but is totally unpretentious. She is an upper-middle-class black leftist who lives her politics and has traveled many miles in doing so: to Stanford University in the early 1970s, motivated by a fascination with the civil rights and black power movements; to Jamaica, where she spent much of her childhood and then returned to work for the government of Michael Manley; to Cuba, where she obtained a master's degree in public health and became the first U.S. citizen to go through a Cuban graduate school; and, finally, to Nicaragua. Trained in anthropology, Gayle has moved from the theoretical into the practical and is now studying the effects of political and economic change on nutritional levels in the Third World.

This is a woman who is politically aware and strong in her convictions, but who cares not one bit for rigid political correctness. "I'm not here to be like the Nicaraguans. I'm here to do some useful work and live a decent life," she says. At times, Gayle even has had a household employee to help with her two children, but, as she tells it, "At first that was hard to cope with. My empleada acted too much like a servant. She wouldn't even sit in the living room when I was there, but I convinced her that was ridiculous." In many ways, hers is a politics of the heart. As she tells here, she had no intention of adopting a child until she met Germilio, a Miskito orphan who was lying in a ward for malnourished children. But he now toddles happily around the house she rents in the middle-class neighborhood of Pancasan in Managua. A cynical friend once said to Gayle, "I hope you're not doing this as some kind of act of solidarity with the Indians." She replied without missing a beat, "I don't even think any Indians know. I'm doing it because the kid was starving."

Gayle is outspoken but thoughtful. She is enthusiastic about the Sandinistas' experiment, but doesn't hesitate to blast them for the flaws she sees, such as poor living conditions in the Miskito relocation areas, and she brings others on the left to task for whitewashing these problems in misguided loyalty. Here is her story as she told it over fruit juice one humid afternoon.

I was born in Chicago in 1953, but when I was six months old my mother took me to live in Kingston, Jamaica. That's where I grew up, in an upper-middle-class black family. We made the move because my mother—the daughter of a Jamaican mother and a North American father—refused to raise her child in the kind of segregated society the U.S. was at that time. When I was about ten, I began to be conscious of the differences between rich and poor, between my life and those of poorer children. I was always wanting to give things away. I would think about being religious, but it just didn't work because the only option presented to me by the church was going to Sunday school and I didn't see how that helped poor people one bit. Still, I never accepted the class divisions in Jamaica, which are very strong. Before I knew what I wanted to be as an adult, I knew I wanted to work against poverty.

As a teenager, I went to England to boarding school and my perspective changed again. I had grown up with this idea that European culture was superior to non-European, and when that myth was shattered I developed a much better view of myself. I did very well in school. I met people from all over the world. I was all set to go to Cambridge or the London School of Economics, but then I decided I'd rather go to the States because I was very interested in the civil rights and black power movements. I was fascinated by the young people in the States and by all the social change going on there. So I disappointed my family by going to California instead of Cambridge. I ended up graduating from Stanford University in Palo Alto with a degree in anthropology.

But, besides disappointing my family, I disappointed myself, too, because I didn't enjoy Stanford at all. I had a lot of cultural problems. To put it gently, Californians are not used to seeing someone of my color with an upper-class British accent. So I got teased, and I got shifted into special minority programs, which I didn't need because my background had not been at all underprivileged. Many of my classmates in the minority program had inferiority complexes and didn't know how to write papers, and here I had been studying in England. It was ridiculous. At the same time, I was very political and a leftist, so I wanted to be accepted by the black students, but they didn't understand me. I mean, I didn't know how to dance, so they just couldn't relate.

My personal life was really screwed up for a while, but politically I always stayed on the left. A lot of black students I knew went through a very extreme nationalist phase and then went very bourgeois and got into standard politics. I never did. I saw right through the co-optation game and stayed pretty much faithful to my original ideas.

After Stanford, I went back to Jamaica for two and a half years and worked with Michael Manley's government. Even though I'm a North American, Jamaica has always felt like home. But I was an American citizen and, around 1976, when the right wing started gaining power in the Manley government and the Siaga forces got more and more consolidated, I began getting hassled because I was a politically active Jamaican resident but not a citizen. I was threatened by right-wing security forces. It all got very uncomfortable. So I went back to California to visit. While I was there, I found out I was pregnant with my daughter, Sasha. So I decided to stay in California because, at the time, they had a lot of good social welfare programs like free child care, Lamaze childbirth classes, and so on.

This also seemed like the right place and time to go to graduate school. I was feeling the desire to move in a practical direction with my anthropology, so I enrolled in a medical anthropology program at the University of California at Berkeley. Well, not to overdo the practical side, what I got interested in at first was traditional Egyptian medicine and the possibilities for integrating it with Western medicine. I started studying Arabic. I got really into it. But then I said, "This is ridiculous. I already speak Spanish. Why not study somewhere in Latin America and not make this thesis a lifetime ordeal?"

So, in 1979, the year of the triumph of the Nicaraguan revolution, I came down to check it out. It was Christmas vacation, and I had a boyfriend who had been living in Central America, in Belize. So we just got on the plane and came down. We didn't know a soul. It was right after the triumph, so there weren't all these solidarity tours running around.

The first image I remember was all these friendly young people in green uniforms at the airport welcoming you to the free country of Sandino. That was invigorating. And the society seemed open somehow. People were into the church. I thought it had a chance to avoid the kind of bureaucratization and dogmatism that some would argue was necessary to defend the Cuban revolution. And because so many people have racially mixed backgrounds here, I felt hopeful that it could avoid being a polarized society in terms of race. Actually, we did have one nasty encounter with racist overtones. A group of twenty or thirty kids started shouting, "Moreno, moreno," which means dark-skinned, and they were laughing. Afterwards, people explained that the kids probably thought we were Indians or Creoles from the Atlantic coast, and their attitude might have been more curiosity than ridicule. But it was very disconcerting.

That first visit, things were absolutely chaotic. We talked to a lot of people who were not in favor of the Sandinistas but were trying to stick around—but by our next visit many of them were gone. There was a sense of sheer exhaustion and devastation from the war. There certainly weren't the discotheques and so on that you see now. Even the restaurants were quiet. I remember we ordered some cake in a restaurant and the cake had a huge cockroach baked into the batter. We tried to say something politely to the waitress, and she just exploded. She said, "You don't understand. We've just been through a war. My son was killed. We didn't even have plates. We barely had food. What do you want?" And of course she was right. We had no comprehension of that experience.

I went back to the States quite supportive of Nicaragua—so much that I spent the next couple of years working as a bilingual receptionist for Casa Nicaragua, a solidarity group in San Francisco. And I kept thinking about coming down to stay a while. My daughter's father ended up moving to Nicaragua, and she spent some time with him, so I would come back to visit. While I was making up my mind, I decided to balance out my humanities background with more science by getting a master's degree in public health. And I decided to get it in Cuba because I liked what I'd heard about their approach to public health. They see it as a social, political, and economic problem rather than as solely a biomedical one. So they've cleaned up the environment, raised people's living standards, established equal relations between men and women, worked on eliminating racism—and people have gotten healthier.

So there I was, the first U.S. citizen to actually go through a Cuban postgraduate program. But I look enough like a Cuban that I could blend into crowds and travel around like a native. I hung out with a lot of people who were far from being Communist Party types and got a pretty broad view of the society, and I was favorably impressed by the degree of freedom. And more, one of the greatest things for me was the academic rigor. Students really are considered the hope of the future and treated as a privileged class. And the teamwork! We even had to write major papers as a group—five or six of us sitting up all night writing a sixteen-page paper, sentence by sentence. It taught me to be very disciplined, and it showed me how a scientifically planned, centrally organized society really works. There are a lot of frustrations for a person who's not used to it, but in terms of human relations they're far advanced. You have doctors and nurses who really work to serve the people, for example.

Anyway, after getting that master's degree, I decided that Nicaragua was the place to do my doctoral research. One thing that finally got me down here was an encounter with Tomas Borge, the minister of interior, the comandante who runs the police and the security forces. I met him on a visit here, and he asked me what kind of work I did. When I said I was a nutritionist, he got very excited and said, "We badly need a nutritionist in Matagalpa. You should come down." He was right in touch with the country's needs. Could you imagine the secretary of defense in the U.S. talking to someone about malnutrition in New York? That convinced me. So I finally came here to live in May of 1984.

By that time, I had finished the requirements for my Ph.D., passed all my exams, and received a fellowship to work on malnutrition down here. My original topic was the effects of land reform on nutritional levels. The research plan was approved and everything. But at the last minute I got a phone call from the foundation saying, "We urge you to go anywhere but Nicaragua." I couldn't pin them down on their reason, but it was pretty obviously political. So that presented me with a tough moral dilemma. I could take the money and go somewhere else and shut up. I could refuse the money on ethical grounds because it's a violation of my academic freedom to pressure me not to go to Nicaragua. Or I could take the money and do a comparative study between Nicaragua and Costa Rica, which is what I decided on, even though that presents some serious research problems. Nicaragua has a war going on, but Nicaragua has also had much greater land reform. Costa Rica, on the other hand, is generally a more affluent society, so there are all kinds of questions about what it means to be poor in a society that's affluent by Latin American standards instead of in one where the vast majority is poor. My plan is to do some research here and then go to Costa Rica, but to keep Sasha in school in Nicaragua so she won't have to move around so much.

One of the first things I did down here was to accept Borge's invitation to come to Matagalpa and work for the Ministry of Health, setting up a nutritional program. Matagalpa is a beautiful old city, in some ways more cosmopolitan than Managua. But the housing situation is so tight that I ended up sharing the home of a Nicaraguan family, and that's an abrupt change in lifestyle for a mother with a daughter who's used to coming and going freely. I was there for several months sizing up the situation and designing the program to measure levels of malnutrition and figure out ways to improve them. I have a lot of regrets about things that weren't possible in Matagalpa. A lot of the data gathering had to be shelved because of the war, but at least I was able to give them the outlines of a program they can implement when things get better. I also managed to administer an already established program to distribute packages of food on a monthly basis to pregnant women, nursing mothers, and children: milk, flour, oil, and canned meat. But, you know, that's not the approach the Sandinistas want to use—giving handouts. They want to help the people produce more.

I also did some work in a hospital advising the people in the kitchen about how to prepare a more nutritive diet. There's a lot of ignorance about what people should eat. Some rural people have useful knowledge about natural healing—they know that garlic has natural antibody producing qualities—but there are also some dangerous beliefs floating around, like the idea that when a child has diarrhea it's wrong to give fluids.

Right after the revolution, Nicaragua made a lot of steps forward in terms of health. Polio was eradicated. Measles and mumps have fallen way down, and so has malaria. One of the reasons I've enjoyed working here is that the government is really behind these efforts to improve nutritional standards. Instead of pushing Nestle baby formula or something, they've got a billboard campaign to encourage breastfeeding! But the aggression has really taken its toll. U.S. companies have been refusing to sell Nicaragua medicine. One of the main strategies of the counterrevolution has been to attack health centers and health workers, to ambush food trucks, to attack farming cooperatives and burn crops. Health and nutrition have suffered a lot.

Nicaragua, like Cuba, is viewing public health as an environmental problem. To prevent disease, you improve people's environment. You give them decent housing, garbage disposal, fresh water, sewage treatment. The government has a commitment to do that, but, since the war began, it hasn't had the funds because everything is going into rebuilding all the facilities that the contras destroy.

Working in Matagalpa was very stressful. The medical people developed a kind of battlefield humor, especially when they had to go out into areas frequented by the contras. People would say, "You're going out into the campo? We won't hold dinner for you, ha ha." It was really petrifying. People would show me places on the road where health workers had been attacked, and once our car broke down right where there had been an ambush.

One of the contras' favorite targets were the antimalaria campaign workers. A driver from the Ministry of Health office where I worked had been kidnapped by the contras and kept nine months. They dragged him around barefooted without proper food. Finally he escaped or was let go, but he couldn't work. To this day, he just sits around the house. He was psychologically destroyed.

I worked with an Argentine woman who was an epidemiologist, and she had been in a small town with a French doctor. He was there to do a survey on some exotic disease. The contras attacked the town, and they were hiding out in her house, lying under the bed. He lifted up his head to say, "I thought you said this was going to be a quiet trip," and a bullet got him right in the brain. She's never gotten over that, because he lifted his head to talk to her.

Early in my time here, I went into the hospital in Bluefields to look over these special wards they have for malnourished children. Actually, they're trying to do away with these wards, because people have a tendency to abandon kids there. Anyway, while I was there I broke a cardinal rule of working with underprivileged kids by falling in love with this little Miskito Indian boy. He was lying there, in worse condition than any of the others, and nobody seemed to know much about him. I was told he was in such bad shape because he was an orphan, and the hospitals here rely on parents to help care for the kids. So he was lying there naked and filthy. I sensed that there was an ethnic thing going on, that this kid was being treated like absolutely nothing by the black Creole nurses because he was Miskito. So I made a big thing about it in the hospital and ultimately decided to adopt him.

I marched into the Ministry of Social Welfare, assuming it was just a matter of doing some paper work, and they thought I was out of my mind. Down here, people only adopt kids if they can't have their own. I also ran into resistance because there's a history here of foreigners coming down and buying children and putting them into child prostitution rings in the U.S. There was a big scandal about that during the Somoza era. So things were put on hold for a while. I sent him money, but I convinced myself that he'd found a home and was happy. I tried to put him out of my mind. But then I went back to Bluefields for the baptism of a friend's baby, and of course I stopped by the hospital. Well, he'd been released into the custody of a family who were simply too poor to take care of him. I went to visit, and he was lying in bed filthy dirty and coughing this horrible cough. The mother said, "Can't you get him some medicine?" Well, the upshot of it was that I took him back to Managua with me, and he's never left. Ultimately, I convinced the authorities that my feelings about the child were genuine, and they were extremely cooperative from that point. They confirmed my initial conviction that the revolution really does want to help all the children, regardless of their ethnic background.

I should have taken pictures of how he looked at first. He had this huge belly filled with parasites, and his skin was really horrible. We thought he was two, but it turns out he's three. At first he didn't say anything, and then all he knew were bad words. Then we gave him medicine for the cough and the parasites, and he started eating like a little garbage disposal, everything in sight. Finally, the day came when he said, "I can't eat any more," and I almost fainted. Then we knew he was better. And now he's fine, talkative, intelligent.

It's worked out very well. One of my friends said to me, "I hope you're not doing this as an act of solidarity with the oppressed Indian people or something." Well, because of my own ethnically mixed background— I'm half American Indian—I don't look at it that way. I'm doing it because whatever I can give him will be better than what he had.

In the process of the adoption, I learned something about the so-called forced relocations that have received so much bad press. The government has been making people leave certain areas, and providing them housing in other areas, in order to create free fire zones so they can really go after the contras. There have been all kinds of allegations of mistreatment, just like in 1981 when the Miskitos were moved, but very little hard information has been available. Anyway, I went into the Ministry of Social Welfare in the spring of 1985 to talk about this adoption again, and they told me I'd have to come back because every social worker they had was up working on the relocation thing. Now, that shows you something about the country. If they were just herding them onto trucks, they would not be needing those social workers.

This relocation business has been hard for a lot of people and divisive for the country. It's true that the Sandinistas are burning down houses, and that's not going to win them any friends. But what are they going to do—leave the houses standing for the contras to use as safe houses? I find some American journalists covering this story incredible in the judgmental pronouncements they make. They seem to start from the premise that the Sandinistas have some kind of evil plan. Spare me.

While I was based in Matagalpa, I traveled to the Miskito relocation area to visit some health centers and saw some of the living conditions. I'm not going to lie: the conditions are very bad. The houses are like barracks. They're very crowded. And a lot of people don't have toilets. I found the nutritional status of the children very poor. We were in one camp for a Miskito feast, and you could tell the people were really anxious to get at the food.

I think it's a mistake when the Sandinistas try to say the Miskitos were living in squalor before and they're in paradise now. It makes much more sense to say, "We had no other option. We had to move these people. We're doing our best. They're in the middle of nowhere and our supply trucks keep getting attacked." But, even though it's depressing, it's definitely not some kind of concentration camp. People can leave—I've seen them walking along the road. It's just that the move was definitely military and not social in its emphasis. At the beginning, they didn't think about the cultural problems: these people who are used to living in isolation and eating fish and coconuts are brought into this crowded settlement and fed tortillas and beans. But the Sandinistas have always been good at admitting their mistakes and attempting to redress them.

I've spent a lot of time with a journalist from the BBC, and he's introduced me to people I'd never have met otherwise, like Brooklyn Rivera, the head of one of the Miskito factions that was fighting the Sandinistas. And even Rivera said to me that he thought the Sandinistas were doing the best they could with respect to the Indians in the relocation camps. He said he cries, viewing the situation of his people, but he could see the limitations of moving them back to their land with the war on.

The war and the absence of international aid have touched everyone here. Since I came, consumer prices have tripled. I mean, it's hard for me, and I have a lot more money than the average Nicaraguan. There are shortages of all kinds of things: light bulbs one month, toothpaste the next, pencils and paper all the time. They have a ration card system to assure that everyone will get the basic foods, but there are lots of snarls in the distribution system. There are fewer and fewer buses on the road for lack of spare parts. New housing construction is just about at a standstill because you can't get cement or wood. People keep saying how bad it is, and it keeps getting worse. It's amazing.

As for my personal life, it's comfortable enough and the work is very rewarding. I live in Pancasan, a middle-class neighborhood. It's very quiet. There are vendors walking past all the time selling food, so you hardly have to go to the market. Most of the people around here work for some aspect of the state. Sasha goes to the American school, and Germilio goes to a day care center part-time. As I said, there are scarcities, but they don't bother me too much. The worst things are the heat and dust, and the fact that Managua is not a very cosmopolitan city. I go to some foreign films and cultural events, and I've made some good friends. But somehow my most enduring friendships have been with people from the Atlantic coast. I think they're more international in their outlook, and we share the Caribbean connection. Many of them have relatives in the U.S., too.

You see, I don't have any illusions about trying to live like a Nicaraguan. I think that what Nicaragua needs from people like myself is that we work to the best of our ability to help develop the country, instead of idealizing the place and becoming uncritical cultists. Progressive, independent thinking is what the challenge of this situation needs. All I want is to live a decent life here and do some good work.

Joy Crocker

While some North Americans can lay out detailed, intellectually meticulous arguments concerning Nicaragua's strengths and weaknesses and their reasons for being there, Joy Crocker operates on a very different plane. Intuition runs her life, and has run it very well so far. Joy "always knew" she would play the piano and has found plenty of performing and teaching projects to keep her fulfilled. From her years at Yale in the 1950s through marriage, motherhood, and divorce, she has kept growing and trusting in the universe to provide new challenges.

A highly personal quest brought Joy to Nicaragua. Her daughter, a member of Reverend Sun Myung Moon's Unification Church, had become an outspoken supporter of the contra cause. Hearing news from travelers to Nicaragua that reflected a much more positive vision and torn between conflicting views, Joy decided to go see for herself.

She went for a two-week visit. She returned to her San Francisco home three months later to pack and say goodbyes before embarking on her newest musical project, teaching piano at Nicaragua's national conservatory. The "guardian angel" who runs her life has come up with a good assignment this time, Joy says with a chuckle.

Over the years, Joy has found a number of innovative ways to bring cultural riches to people who have lacked access to them, and this is a strong priority in the Nicaragua she stumbled into. This revolution says its vision is the "democratization of culture," in the words of poet-priest Ernesto Cardenal, under whose direction the Ministry of Culture has created rural arts centers and theatre troupes, splashed murals around the cities, and subsidized tuitions to make music and art training generally affordable. It has sparked controversy among international critics by espousing a highly politicized view of what art is: it is "the trigger of revolution," according to one popular aphorism. Nicaragua's government has taken on the tough task of encouraging arts that are both revolutionary and artistically sophisticated, and has gotten mixed reviews in that attempt.

To teach piano in a nation that is just pulling itself up from illiteracy, to bring musical riches to a nation that is still fighting a thousand forms of poverty—this is the challenge offered to Joy by her playful guardian angel. She has accepted it, and immersed herself in Nicaraguan life with a refreshing lack of expectation.

Anyway, after spending some time in that yogi's ashram in Vancouver, I came back and devoured books on spirituality; even audited courses at Graduate Theological Union in Berkeley; had long talks with my minister until neither of us could keep our eyes open. It was very heady stuff.

Partly because of these changes in me, Dick and I decided in 1975 that he would start a new chapter in his life, namely new love, and I would start a new chapter in mine, namely learning about the transcendental world. So we parted in good faith.

I don't like to think of myself as deeply religious—certainly not as a church-going little old lady. The chief thing I do have is a very strong faith in reincarnation. I also believe that life is to be lived in such a way that you hurt none if possible and help others as much as you can.

In a way, although I had married for life and planned to go on being a conservative professor's wife and a piano teacher, the breakup really seemed to free me to explore. I did an awful lot of reading of mystic literature: Sufi, Zen, the books of Seth. By about 1982, I had gotten to the same point in this exploration as I had ten years before with outward travels: where do I go from here?

Around the same time, things began to get tense in the church where I'd been calling myself minister of music. The ordained ministers did not like someone else talking about theology, as I'd begun to, especially since it was not always the same theology they preached. After one particularly intense project, I suddenly thought it was time to resign.

For the first time in my life, the phone did not ring a week later with another juicy project. I played and went to concerts but didn't really get into anything. Then a friend suggested that we go back to visit San Antonio, which had been a sleepy mission town when I left it in 1946. So we made plans.

Meanwhile, a number of people in our ecumenical church group in Oakland had been going to Nicaragua and saying what a neat place it was. It was getting deadly assaults from the press and the administraton as totally evil, a communist blight, etc.

I was drawn into the debate for a particular personal reason. My daughter, who had joined Reverend Sun Myung Moon's Unification Church five years ago, was one of those who were saying Nicaragua was communist and a threat, and I learned through her that the church was actively supporting the contras.

Martha joined the Moonies when she was seventeen. She had been hitchhiking around the country with a dime in her jeans and her guitar on her back and, when she got back to Berkeley, these people invited her to dinner. She found real companionship. I could have pulled her out, but I couldn't think of anything I could offer her that would have made her as happy. Dick said he wouldn't make the move to pull her out as long as I stayed on top of the situation. I visited her for a weekend and was quite taken with the group as being very spiritual, intellectually active. Of course, anything in Berkeley is unique. I spoke to a number of people at length about their theology, and was sort of satisfied that there's more than meets the eye. Of course, some Moonies, like some Christians, think of reality as a box two inches square. But, for others, there is no end to the possible interpretations of theology.

I was vaguely aware at the beginning that their attitude toward communism was pretty rigid, and I suggested at the time that not all communist countries were the same. But, in 1979, it didn't seem to matter. Then, when Martha came back to visit in 1984—I was already thinking about going to Nicaragua—she had become much more outspoken about the communist problem. She said, "We don't like dictators, of course, but dictatorships can change, and countries under communism never come back." She quoted some stunning number of people who have fallen to communism, which in Moon's theology represents the anti-Christ. They feel that the coming of the kingdom of God is hindered by the presence of communism in the world and so it must be fought—militarily in Nicaragua's case.

When we talked about Nicaragua, I pointed out that it's certainly not a godless place. It's one of the most Christian countries in the world, according to our Christian friends who have been there. But she wasn't convinced.

I kept thinking, "Why not visit Nicaragua on the way to San Antonio?" Now, Nicaragua is not on the way to San Antonio. My friend Dorothy was not wildly enthusiastic about the detour, but she agreed. We signed up for a week's tour, and I came down a week early because I like banging around a new country by myself.

During that first week, I wandered into the conservatory in Managua and mentioned that I'm a pianist. People asked, "Where did you study?" I said, "Yale." They wanted to know if I'd taught at the conservatory level. I said yes. "Will you stay here and teach our teachers?"

I'd never even studied Spanish. I thought I was imagining it. I said, "I'll come back tomorrow with a translator." But the invitation was as clear in English as in Spanish. I protested that I had commitments back in the States—teaching and so on—but they were absolutely uninterested in that. Pablo, the director, said, "You can rent a nice room with one of the other teachers, and we'll pay you ten thousand cordobas a month. Won't you stay?"

There was this pause, and I heard myself saying yes. It felt totally unreal, but as I thought about it I realized that my guardian angel had just been a little slow this time.

My job is teaching advanced students and teachers. The conservatory, along with an art school and museum, is in a lovely medieval looking complex of buildings overlooking Lake Managua. You can look out and see people cutting the grass with machetes and students practicing their instruments all over the lawn.

Like everything else in Nicaragua, the conservatory appears to have been outfitted by a trip to the Salvation Army store. Even the concert grand in the auditorium usually has eighty-five to eighty-seven notes working. You know, playing the piano can be one of the great sensual delights of life, but it's less so when the ivory on the keys is worn off. There's a shortage of music, a shortage of books. But the people are so appreciative of whatever they get.

The conservatory is funded by the state; pupils don't pay anything. But the student body is still small. You have to understand that these people have been too concerned with simply surviving to afford luxuries like musical training. I've gotten into conferences about pupils with problems, and another teacher will tell me, "No, there's not a piano in the home. In fact, there's nothing in the home." That's the reality.

When I was interviewed for the job, Pablo asked me to review my music and teaching credentials. About five minutes of that seemed to suffice. Then, he asked me for a political resume. I said, "Huh?" It turned out, he needed to know if I had worked with a solidarity group or done any kind of progressive work. I said, "I guess I worked for Ron Dellums a little." He said, "Could you get a letter of reference from him?"

They were serious! But that seemed okay to me. In fact, it kind of fits in with my monistic view of the world—that everything is connected. Revolution is not something you do with guns. It's struggling to bring out the best in yourself and your country in every respect: politics, culture, religion. There are seminars at the conservatory on "Revolution and Esthetics," and I love that. And religion fits in there too. At one point, the lecturer in that seminar expressed the opinion that God didn't have any place in a discussion of esthetics. But Pablo, the director, said, "How can you think about art without thinking about the source of art?" It's exciting just to be in a climate where all this is discussed so vibrantly.

Even with the war going on, I have a great sense of safety here in Managua. There are lots of police and soldiers, but they are obviously part of the people and not working against them. Even the guns on their shoulders seem more like guitars.

My first weeks here, I fell in with a group of internationalists who were in Nicaragua for many different reasons but had gravitated toward each other. Each morning around seven, we'd gather for breakfast and exchange information about what we'd learned the day before. I was amazed at the level of political knowledge many of these people had! Every day, there would be someone new showing up—maybe from Bolivia, maybe from Holland—and new stories to hear, sometimes from the war front.

There was one particular guy who had a lot to do with awakening me to the brutality of the contra war and its impact on people's day-to-day lives. He was a young journalist, a striking, handsome, blond fellow, Scandinavian-looking. He had been around a lot. He had a sardonic, brittle humor. You knew and he knew that he was being funny to keep from crying. He would talk about various uses of the knife to slice people up. He'd seen bodies and burials, he'd seen people's eyes ripped out by the contras.

But it wasn't as much the specifics of his stories as the intensity of this young man. He couldn't have been more than twenty-one, but he had the wisdom of having seen much more than kids that age should. Remember, I grew up in the generation that thought college was about playing pranks and joining sororities. This kid should have been out waltzing, instead of taking these pictures and looking at the world with eyes that knew too much.

After I said yes to staying here, I taught three months on a short-term visa and then went back to the States to settle my affairs. Of course, I saw my daughter. I did everything I could to convince her that she and her friends have got to stop picking on my buddies down in Nicaragua.

I tried to argue that the contras didn't represent a Christian or human way of doing things. She said, "War is hell. The contras have been guilty of the abuses but so have the Sandinistas." Her deeper point seemed to be that the end justifies the means. I wanted to cry. I wanted to kidnap her. I got into a shouting match with the guy who runs her house. It was awful.

But I'm here and the work is very, very satisfying. I brought back some Debussy sonatas for one of the other teachers, and she was in seventh heaven. Everybody seems to want to learn music. I brought down a little two-hundred-dollar Yamaha portable organ, one of those things that plays the whole band, and everyone wants to try it. It's wonderful to work with people who have been denied cultural advantages for so long. When my Spanish gets good enough, I just might try to start another literacy campaign, this time with music.

Bill Gasperini

Bill Gasperini has learned the art of maintaining calm in the middle of chaos and lives a life unusually open to change. As a journalist and researcher for a "liberal think tank" in Managua, he is able to travel widely in Nicaragua, just as he has in other countries as often as possible.

A student-exchange program in Brazil ten years ago stands out as the major turning point in Bill's life, the experience that turned him on to Latin America with a fervor that has yet to be turned off. In Brazil, he lived with very poor people who worked to their limit but stayed poor. He also met "liberation theology" clergy who were trying to help these people analyze and change their situation. He returned to the United States with a renewed appreciation of the depth of the structural problems that maintain the rift between rich and poor, an appreciation that was enhanced by travels in the Middle East, ecological field work in Mexico, and, finally, graduation from Cornell University's program in rural sociology.

Bill's flexibility has not only taken him across continents. It has allowed him to make change after change in his career and external image without apparent threat to his underlying sense of security, so focused does he seem on the problems of wealth and poverty. He has worked in a longshoremen's hiring hall, built latrines in Brazil, been a paralegal in New York, worked for a wire service, and taught bilingual children. Along the way, he has found time to become an accomplished singer and guitarist, with a strong interest, of course, in Latin American music.

Bill had recently crossed the line into the over-thirty generation when this interview took place. But, as he evaluates his life in Nicaragua and the changes he has witnessed in that country, he gives the clear impression that his past adventures are only a beginning.

I grew up in a New York suburb called Mount Kisco, and I was always very sensitive to people saying, "Oh, you kids from the suburbs. You've got all you want. You don't really know what the world's all about." I hit high school in the late 1960s and was very much influenced by the social movements of the era. I went to school in a very homogeneous community—ninety-nine percent white, upper-middle-class—but my social life was in another town that was much more cross-sectional. That led to a very divided, schizophrenic lifestyle. But it was worth it. I've always had some sort of identification with minorities or people who are not, shall we say, typical.

I've always been politically minded. I worked with a campus peace group during the Vietnam years. That was in Gettysburg, Pennsylvania, which most people think is just a Civil War battlefield, but where I, sure enough, spent two years in college. Gettysburg didn't do a whole lot for me, and eventually I left, went through a lot of changes, and hitchhiked across the U.S. That's another thing about me. I've never liked staying in one place very long.

If I had to characterize my politics, I guess I'd use the term "progressive." I believe there's a lot of injustice and that we must work together to find a better way. But labels like "socialist" and "Marxist" don't work for me. I've read a lot of different social theories, but I believe there's a lot lacking in any theory. Reality is something you have to deal with as such.

After Gettysburg, I took a number of odd jobs, including one in the longshoremen's hiring hall in Newark, New Jersey, where I had a lot of contact with Spanish and Portuguese people. My brother was in India that year through a student/youth-exchange program, and I applied to the same program and was sent to Brazil. The day I received that letter was a complete turning point because it was the first time I thought seriously about Latin America, and I haven't let it go yet.

I don't think any amount of studying can prepare you for arriving in a place like that, with beggars everywhere, slums totally covering the hillsides. I had read enough that these things weren't a shock, but I remember thinking kind of soberly, "My God, this is the reality." I spent Thanksgiving of 1976 in a poor, drought-ridden part of Brazil, with a family that was just about out of food. Because I was a guest, they made tortillas and broke out their little supply of beans. They had to bring water on a donkey from an oasis about two or three miles away. I kept thinking of everyone in the United States eating fabulous Thanksgiving meals and realizing I was pretty far away from what I grew up with.

Now, those people aren't poor because they're lazy or something. They work constantly. But they're sharecroppers. Half of what they raise goes to some doctor or lawyer who owns their land. I came to realize that no matter how industriously you follow the Band-Aid approach—the Peace Corps approach—to poverty, nothing is going to change until basic structural changes occur.

The Latin American culture gets into your blood, and the sense of transition and growth. It made it difficult when I finally went back to come to terms with the static lives people lead in the U.S. I left Brazil in 1977—I had some family problems to deal with—and worked in New York as a paralegal for a while. You may think there's culture shock in adjusting to Latin America, but the real shock is when you return. You fly into Kennedy Airport and drive into Manhattan thinking it's pretty much the same. But subtle things about relationships with other people changed for me. Old friends were different. I was different. The people in this law firm were mostly into their own upward mobility, and the only person I felt really close to there was a guy from Chile.

After saving some money, I finished my undergraduate education at Cornell University, studying rural sociology, which is kind of like development studies. In 1980, I graduated and was fortunate enough to be hired by a couple of Cornell professors to accompany them to Mexico as a research assistant. I spent three months with them, studying a particular species of ant and its effect on crops—a very practical project, as it turns out.

These professors were part of a group called New World Agriculture, a network of socially conscious scientists who are, in fact, doing a number of projects in Nicaragua, such as helping the country cut its dependence on pesticides. I was fascinated with the ancient cultures of Mexico and with that project, and glad to be back in closer touch with the realities of Latin America.

I had become involved in support work for Nicaragua during my time at Cornell, raising money to help the literacy campaign after the insurrection. After years of denouncing Somoza and screaming about repression, now there was something positive to get out and talk about: teaching people to read and write. The response had been tremendous. So, when I finished my work in Mexico, I decided to sell my return ticket to the U.S. and make my way down here for a visit. The month I spent was one of the highlights of my life, ever. After two years of studying Nicaragua in the States and supporting it, to come and be here and feel the people's acceptance was very moving.

During that visit, I also traveled to the Atlantic coast, knowing that was a completely different reality and one you need to confront in order to understand Nicaragua. These are people who have always been exploited from the outside, first by the English and Spanish. Somoza left them alone, but he let the North American companies run rampant, like the timber companies in northern Zelaya. You can see even today areas that have been razed by the timber industry.

So then the Sandinistas came parading in, saying, "We're here to help you. Here's a new government, and this is what we're going to do." A lot of people resented them, especially in the more remote areas. Cuban teachers had been brought in, and some people, having heard years and years of propaganda about Cuba, didn't want Cubans teaching their children. There was a lot of cultural insensitivity and misunderstanding on the Sandinistas' part, contributing to the resentment. It didn't really explode until a little later. But, just a few days after I was in Bluefields, there was a riot there, directed at the Cuban presence.

A lot of the early hostilities were the results of misunderstanding and the inevitable difficulties of any kind of change. For example, the land reform institute came in and pretty much took over the role of middle man in agriculture. There were new layers of bureaucracy. Fishermen had to come and sell their catch to the new government fishing agency, reorganized from the one Somoza ran. They were paid by check instead of cash, which meant they had to come into town and probably stay overnight to get to the bank to cash it. When you change lifestyles that have been in place over centuries, it's not the easiest thing.

Adding to the Miskitos' hostility was Steadman Fagoth, this charismatic, captivating leader who got very involved in fomenting divisions and arming the Miskito Indians who fled into Honduras. Ultimately, the attacks by Fagoth's bands of Miskitos against those who stayed in Nicaragua led to the government's decision to evacuate ten thousand Miskitos from the Rio Coco area. And that controversy still hasn't completely died.

On that visit, I hoped there might be other possibilities of staying and working, but I knew it was difficult for people without sought-after technical skills. I had ideas about becoming a journalist, but I wasn't one yet. And, at that point, I began to feel a strong desire for some roots. So I left Nicaragua and established myself in the San Francisco Bay Area. I worked as a translator and writer for a news service and then as a teacher in a bilingual children's center.

I came back briefly in 1983, just to attend a New Song festival—singing and guitar playing being avocations of mine when I can find the time for them. Again I thought, "Wow, I still hope to be coming back to live." Some of my friends were trying to work as journalists in Nicaragua, so I decided it was time to try it if I was going to. I closed up shop in the Bay Area, spent a few days with my mother, and came down here to stay in February of 1984.

Pretty much by accident, I came by the Social and Economic Research Institute (INIES) here and found out they were looking for someone to help work putting out an English version of their magazine, *Pensamiento Propio*. Literally, it means "proper thinking," but the real sense is not so heavy-handed; it's more like "good thoughts." It's a semi-academic monthly bulletin which deals with socioeconomic issues that affect the various Central American countries. So that's my full-time job, with freelance journalism on the side.

When I came back to live, I arrived for the commemoration of the fiftieth anniversary of the assassination of Sandino, a big national holiday. There was great euphoria and fun all week. I tried to experience everything: press trips to the border, ceremonies to award land titles to the peasants, the tremendous rally in the plaza when Ortega announced the date of the elections.

When I first arrived, I lived in a house about ten blocks away from my office with a bunch of internationalists. Then, in December, I moved in with a family very close to my office. I'm pretty much a boarder there. I'm just too busy to spend much time at home. I don't have many possessions or think much about material needs. I mean, any time you spend more than a couple months in a place you tend to accumulate books and papers. But, really, as far as possessions, I've got two suitcases and a backpack worth of stuff, and a little library. No furniture, no pots and pans. I don't like to accumulate that stuff.

Pretty soon, I began to sense a change from 1980. Except for the celebration weeks, the euphoria had worn down. The long hard haul had set in. People began to understand that making revolution was not just overthrowing a corrupt government. A revolution is an ongoing process that can take centuries.

On short visits here, people can go home with the idea that everything is—wow—marching ahead as it should: women are being liberated, young people are moving forward, and everything. When you live here, you begin to realize that this process is going to take a heck of a long time.

The country is facing a very serious situation economically. There has to be a tremendous expenditure on defense, and that means having to put all the revolution's grand projects on hold. When I came down in 1980, that was "the year of literacy," and everyone was talking about 1981 as "the year of health." Each year there was going to be a major effort like that. But before you knew it 1983 became the year of defense and production and the next year was the year against aggression. As long as this contra war continues, everything but the bare essentials will keep being put on hold.

One wonderful thing about being here is the degree of culture all over the place. I remember a year or so ago, visiting some friends in a barrio out near Carretera Norte in Managua, when a delegation of trade union people from the U.S. arrived. These local kids started basically putting on a show for them, with puppets, music, the whole works. It was so good—the quality of the puppets, the way they manipulated them, everything—that people were blown away.

I think that, in Nicaragua, as in Cuba, culture goes hand-in-hand with revolution. There's no way you can separate them. It's like a renaissance, you know? A cultural renaissance. You have an explosion of social/political/economic change. You've got people whose creativity is being extended beyond its normal levels. And, consequently, you get a tremendous flowering of all kinds of art forms. It's like they say, "Culture is the artistic weapon of the revolution." And that has great implications, not just in an already revolutionary society. At this New Song festival I attended, there were representatives from all over Latin America, including from countries like Chile, Argentina, El Salvador, Guatemala—many of them now in exile. But their music expressed the aspirations of those people in incredibly eloquent ways. The festival was held at Lake Tiscapa—which used to be a body dump for Somoza's Guardia—so there was symbolic significance besides the fact that it's a beautiful place. The atmosphere was one of tremendous unity, with these people from all over Latin America gathered together—almost surreal.

A lot of reporters talk about the abstract stuff: what did Daniel Ortega say, or what did some famous economist say? Most of all, I'm interested in letting people know about daily living down here. When I was getting ready to come down, people in the States would ask, "What's it like to be at the big rallies? What's it like to wait in line for gas because the ship bringing crude oil from Ecuador couldn't get there? What do Nicaraguans think about Americans?''

So, what do Nicaraguans think? How do they feel? There's a tremendous sense of unity and pride about the country. They feel that this is their thing. Working at INIES, whenever there's a big rally or event, everyone leaves the office early and heads down there. Now, they're not forced to go. But they want to. They close the government ministries early, and those people are expected to go. But everyone else just goes.

There's the same feeling about going to help with the coffee harvest. A few non-essential government ministries actually closed their offices and sent their employees up to work during the peak of the harvest, but mostly people were free to volunteer and they got their salaries just the same whether they cut coffee or stayed in Managua. I went to one of the send-off ceremonies for people going to help withthe harvest, and it was almost the same spirit as in the literacy crusade. People were saying, ''We've got to help with the coffee. We've got to help bring in dollars for trade.'' Some of them are still up there, months later, still picking.

It wasn't too long after I got here and got settled that it was time to start covering the election campaign. I made a point of attending at least one rally of each opposition party to really get a good sense of what was going on, and I'll tell you, it's hard to translate what has gone on in Nicaragua into terms U.S. people can understand. The two systems are hard to compare. In the U.S., we tend to think in terms of a balance between parties; the Democrats and the Republicans theoretically have equal potential to get a candidate elected. In Nicaragua, the spectrum of ideologies represented was quite broad, but there was some truth to the charge that the opposition parties were at a disadvantage; they had the three-month campaign period to put forth their programs, while the Frente had had the previous five years to propagandize. But that's inevitable. The Frente is more than a political party; it cuts across all kinds of lines. It's really more like a movement. It's a whole way of thinking that people participate in. So it does have an advantage.

On the other hand, the opposition parties that participated had complete liberty to say anything they wanted. I went to all these rallies, from conservative democratic to off-the-wall, extreme left, and they were saying, ''Down with the Frente.'' They were blaming the Frente for the economy, for the draft, for the war. They were saying that, if the government weren't totalitarian, then the contras wouldn't be attacking. On TV they were able to say these things!

As it ended up, the parties that went through with participating in the elections did gain ground. The Conservative Democrats (PCD), who are the second largest party in the country, and the Liberal Independents, the third largest, are both seriously split as to whether they should participate in the electoral system or abstain. Both of those parties had conventions in late October and had bitter battles about that. The faction of the PCD presidential candidate, Virgilio Godoy, voted to pull out. But the vice presidential candidate got on TV and said, "We've gone this far, we want everybody to vote." And they came in third. Not bad.

On the other hand were the groups that didn't participate, the so-called Democratic Coordinadora—four political parties and various labor unions. They refused to register, even though the Frente extended the deadline for them, because they said the press was controlled and fair debate wasn't possible and so on. But that, it appeared, was manipulated partly by Washington. Arturo Cruz, who was their candidate, is now openly aligned with the armed counterrevolutionary groups, as is Pedro Joaquin Chamorro, who owns *La Prensa*. Things have gotten a lot more polarized.

The other thing that got a lot of press were the turbas, these mobs who would come and disrupt Coordinadora activities. I was at a PCD rally in a little town south of here called Jinotepe when there were problems. Out in the street, there were some Sandinista youth who were offended by what they had heard. They started shouting, "No pasaran," the slogan you hear all over that means, "We won't let the contras in." The PCD people started shouting back, "Down with the Sandinista communistas."

People got riled up. Eventually, some PCD people found some boards at the lumber yard nearby and brandished them. People picked up rocks and the soggy plastic bags that cold drinks had been sold in. And before you knew it, there was a riot. It erupted in about two minutes flat. I kept thinking, "Hey, Sandinistas, this is not going to get you good press."

But the thing is, you can't boil it down to a simple explanation. You can't just say, "These Sandinistas are out provoking riots." You have to consider the context. There are certain people in the mass organizations who are provocateurs, who are fanatics, who are clearly opposed to any pluralism. And there are people who have sons and brothers and sisters who are fighting in the war. And they just get angry, they react from the gut. It just gets to that breaking point.

The issue of press censorship is also really complex. It's wartime, and there are restrictions on information, which doesn't make my job any easier. Just recently, there have been new layers of bureaucracy imposed on reporters. You have to apply for permission to go to certain areas where they say there's fighting. Just this weekend, a group of us was denied permission to go to one rural area where they said there was danger of contra attack. But I think it might have been because villages were being relocated, and they weren't too keen on us cruising in and just interviewing anyone.

See, they're moving people out in the countryside to areas that are (a) safer and (b) where the revolution can provide better services. I talked to a woman this morning from the Ministry of Social Welfare, and she told me there are presently about 180,000 displaced people in Nicaragua. Some forty thousand of them are immediately in need of shelter. Ten thousand are Miskitos from the Rio Coco area.

But these forty thousand are pretty much people from the Pacific side who are having to leave their homes because of the fighting, directly or indirectly. In some cases, such as up in San Juan de Limay, some people are being moved because the government claims that they had long provided support for the contras. In fact, an army official admitted that the contras have a social base in that region.

These campesinos live a very simple life. They're very isolated. They just raise their corn and their chickens and try to stay alive. Some of them said to us, "What are we supposed to do when the contras come? They're armed, and they say to us, 'Give us food.' So we give them food. So then the army comes and says we're collaborating with the contras because we've given them food." We interviewed twenty-four men who had been in prison for two and a half months as suspected collaborators, and that was the picture they painted.

Speaking of prisons, as far as I know, there have been no criticisms of prison conditions in Nicaragua. Prisoners are treated in a very fair manner. They work. The prison I saw was very clean. The common criminals who were there were making chairs, planting corn. That's one charge I don't think anyone can make against Nicaragua, that there are torture chambers or anything.

But they are moving people from their homes, and it is definitely a mess. The idea is that they can give the people better services and keep them out of the line of fire in case of a major offensive. What that means is, they can go anywhere they want if they don't like the resettlement areas, but they can't go back home. In fact, tragically, the government has been burning some of the homes to keep people from moving back and to keep the homes from being used as safe houses by the contras. One of the most heartbreaking sights I've seen was the charred remains of somebody's house, with a kitten meowing in the rubble.

The life here is a very agitated one. If you're a journalist and you have duties to a magazine and you're generally committed to following what's going on, you tend to be rather busy. And, as an internationalist, you're always an outsider. No matter how much you claim to be living with the people, you can always leave. Certainly that's true for the press corps. For the most part, they don't identify as part of Nicaragua, and that's a different dynamic from being here forever. If your salary happens to be in dollars, you can eat lobster for dinner every night down here. Many reporters are very conscientious, but I don't think they really feel in their gut what's going on here for the poor, and that has to affect how they report the news. For example, TV crews who live in the Hotel Intercontinental—how can they relate to people up in the mountains who are barely surviving?

Rebecca Leaf

Engineering is a field peculiarly concerned with means and oblivious to the ends for which those means may be developed. Engineers—often proudly—define their work as figuring out how other people can do what they choose, be it building bridges or bombs. Rebecca Leaf is a defiant exception to that rule. An MIT-educated engineer, she could be shopping for river-front condominiums in Cambridge if she chose. Instead, she daydreams of finding a house in Barrio Riguero, a working-class area in Managua where four walls and a tin roof can be had for about two hundred dollars. Nicaragua, where Rebecca is a power plant engineer for the country's department of energy, has offered her a combination of satisfactions that her native New England couldn't quite match. Her work is fulfilling in the doing and serves to empower the poor rather than to maintain the status quo. And she finds in the culture in general a strong sense of community and cooperation that, back home, was more easily found in the counterculture.

Rebecca's is the story of a woman who began her adult life reacting against things that offended or constrained her—academic competitiveness, a consumer culture, a too-narrow world in the suburban Massachusetts community where she was raised. After considerable travel and experimentation and a long look inward, she began shaping a path toward positive goals, and chief among these was helping to eliminate poverty rather than just ministering to its victims. Stumbling on the awareness that she enjoyed designing and building equipment, she was nearing thirty when she chose engineering as her path.

With a gift for understatement, Rebecca tends to describe her life's greatest outrages as "not too pleasant" and her joys as "real nice." But the depth of her commitment and the strength of her vision show in the concrete choices she has made and the seventy-hour weeks she has worked to make her dreams reality. Here she tells about these developments, and about the fulfillment and challenge she has found in Nicaragua.

I grew up in an affluent white suburb of Boston called Winchester, Massachusetts, and by the time I had finished high school in 1967 my chief desire was to get out of there. I had been a typical, smart, suburban kid, oversaturated with high-pressure schooling demands until I decided that the image wasn't worth the pain.

The larger world came in through the news media, and it seemed unfair to remain so protected from it. I couldn't stand the direction my classmates seemed to be moving in, of getting out of school and looking for the straightest path toward riches. I was angry, outraged, and tormented by news of war and poverty in other parts of the world.

I became a VISTA volunteer in New Mexico, in a program for Hispanic farmworkers to develop opportunities for education, jobs, and housing. There I did get to see some more of life—the hard life of people who live in a depressed rural area and are also foreigners to the culture around them.

Poverty and hunger are very obvious when you're in the middle of them. In New Mexico, I got involved in some activities for black kids in the town. We would truck them up to a farm in the mountains on weekends to do farming and recreation. Well, at one point, a couple of little boys sold something and got hold of a couple dollars. They asked me to drive them in to the store. I figured that they wanted to buy some candy, but they came out with two loaves of white bread, sat down on the sidewalk, and just crammed it into their mouths because they were so hungry all the time.

VISTA gave me the broader view I was seeking, but it didn't teach me what to do with it. So I spent some time bumming around Europe and Israel. I washed dishes. I made jewelry. I lived on a kibbutz. I worked as a chambermaid. My father is from a Jewish background, so Israel was sort of a search for roots.

Eventually, I wound up back in the U.S. and enrolled at MIT. I felt the need to do some serious learning in order to change some of the injustice I was seeing. I got involved with a small group of faculty and students who were starting a center for world hunger studies.

Two things caused me to get disenchanted. First, the Vietnam War was going on, and I wasn't pleased with MIT's connections with the military. A group of us students went around snooping out weapons projects. One that particularly disturbed me was research for a radar system called a "moving target indicator." It would be mounted on helicopters and used to detect objects four to six feet tall moving about one to two miles an hour in a background that resembled jungle grass—in other words, poor people in Southeast Asia. It seemed incredibly ugly to use all this sophisticated science and technology to kill peasants who were practically defenseless.

We tried to have meetings with students about all this, to get them to realize that they faced a moral decision about the kind of work they would do. But the predominant attitude was, "We're going to study whatever is handed to us and take whatever job is handed to us and we really don't care to think about the consequences of our work."

The other thing that hit a nerve for me had to do with the group on world hunger problems. What developed was a center where different

Third World countries could come seeking advice to solve their hunger problems. The first country that applied was El Salvador. From my New Mexico days, I knew more Spanish than anyone else in the group—which wasn't much—so I got the job of translating all kinds of reports on food production and distribution, health indicators, and so on. It was really obvious from the land-use patterns over the years that more and more land was being used to grow cash crops like cotton and coffee, which benefited only a few large growers. Less and less was used to produce food. The obvious solution would be to give back some of the land to peasants to grow more food. But the way our professors saw it, and the way the report was finally written, was that they should get some nutritional additive to mix in milk for school kids.

At that point, I decided this was not really the way I wanted to spend my energy. I wasn't an empowered enough person yet to confront the professors on the idiocy of what they were doing, but I was together enough to know I didn't want to be part of it.

I've never tried to categorize myself politically. Any policy that seems to be directed towards improving the lot of people in need is probably OK with me, and policies that ignore people's needs generally aren't. It became very important to me to figure out a means of making a living without contributing to the latter kind of policies.

One of my major sources of support and stability during those years was the fact that I lived in a very close-knit group house. Another woman in the house was looking for a creative way to make a living, and I was looking for a business that would allow me to be independent of the larger social system, so we ended up starting a pottery business together. That was my livelihood for six or seven years.

Pottery was never an exciting creative pursuit for me, and eventually I developed a problem with my wrist which told me it was time to find another career. I had enjoyed cultivating my building skills by fixing up my studio—all from scavenged materials, doing a little carpentry, plumbing, electrical wiring. I had also built a couple of little experimental kilns to fire small pieces of pottery with solar energy. I found that I really enjoyed designing equipment and building it.

For a long time, I'd been aware that more education would help me contribute more powerfully to solving some of the problems I saw in the world. In particular, I got to thinking that a strong technical background would make me more useful. As a woman, I guess I had never figured I could build something that would really work well. But meeting strong women who were taking charge of their lives and working things out, I was encouraged to take greater risks myself.

So I decided to go after the best mechanical engineering education I could lay my hands on, with the idea of taking it to a developing country where I could put it to good use. I enrolled at Northeastern University, a school where students alternate six months in the classroom with six months at a "coop" job in their field of study, because I wanted to get a taste of what work would be like for an engineer. I had been living quite a counterculture life there in my little garage, heated with my woodstove and the pottery kiln. Putting on a new suit of clothes and going out to a "straight" job was a strange transition, but I found that if I acted like I could carry it off, then I could.

At Northeastern, I was a good bit older than my classmates and one of usually only two or three women in my classes, so I'd hang pretty tight with the other women. Then, as people noticed that I was getting A's all the time, they started asking me questions, which was good because it gave me a chance to talk engineering. It's hard to describe how isolated I had become during those years in that garage, kicking that potter's wheel. Human interaction is an important part of being an engineer, so I needed to exercise my mouth a little.

Then I began to hear about innovations happening in energy technology at MIT. I opened up a catalogue and spent the night trembling at the variety of exciting courses, so I transferred back there. The chance to study all this new technology opened up horizons for me. The professors there are excellent and, because the labs are so well equipped, you can really see and hear and touch the concepts you're studying.

I graduated from MIT in 1982 and started looking for work, figuring that I'd give myself a little breaking-in period in the U.S. and then go overseas. I had gotten really interested in renewable energy sources; they seemed especially important for Third World countries because buying petroleum cuts into their foreign-exchange resources so badly. I also understood that a poor country can't afford to gamble on an untested technology, so my plan was to learn as much as possible about assessing the feasibility of renewable energy projects and then share that knowledge with some developing country where it could help people.

I sent out resumes to every solar company I could find an address for. But there were a lot of people looking for jobs in that field, and the industry itself was undergoing a major shakedown. I got a few job offers, but they were all unsolicited offers from the military contractors whose presence had driven me away from MIT my first time there. I was again frightened by the extent to which an engineering background can lead you into destructive applications.

Well, instead of sitting around Boston getting discouraged, I decided to come down to Nicaragua to visit a friend who was teaching forestry. Besides getting consolation and a change of scene, I thought coming to a developing country could give me a more realistic picture of the skills I should be cultivating — even though I thought my big move would be years in the future.

When I arrived, everybody said, "You've got an engineering degree. Oh wow! There's a tremendous demand for engineers. Stay and work."

I would protest, "No, I just graduated, I don't really know anything." But it became clear that just having an engineering degree is a rarity down here. Even with my halting Spanish, a guy at the university wanted to hire me to teach. I was aghast.

I had made it a point to come down with some projects that would give me an excuse to meet people, practice Spanish, and feel useful. I brought down some information for the appropriate-technology research center outside Esteli. That center has a research and development group working on practical projects like farm equipment, fuel-efficient woodstoves, and pumps for getting water from deep wells. People from agricultural communities and cooperatives would come and live there for a month or two to learn these technologies, and then go back to teach their neighbors. That seemed to be a great way to organize.

Just walking around Esteli, where the center is located, is an experience. It's nicknamed "Heroic Esteli" because it was under a brutal siege and had fierce fighting three or four different times during the Somoza era. You can still see bullet holes in lots of buildings. And now the contras are pushing for it. I saw Sandinista soldiers everywhere, but I was impressed that they were regular people who didn't seem interested in throwing their weight around. They seemed to be part of the population, not against it. And everyone I met was open and frank about their life stories, some with complaints about current conditions—no hesitation, no wondering why I wanted the information. None of this seemed like what I'd find in a totalitarian state.

I also brought medical supplies and some materials for a sewing cooperative another friend of mine was working with. Some of the workers on these cooperatives are refugees from El Salvador, and I was impressed with the way Nicaraguans were treating them when their own situation is so tough. There was a clear effort on the part of the Nicaraguan government to integrate Salvadorans into this society by giving them land and helping them start cooperatives if that was what they wanted to do.

Here's a story to show you one aspect of what the Nicaraguan revolution means. At one point, I joined a building brigade to put in some plumbing in a poor community in Managua. The government provided pipes, valves, and fittings, and the people were asked to provide the labor. Until then, the water supply was one central faucet. The little kids and women would go fill up a big barrel and put it in this cart whose wheels were anything but round, and lug it up a path that became a gully when it rained. So the people, organized in those neighborhood committees that President Reagan is so afraid of, got together and worked a few weekends, with a lot of spirit and laughter and singing. And then they had plumbing in every house.

I reluctantly went back to Boston and finally found a job with a high-tech research and development company in the energy field. Well, I really immersed myself to learn as much as I could. I took welding courses and turbomachinery design courses and learned about vacuum systems. I developed a reputation as a real grubby person, going through more lab coats than anyone else, because I liked to explore the machinery, climb around inside the furnaces, and so on.

After a year and a half, I'd saved up some money for the first time in my life. I began to feel pretty well prepared to be useful to Nicaragua, and it had somehow become clear in my mind that that's where I should go. I also felt, watching the political and military situation deteriorate, that I should go soon if I was going.

So I made the decision and got moving, sending down a bunch of resumes for my friend Linda to circulate. She was able to make contact with a couple of people in the national energy office who were enthusiastic about having me come.

I got here in November of 1984, the week after the MIG scare. It was still tense. People had dug bomb shelters and made evacuation plans in case of invasion. It was just painful to realize that something so wrong could be just around the corner, that so much destruction could fall on this beautiful place, and that my country would be responsible. But, in spite of that, I was delighted to be here. I didn't have many second thoughts.

When I arrived, I had a little extracurricular project to do before starting my actual job. Some friends in Massachusetts had found a sewing factory that was going out of business and had purchased fifty old industrial sewing machines and sent them down here on a boat. They had been unloaded that summer and some had been distributed, but there were problems. Some of the electric machines were being sent out to sewing cooperatives that had inadequate electrical service. Some of the treadle machines needed adjustment. So I spent my first month traveling around seeing how many of those fifty sewing machines I could get working, and waiting for the paperwork to be finalized for my permanent job.

My job is as a mechanical engineer in power plant maintenance for the energy office. There's a small group of us in the main office of Managua, serving as advisers for the power plants around the country. We try to keep the power plants in the national grid functioning—which include petroleum-burning, geothermal, and hydroelectric plants—and solve maintenance problems when they come up.

At first, I wondered what it would be like being a lone woman engineer in a country as steeped in machismo as Nicaragua is. And, in fact, people around me were uncomfortable to see me getting my hands dirty. But, as I've established myself as pretty knowledgeable in certain areas, they've gotten more willing to let me do my job.

Working in the energy field here is not real different from in the U.S., since it's more or less centrally planned in both countries. Here, the stringency of the war situation has caused the government to decide that the energy production center needs to be self-sufficient. That is, we need to buy fuel, and repair, maintain, and expand the electrical facilities on just the money earned from selling the electricity. That's a challenge. It means that Nicaragua hasn't been able to extend the electric grid as much as it would like to. There are lots of rural areas where people don't have electricity. The government would like to get electricity to everyone just as it insists on getting rice and beans and education and health programs to everyone. But it's difficult.

A big part of our job is figuring out how to get spare parts built, since there aren't enough dollars to import them. Since I've got the strongest background in heat transfer, I end up doing analysis of heat exchangers when they're falling apart and seeing if we can rebuild them using whatever materials are available. It's exciting work for me because it involves not just the heat transfer, but helping with other mechanical problems. All those late nights in the lab are coming to fruition. I'm even doing some teaching around the office, because other engineers and technicians are interested in the analyses I do and ask all kinds of questions.

I am employed, not by any international aid agency, but directly by the Nicaraguan energy office. This gives me something of an insider's view of one of the largest state institutions. The orientation course for new employees was especially revealing. A group of about fifteen of us—cooks, accountants, truck drivers, secretaries, engineers—were sent on a two-day retreat. We got to know each other a little bit, and we discussed issues that would be important in relating to each other and our work: the dialectic process among the individual, the group, and society; and the differences between work discipline in the old and new societies. Many people had stories from the Somoza era of being treated like absolutely nothing at their jobs, and one man said he had actually been slapped around by his boss. Now there's an effort to teach people about cooperation for the first time, and it's taken very seriously.

For instance, we have frequent assemblies for all employees in which the administration reports to the workers on current problems confronting the agency, the status of the budget, and so on, and at which labor-union representatives present their reports. At that orientation, we were invited to join the union and the internal militia of the energy office, but no pressure whatsoever was applied.

A big problem for this country, technically, is that lots of highly trained engineers left after the revolution, and many who are working on power plants now are just getting out of school. And university education suffers from a shortage of books, well-prepared teachers, laboratories. To complicate matters, all the major power plants were designed by outside companies which would build the thing, leave a few operating manuals, and say, "so long." When problems arise, people find that information they need is nowhere to be found.

Of course, the war and the U.S. economic sanctions are having an effect. The sectors hardest hit by the sanctions have been medicine and agriculture. The major equipment of the energy infrastructure is mostly European. However, the war situation in the hilly northern part of the country and the U.S. pressure preventing loans to Nicaragua from international banking institutions are severely restricting normal development of Nicaragua's hydroelectric and geothermal energy potential.

Aside from the tension of my first weeks here, I personally have only had one major scare. I was sitting on the patio of a restaurant in Managua having a late meal with some friends. It was a placid scene—palm trees around and big red parrots in cages on the patio. Then, out of nowhere came a big BANG and what sounded like battlefield noises, followed by a huge flash up on the hill very near. Then the electricity went dead and everybody scattered. It was a tense scene, especially because the explosion came from the main military hospital in the city. My first thought was that there had been some kind of sabotage. It turned out to have been a gas explosion caused by faulty electrical wiring, and the hospital had had enough warning to evacuate everyone. It was not a major contra attack in the heart of Managua. But it was a reminder of the dangers people face all over this country, and I wasn't the only one who felt it. All over town, people were lining the streets, gathered around radios. Militias were all out.

I've seen some unfortunate changes since my first visit—not the fault of Sandinista policies, but of the aggression our own country is carrying out. There are more beggars—there were almost none when I came before. It's also disconcerting to see Sandinista propaganda get more and more strident as the war heats up. You'll hear on the radio that all of Sandino's men must go to the front, stuff like that. It clutched at me at first, the militancy of it. But the more you hear of coffee harvesters getting bayoneted to death and wedding parties getting machine-gunned and doctors getting killed and hand grenades being thrown into day care centers, the more understandable it becomes. What's happening here is a systematic destruction of the infrastructure that's meant to be supportive of the campesinos. There comes a point where people have to fight back.

On a more personal level, one of the hardest things has been finding housing. Apartments don't exist. A whole house is too expensive. Poor families don't really have enough space to rent you a room, and well-to-do families don't appreciate why I'm here. I am now living in an overly expensive pension, but still looking for a simpler place that's better integrated into a neighborhood.

Apart from that, I'm getting pretty well settled. I bought a clunker of a car from another North American who was heading back. I don't get a chance to feel isolated from home because people from the States are passing through all the time and sending me little packages with parts for the sewing machines and candy bars and things. All in all, this is as close as I can imagine to the life I've wanted.

Nancy Donovan

Under Fire

Sharon Hostetler

Under Fire

As these stories have unfolded about the dream that has drawn these North Americans to live and work in Nicaragua, we have inevitably heard reference after reference to the unraveling of that dream. Against the backdrop of plans to educate a new generation, we hear that there are not enough pencils. Against the news of land reform, we learn that peasants are frightened from their cooperatives by raids from Honduras and Costa Rica. A vaccination campaign has wiped out polio, but it has fallen short of eliminating malaria, and much of the reason is the effective threat of contra attacks on rural health workers. And, perhaps the saddest aspect of all is the inevitable failures of the dream itself under pressure—press censorship, the military draft, periodic flareups with churches over political loyalties, alienation of some private producers, and the mistrust of the Atlantic coast population surrounding the relocation of ten thousand Miskito Indians out of combat areas.

In the first five years after the overthrow of Somoza, the "new Nicaragua" found itself enmeshed in a number of wars whose basic thrust is as old as history. The battlefield war that began as a series of raids across the Honduran border by defeated members of Somoza's old National Guard has become an organized, well-financed military engagement which has also involved forces on Nicaragua's Costa Rican border. Since the U.S. public first began hearing reports of training camps for counterrevolutionaries in rural Florida in 1981, our government has played a key role in bringing together isolated anti-Sandinista forces, equipping them, and giving them strategic assistance in what the Reagan administration admits is a campaign to overthrow the Managua government. By the end of 1984, deaths from this war included 2,812 Nicaraguans and 4,760 contras. In addition, 3,720 civilians had been kidnapped, and their whereabouts are not known. Nicaragua has sustained a stunning $445 million in damages, an entire year's export earnings.

The devastating impact of this war lies partly in the predominance of civilian targets—which account for one third of the deaths—and the cruelty with which the contras operate. The substance of several eyewitness accounts presented in the following section is repeated, with many others, in a report compiled by former New York State Attorney General Reed

Brody, "Attacks by the Nicaraguan 'Contras' on the Civilian Population of Nicaragua," the fruits of four months of research, published in March of 1985.

The contras' pattern of targeting civilians involved with democratic reform and government services—and of kidnapping and mutilating as well as killing victims—is confirmed by Americas Watch, a human rights organization which has sharply criticized the Sandinista government for isolated offenses. Americas Watch describes the contras' behavior this way. They "have systematically violated the laws of war throughout the conflict. They have attacked civilians indiscriminately. They have tortured and mutilated prisoners. They have murdered those placed hors de combat by their wounds. They have taken hostages. They have committed outrages against personal dignity."

When a band from the FDN (Nicaraguan Democratic Force, the Honduran-based contras) was interviewed by two Belgian journalists the day after the infamous Wedding Party Massacre in Wiwili about the appropriateness of such tactics—seven civilians were shot in cold blood, including the bride—a spokesman said without apology that whatever steps were necessary to fight "communism" were acceptable in this war.

In spite of these no-holds-barred tactics and more than one hundred million dollars in U.S. aid, the contras have been unable in five years' operation to capture any populated territory in Nicaragua. Their long-term effect, beyond the terror they instill in the population, is likely to be in cutting off the people from the programs of the new government by selectively targeting local leaders, cooperative workers, health care specialists, union organizers, road crews, and others who are working for practical reform.

But a second war may have a broader and longer-range impact on the Nicaraguan people, even in Managua, where "la contra" exist mostly as a haunting presence on the daily news. Nicaragua is fighting for survival economically just as much as it is militarily. And here, too, our own government has made many decisions that will shape this small country's destiny. In its first months in office, the Reagan administration cut off wheat sales to Nicaragua, terminated payments of aid approved since the revolution, and articulated a policy of pressure on the Sandinistas to force conformity to U.S. political and economic norms. In Reagan's first term, that campaign came to include blocking major loans by several international lending agencies—loans of a type routinely relied upon by Third World countries. Press reports indicate a number of cases of pressure against our allies not to sell Nicaragua key commodities such as oil even before the announcement of a package of economic sanctions in the spring of 1985. These formal sanctions included an end to purchases from Nicaraguan exporters; an end to sales of goods and services to the Nicaraguan government or private sector; closing of U.S. ports to Nicaraguan ships; and closing of U.S. airports to Aeronica, the Nicaraguan airline.

If these steps had been taken against a fiscally healthy country, they might have required some adjustment but would not have led to major disruption. That is, they might have constituted the kind of pressure the administration said it sought. But, when the Sandinistas marched into Managua, they inherited a country devastated by the war and the earthquake. They also inherited a treasury that had been looted as the departing Somoza's last official act. He left a paltry two million dollars and a national debt far higher, much of it accumulated in the course of his private business dealings. By agreeing to pay back that debt, the new government bought itself the respect of many nations, but it also took on a task that may be harder than winning the war against Somoza. Five years later, daily life in Nicaragua is shaped by the scarcity of consumer goods, shortages of repair parts for transportation and industry, even the need to do without such basics as medicine and fertilizer.

Hunger and frustration are profoundly effective weapons. Are these economic pressures having any effectiveness at all in pushing the Nicaraguan government into positions more favorable to Washington, as the Reagan administration hopes? Or might they be doing the opposite, as suggested by President Daniel Ortega's ill-timed visit to Moscow in the spring of 1985, when the country was desperate for funds to plant the season's urgently needed cash crops and aid from the Inter-American Development Bank had been held up by our own government's parliamentary moves?

Nicaragua sees itself as under fire both militarily and economically, and the following testimonies will clarify the human impact of that situation. But the least-understood war, and the one that makes the other two possible, is the information war taking place in the international arena. Is the United States' hostility a result of Nicaragua's military buildup, economic disarray, and press censorship, or has it created these problems? Has the counterrevolution become a popular cause, as broad-based and charismatically led as the revolution against Somoza was? In the experience of those the Sandinista revolution was meant to help most directly, the poor who are Nicaragua's majority, have the gains since 1979 outweighed the losses? And, if they haven't, who is to blame?

The stories in this last section are in many ways the most difficult to come to terms with. They are the stories of North Americans for whom the war is a central reality, either because they live in areas where contra activity is a fact of life or because their work involves observing and reporting the mounting casualties.

Coming from a variety of religious and scholarly backgrounds, these people may be most remarkable in their similarity to folks one could meet in small towns and cities here at home. They do not see themselves as visionaries or as martyrs, merely as individuals who by unique combinations of circumstances have something special to offer and are willing to give it here, in the heart of the conflict.

Sharon Hostetler

Sharon Hostetler is in Managua as a staff member of Witness for Peace, a group of Christians and other religious people who are standing up against the war in Central America in a uniquely powerful way: by visiting the war zones to bear witness to the nature of the fighting, the casualties, and the impact on daily life. Witness for Peace delegations—often representing a particular church, union, or community group—travel first to Managua for orientation and then to one of the many outlying communities. They live with the Nicaraguans in every sense, sharing their hospitality, helping them with their work, and experiencing the same risks they do. Delegations, with the help of the long-term staff in Managua, also travel to the sites of battles and atrocities to collect eyewitness accounts and to grieve with the survivors. By entering the Nicaraguan reality rather than observing it from a safely neutral perspective, these witnesses hope to accomplish several things: to send home reports that are both accurate and emotionally compelling; to offer direct material and moral support to the Nicaraguan people; and to increase the political cost of contra attacks through the presence of U.S. citizens who knowingly place themselves at risk.

I met thirty-two-year-old Sharon Hostetler at the house where Witness for Peace bases its operations and lodges its many international visitors. On a quiet street lined with pink and purple bougainvillea, the house is humble but infinitely hospitable. Members of a new delegation from the Midwest ate rice and beans and salad cafeteria-style, then congregated on the patio to continue a daylong orientation. Partway through our talk, Sharon was called to address that group, and I was privileged to see her in action as she described the reality of life as a peace witness. In painful detail, she told of a conversation with the mother of a thirteen-year-old girl who had been killed in a U.S.-aided aerial attack on a military training school where the girl had been selling pastries. At one point, her voice broke and tears came gushing. But she kept on with the story, not bothering to hide the emotion and remarking, "It never gets easier to do this work. It's what we call the painful privilege of being here."

The message I found in Sharon Hostetler's words goes beyond the anger and horror that the Central American war can inspire. It is a message *of moral authority, of great faith in the power of individual action, of love for the Nicaraguan people and culture, and of hope that abides.*

I was born in Plain City, Ohio about twelve miles west of Columbus, in 1952. Our family had ten children, so there were twelve of us including Mom and Dad. I grew up on a farm. My early recollections are of being outside, playing softball every afternoon in the summertime with all my brothers and sisters. We had quite a softball team. We also did a lot of other things together. We helped with a lot of farmwork. I grew up driving a tractor. I went to a public school. My family belongs to the Mennonite church, and that had very strong implications in my formation. The Mennonite church is what we call a peace church, a traditional peace church, meaning that we do not participate in military armed force of any kind. We are also concerned with the broader implications of peace and justice through nonviolence in bringing about social change.

Being in a big family in a small house taught me a lot about being together, the importance of family, sharing through hard times. The Mennonite church, being a community-type church, reinforced those values—the importance of a community and the religious values of love and justice. I think one of the most important ways I learned those lessons was in looking at poverty. I was going to a church where we obviously had concern about poverty—at least a concern that led people to give out of the pocketbook or the bank account as long as we all had enough. My family was far from wealthy, but I always wondered why we had and other people didn't have. I also wondered why the church itself was not spreading out and bringing more people in under its umbrella.

I guess I've always thought a lot about what my own religious commitment really means and what the church stands for. I remember being taught about nonviolence and the concept of refusing military service for moral reasons. As Mennonites, we're taught that we're all brothers and sisters and therefore to use violence to end the life of someone else who is also God's creation is not appropriate. In eleventh grade I wrote an editorial in English class, and it was not particularly popular. I argued that a peace church had to say more than "Don't participate in military force." It also had to be more concerned about broader issues of social justice and combating institutional violence. That made people stop and think, and it also made me stop and think as I wrote it.

After I graduated from high school in 1969, I went to a Bible institute for two years. Then I went to Ohio State University for one quarter. In 1973, the executive secretary of Rosedale Mennonite Missions called me and asked if I would be interested in going to Nicaragua to work with the Mennonite voluntary service program in a rural clinic. The job was in community health organizing, working in a pharmacy as an assistant to the nurse. I wasn't exactly sure what I wanted to major in, and I was interested, so I decided to do it. I took a short course in nutrition, spent a few months in Costa Rica studying Spanish, and finally came to Nicaragua in October of 1973.

I loved it here from the beginning. I like Spanish and I like the people. But don't think that my initial motives were some strong, pure sense of political awakening or social justice. I came down because the executive secretary of the missionary program invited me and I said sure.

That first period here, I was working in Nueva Guinea, an area which was being "colonized" as they called it—part of what was known as land reform during the Somoza regime. They were moving people who had been displaced by the 1972 earthquake, by other natural disasters, or by the consolidation of large landowners producing cotton or coffee. For whatever reason, these people had been pushed off their land, shipped out, and dropped into the middle of the jungle.

On my way out to Nueva Guinea the first time, I got off in this little town where the bus dropped me, not speaking Spanish but confident because someone was supposed to meet me there. I particularly remember that I wore these white tennis shoes, although I don't know what possessed me. Well, it was pouring down rain, and the person came to meet me on a mule. I had never been on a mule in my life. We drove tractors back in Ohio. So there we are on this mule for three hours along a little path with mud four feet deep. It was such virgin jungle that there were monkeys all along the trail. That was my introduction to Nicaragua.

The village was really poor. It had no electricity. It was three hours by mule to the nearest town, where you could catch a bus to Managua. You had a main street with houses along both sides and that was about it. We did have running water during the rainy season, using a system of barrels. During the dry season we had no water. It was a subsistence-level existence, pretty poor. We'd bathe in the river during the summertime, wash our clothes in the river. The clinic did have a motor for emergencies. But it was primitive. Still, those were three of the best years of my life, just living out there with campesinos. They took care of us like we were their children.

After I learned some Spanish and started reading the history of Nicaragua, I could analyze the situation more deeply, stepping back from my culture enough to see into theirs. Then I started to think about the wider issues of justice. Why are the people in Nicaragua so poor? Why is my family not poor? Obviously, within the United States there's a lot of poverty. But that experience made me look at the wider issues of underdevelopment, capitalism, socialism, other forms of government. I realized there is probably no ideal form of government, but I also came to understand that capitalism may have shaped my perspective in ways I might not want. I came to realize that the people in Nicaragua are poor because of the years and years of exploitation, starting with colonization by the Spanish. You had these Spanish conquerors coming and claiming in the name of the king vast areas of land. And then they would force the native people to work for them, but all the wealth would go back to

Spain. After Spain, it was England. After England it was the United States, taking out the raw materials.

I was acutely aware of the struggle against Somoza in those years. Being here during the time of the National Guard and seeing how the campesinos were treated, I couldn't help but have my eyes opened. You know, my father's a farmer, so when I saw the campesinos in Nueva Guinea working their land and not being able to get their grains to the market, or getting a very poor price I would say, my God, that could be my father. That drove home the fact that there was really injustice here.

I was here from 1974 to 1977, then I went back to the United States and finished my undergraduate degree at Eastern Mennonite College. It was a B.A. in social work. From there I went directly into graduate school at Ohio State University, where I graduated with a master's in social work in 1982.

Probably as a result of that early exposure to Central America, I got interested in the Latin American studies program at Eastern Mennonite College. They had a program in Costa Rica of students who wanted to do social work internships abroad, and I became director of that program. I usually had students here in Nicaragua, so I had an excuse to visit here and maintain my ties. By now, we're talking about the early years of the counterrevolution, which I knew full well was supported and financed by my government. As I spent time here, I developed a close relationship with Witness for Peace, working with them when I had time and filling in while they looked for a permanent coordinator. They talked me into helping two weeks a month with the logistics for the short-term delegations: Where are these people going to sleep? How will they be fed? Then, in May of 1984, I came back here to work with them full-time. It just seemed a natural thing for me to do, having lived here under Somoza and seen the popularity of the insurrection, and then knowing that my country was working to undermine it.

My life here is really very satisfying. The permanent staff of Witness for Peace all live in this house on the edge of Managua. Ana Louisa, our cook, is like a mother. She cooks wonderful rice and beans and vegetables. It's a relaxed neighborhood—lots of doors are open in the evening, so it's easy to visit. We have a hammock here on the porch where I love to watch the sun go down when I have time.

Of course, I've been scared at times. Once, on a trip with a Witness for Peace delegation up to Jalapa, where there's been some of the worst contra activity from the beginning, I was acutely aware that the road had been mined in the past, and there had been ambushes. But, for me, that fear is overshadowed by a commitment that I feel not only to the people of Nicaragua but to my own people back in the United States and to the whole cause of self-determination.

On that trip to Jalapa, I visited this humble little gallery that's maintained by the Mothers of Heroes and Martyrs, a group of women whose sons have been killed defending Nicaragua. On another visit there, I met an elderly gentleman whose son had just been killed in combat, and our whole delegation was invited to the wake. It was Christmas Eve. We all stood outside this old man's house and said a prayer, feeling a bit like outsiders. But the father invited us right in. That was my first direct contact with these casualties. The father said, "This is the second son I've lost, but there are still two of us left and we will be here." And then he prayed: "We realize that many people's hearts are made of stone, but we know that someday you are going to turn those hearts of stone into flesh and blood." That made an enormous impression on me, that this simple farmer would even see his enemies as human beings capable of change.

The unbelievable thing is that, for all the Nicaraguan people have been through at the hands of the U.S., they are still warm and accepting when U.S. visitors come down to help. It's very important that folks back in the States realize that people in Nicaragua want peace with the United States. They love and respect the North American people very, very much. It's impossible to see that love and not to want to return it.

Too many people in the United States are unaware of how much these people have suffered: earthquakes, a horrible dictatorship for forty years, and now another war for five years. People have asked me in the war zones, "Why doesn't Reagan come down here and see what's happening to us? Why doesn't he come see the atrocities committed by these contras he's supporting?" If he thinks the Nicaraguan government has betrayed the revolution and it's his place to pressure it back into line, he is using a very violent and immoral means of pressure. As far as I'm concerned, it is the decision of the Nicaraguan people what form their revolution will take. There is no justification for invading another country like this.

Whatever the shortcomings of this revolution, it has moved people much closer to democracy and dignity than they were before. I talked to one farmer, who was not particularly supportive of what we call the revolutionary process, but he still said to me, "The difference is that, before, I used to feel like a dog. Now I don't. Now I can raise my head." That's the biggest difference, the pervasive sense that people have the right to express their opinions. They can complain about the government out in the middle of the marketplace, in front of the police. That was never true here until now.

On the other hand, there's obviously press censorship here. I wish there weren't, but I realize also that this country is at war and most countries at war will censor any kind of military information and some kinds of economic information.

I was here for the elections. I was also here for the elections during the time of Somoza. It's a huge difference. During the campaign, you could sit down at 6:30 and watch the fifteen-minute time slots each party had to present its positions. I was amazed at some of the things they were saying on television—very harsh criticisms of the Sandinistas. As far as individual liberties are concerned, I personally have not come across any cases of oppression. I'm sure there have been incidents, but the important point is that they're isolated and not systematic. There's obviously religious freedom—you can see people going to church all over the place.

The biggest violation of human rights here is what the contras are doing to the Nicaraguan people. One memory that still makes me cry is a trip I took to Santa Clara, a town which was attacked by air on September 1, 1984. We were preparing to take a short-term delegation of Witness for Peace up to Quilali, so we needed to go out to confirm a few things. It was a very beautiful area with rolling hills. Driving along in the sunshine, I said to myself, "When this war is over, I'm going to come back here and ride a horse through these rolling mountains and discover the countryside because it is just absolutely gorgeous." It was that kind of day—butterflies in clusters and flowers everywhere and lush greenness.

On the way back, I noticed that a lot of people were standing out in their yards. I remember thinking, "There's something strange going on here." Eventually, we got to a group of soldiers standing by the road who stopped us and asked us where we had come from and where we were going. When we told them, they said "Okay, go but go quickly." So I thought, "Oh my God, something did happen here. What happened?" Later on, we picked up some hitchhikers and we noticed one woman who had a bandage on her cheek. She told us there had been an aerial attack on the military training school at Santa Clara and that some people had been killed. It was too late to go there that day, but the next morning we took the truck back across the river to confirm the reports. Three young girls had been killed there, as well as a twenty-eight-year-old farmer from another town. The Witness for Peace group divided up and went to talk to the families of the victims.

I spoke to the Hernandez family, whose thirteen-year-old daughter, Alba Luz, had been killed. She and her cousin, Soccorro, had been on the military school base that day, as they often were, selling baked goods to the men. Well, the selling wasn't going real well, so she had climbed a tree and was picking crab apples when a plane circled overhead and Soccorro yelled up to her, "Alba Luz, come down from the tree. These are not our planes." But before she could come down, a rocket exploded right there close to the tree and a piece of shrapnel got her in the side. She fell from the tree saying, "My God, they've killed me." She did stagger up and literally fell into the arms of a soldier who took her inside a building on the base, where she died.

When we got there and went in to talk to Alba Luz's mother, they had just finished putting the body into the casket and arranging the flowers around it. The family was all standing there, looking into the coffin and sobbing. We stood with them and cried with them for five or ten minutes.

Later, I sat down with the mother and she just poured out stories about her little girl. She and Alba Luz were both Christians, members of the Assemblies of God church. Alba Luz was very devout. It turned out that her favorite hymn was one that I remembered singing way back when I was in Nicaragua before—"The Glory of God fell on Mt Sinai."

Señora Hernandez talked about how responsible and obedient Alba Luz was. Every morning she would go to school and every afternoon she would sell these baked goods, and this was the family's only income. On the day that she was killed, she had her little handkerchief to hold the coins she brought in, and even when she climbed the tree she was clutching this handkerchief with her money. When she fell she still held onto it. Only on the table where she died did this handkerchief with the money fall to the ground. That's how responsible this girl was.

In the end, the mother said to me, "You know, I really don't know what's going to happen to me now. I have no income. I'm taking care of my own mother, who is an invalid. What am I going to do?" And then, as so many Nicaraguans do, she begged us to intercede with our government. People down here often say, "Reagan must have no children or he wouldn't be so callous about killing ours."

When I came down to work with Witness for Peace, I didn't get back home for the first two years. Fortunately, my family is not the kind that requires frequent contact to stay close. They're very supportive. I think my father and mother get a lot of vicarious satisfaction out of my work, and that's great. When I couldn't go home last Christmas, I wrote to them saying that my Christmas gift to them was going to be staying here to protest our country's policies, to make sure that in the future we could always be together at Christmas. That was a gushy way to put it, but they understood.

Christmas here is delightful. The celebration actually starts in the beginning of December, when people set up altars with flowers and leaves all over the country to celebrate the Immaculate Conception. For a week, they go around singing songs to the Virgin Mary. Then, the eighth day is called the Day of National Shouting. Wherever there's an altar, people ask, "Who causes such joy?" And people around them answer, "The conception of the Virgin Mary." They give out little gifts and sweets like sugar cane and sweet lemons. Then, on December 24, the major celebration happens, with families getting together for midnight dinner. You're up all night. Then Christmas day itself is a day for taking it easy. I think we went swimming at the lake. I was feeling a mixture of closeness with the people and sadness for all those who were facing Christmas displaced from their homes, or with family members missing, or worse.

You know, it never gets easy. Sometimes I get caught up in the busyness of the office—calling people up to borrow a bus because ours is broken down, figuring out what to do when the phone doesn't work, running around. You never forget the war, but you forget how deep those feelings are—until you try to talk about some experience and find the tears flowing. We call it the painful privilege of being here.

But there's always something to hang onto to keep on going. For instance, when I read in the newspaper about what's happening on Capitol Hill, and I realize that this war probably isn't going to end tomorrow, usually what I do is go find a good Nicaraguan friend. They're the ones who'll get me back. Going out and playing with children, talking with neighbors—not necessarily talking about the war, but seeing the spirit of these people and their sense of humor. Sometimes I get strength to cope with the suffering from the very people who are suffering the most.

One great source of their strength, I think, is the fact that Nicaraguans are able to see themselves as part of a whole movement, a community, not just as individuals. They can say, "My death is not the end of the movement—my death means a continuation of a movement. My death serves."

One of the customs here is, when they say the name of somebody who has been killed, they say "*Presente, presente, presente.*" They repeat it three times—that person is still here. Somehow, by tapping into the strength of the community, they channel the energy of sadness and suffering into a deepening of their commitment to work for the things they're struggling for.

As I step back and evaluate my own growth, I know that it's the inspiration of the folks here in Nicaragua that makes me ready to go. We can get very, very physically tired. This is work which can keep you in the office day and night if you let it. But the sharing with the people here is what gives us the energy—the simple expressions of determination by people who can say, "My son was killed but he's *presente.*" That's what keeps us going—that, plus the faith that truth and justice will win. I really believe that.

Susan Van Dreser

While many of the subjects of this book were recommended to me for their expertise in some neatly-defined area, it was sheer luck that brought me into contact with Susan Van Dreser—luck in the form of a phone call from a Cambridge acquaintance who asked me to deliver a box of presents to a friend who had gone to Nicaragua for a short course in Spanish and had ended up staying. Each added detail made me more enthusiastic about delivering this package and meeting this mysterious friend. A Unitarian minister, she had taken time off from her parish to attend the Nuevo Instituto de Centro America (NICA), a school on the edge of the war zone which not only teaches Spanish, but involves students in community projects to provide total immersion in the Nicaraguan reality. But Susan Van Dreser had become even more immersed than the average NICA student. Playing along with the matchmaking efforts of the Nicaraguan family with whom she stayed, Susan surprised herself by falling in love with the son of a well-to-do but revolutionary family. Less than two months after their meeting, she married Axel Dávila Bolaños and became the senora of a finca (plantation) in the rolling hills outside Esteli, saying goodbye to her parish back home but not to the ministry.

Susan seems to be approaching her new life with relaxed enthusiasm. But she has already opened herself to enormous change and considerable risk. Battles and contra raids have taken place within a few kilometers of the finca where Susan spends part of her time, although there is still a sense of safety around the family home in the town of Esteli. What's more, while others in this book have come to Nicaraguan with a job to do, Susan's choice is a sharp turn off the career path she had established and means starting from scratch to find fulfilling work. She has time to do this, with a supportive husband and no serious financial worries, and even finds herself "learning to be dependent." And she knows all these adjustments will take time: she is choosing not only to work in a new place, but to adopt a very different way of life.

When I arrived with the long-awaited package, Susan opened it and passed around part of its contents—peanut butter cups—like the rare treat they are in a poverty-stricken country. During our visit, family friends, including a number of government officials and Sandinista soldiers, passed

*through. We found a comfortable spot next to an open courtyard—with
a Michael Jackson record spinning underneath a portrait of Che Guevara—
and Susan spent two hours telling me about the developments that brought
her here.*

I seem to like to wander around, to go to all kinds of different places.
My family visited Scotland once when I was in high school, and I fell in
love with it so hard that I split my college education in the middle to go
and teach for two years there and in England.

I'm sure my parents had a lot to do with my willingness to travel.
We moved around a lot when I was a kid. My father was first in business
and then became a Methodist minister, and he brought us up in a variety
of places in New York State, Vermont, Georgia, and Virginia.

My dad also had a lot to do with the fact that I've ended up a minister,
I guess. I first thought about entering this field when I was about eleven.
I've always been into helping people, and because of his work I was very
familiar with this kind of life.

That doesn't mean my path has been a straight one, though. I finished
my degree in English at Beloit College in Wisconsin in 1976 and moved
to Boston. My first job was working in drug and alcohol rehabilitation with
teenagers. I did that for four years, which is an awfully long time to be
doing that kind of work. Eventually, I realized there was nowhere to move
in my work without another degree. I would be stuck in the caretaker role
forever, and it was burning me out.

I thought I would study more psychology when I began looking at
graduate school programs. By then, I had started going to church again.
I had rejected it for a while, as part of being a good rebellious North
American kid. But it was a familiar atmosphere and a place where I could
go at least once a week to be quiet and get some mental stimulation I
really wasn't getting anywhere else. One day I was sitting in church,
listening to the minister preach, and I thought, "Gee, I could do that!"
My next thought was, "That's absurd," but I knew it wasn't, and a year
later I had received my acceptance to Harvard Divinity School.

At first, I thought I would go into pastoral counseling and stay on
the psychological end of things. But when I did my internships in churches
to fulfill the requirements for my master's degree, I discovered that I really
enjoyed a whole spectrum of activities in the church. I like public speaking.
I'm even a good administrator. Branching out into these areas made me
feel much stronger and more confident, and it was a chance to rediscover
how great and nifty people are. So I ended up, after graduation, being
ordained by the Unitarian Universalist Church in Sharon, Massachusetts
and becoming a regular suburban minister. If there's anything I'm going
to miss here in Nicaragua, it's that life.

My awareness of Nicaragua developed gradually during the late 1970s.
Somewhere on the second page of the newspaper, in among the little blurbs
that outline all the coups and floods and so on in the world, I remember
a little blip saying there had been a revolution in Nicaragua. For some

reason, it excited me. Somtehing was happening. The people were rising up and a nasty dictator named Somoza had been overthrown. I remember—it must have been shortly after that—seeing a photo of the people pulling down the statue of Somoza. I was overwhelmed by the number of people taking part.

My connection to Central America grew in little steps when Archbishop Romero was assassinated and when the four U.S. church women were killed in El Salvador in 1980. During my time at divinity school, several other pieces to the puzzle fell into place. One was the development of my own feminism, which led me to be in solidarity with the women in Central America. And another was discovering liberation theology. I was very much influenced by reading *The Gospels of Solentiname*, which are transcriptions of dialogues among people on these islands in Lake Nicaragua. Ernesto Cardenal, who is now minister of culture in Nicaragua, was the parish priest there. These dialogues are an attempt at interpretation of the gospel by peasants reading them for the first time, without the intervening interpretation of a priest. Now, I think Cardenal did a good bit of interpreting; his Marxist reading shows through. But what they reveal is still very important: that the gospels don't just mean loving your enemy and letting him swat you down. They also mean loving your friends and fighting for them.

Eventually, that thinking led the people of Solentiname to take up arms against Somoza, a decision which some of them regret while others don't. But what's important to me is that it shows a real struggling of people to live with the gospels in other than the white, middle-class way in which I had been brought up. I had been seeing the gospels in one particular way: even "the poor" was a metaphor for people who were not fully human. But, reading Cardenal and studying liberation theology, that simple thing struck me: "This is literal! This means people who are poor."

During those years, I learned to appreciate, understand, and love the gospels more. I started to understand that the gospels of Jesus really sincerely and genuinely request that we work with the poor. But I'm a white, middle-class, bourgeois person. That's my culture. So the challenge was to step outside my own background. It was that understanding that made me open-minded enough to come down here and even to be able to live here.

As for Nicaragua, the turning point in my involvement was the invasion of Grenada in the fall of 1983. I've always been an underdog kind of person, predisposed to pay attention to the little countries. I'm also pretty skeptical of the U.S. government—that's a bias I'm aware of—and especially against the Reagan administration. I had done some work for the Democrats in 1980. So, as the contras emerged into the public eye, I definitely began to see Nicaragua as an underdog pitted against a much bigger dog, the U.S. Intuitively, I said, "The underdogs are the Sandinistas in Nicaragua and the guerrillas in El Salvador." A lot of people I respected were talking the same way. I began really intensive reading on Latin America that fall and became even more convinced that what was going on here was the United States trying to impose its will on supposedly independent countries.

Coming to Nicaragua involved a whole different kind of thinking from picking up to go to England and Scotland. In the Old Country, I was just drawn by pure romance. And there weren't things like a different language and a war situation to complicate matters. Thinking about coming here meant facing the possibility of my life being in danger. But I felt strongly, as I have for years, that the United States should not be intervening in countries such as Nicaragua; that it was my responsibility to support the people in such a country; and that one way to do that was with my presence.

That opportunity came when a Witness for Peace delegation from Massachusetts came down here in March of 1984, and I was able to be part of that team. It was a tremendously exciting trip. I was so stimulated by the way I saw the Nicaraguans struggling that I got involved immediately in solidarity work back home.

I knew right away that I had to come back again. There was no question. It's a missionary kind of impulse. I came because I knew I could share some of the things I had as a North American, and I could bring back to the U.S. more knowledge and sensitivity which would deepen and strengthen my solidarity work.

When I came back down, it was to attend the Nuevo Instituto de Centro America, a school in Esteli that teaches Spanish but also gets its classes involved in community projects to really live the Nicaraguan reality. I was housed with a woman named Chapita and her extended family in a rather crowded place. Well, my Nicaraguan "mother," as I came to think of her, was convinced from the beginning that I should marry a Nicaraguan man, and all the women in the neighborhood backed her up. What's more, they took it upon themselves to find me one. They were all setting me up with their nephews, cousins, brothers, and what have you. Right in front of some guy, they would say, "This is my nephew. Pretty nice looking, don't you think?" It was very heavy match-making!

Anyway, while this was going on, we visited the Dávila Bolaños household one Sunday afternoon. Axel, who is now my husband, was sitting at the table with some friends eating a meal. Mind you, this was when I spoke hardly a word of Spanish. People would have to repeat things fifteen times for me. But we managed to have a little conversation. A few days later, I came back and visited. Eventually, I discovered that he owned a finca, and I was really aching to get out in the country. So I said to one of the women, "Can't you get this guy to take me out to the finca?"

Well, one Saturday, I was supposed to go coffee-picking but the school cancelled the trip because coffee-pickers from Esteli were being killed, so Axel and I went to the finca instead. It's a stunning place, four thousand feet in the mountains. You can see Lake Managua from one of the hills, and there are all these lakes and streams for bathing.

That first day, Axel got me alone on one of the patios and began courting me very heavily. "Won't you give me a kiss? Will you marry me?" It was incredible! I hadn't flirted like that since I was fifteen! I would let him kiss my hand and then yank it away. You don't need a lot of Spanish to flirt—just "no" and "si." So we spent a good part of the day flirting and had a wonderful time!

We got together again the next week, and things developed fairly rapidly. Pretty soon, I moved out of Chapita's house, largely because it didn't seem fair to take up that space when I was spending all my time at Axel's. I was accepted into the family rapidly. They called me "sister-in-law" long before we actually got married.

This family, by the way, has a really intriguing history. The father, Dr. Alejandro Dávila Bolanos, was involved with the Sandinista movement from its inception until he was murdered by Somoza's Guardsmen three months before the triumph. Probably an important factor in his murder is the fact that he was a political and philosophical mentor to many Sandinista leaders: Fonseca, Mayorga, the Orgetas, Borge. In addition, he was a physician who became known as "the people's doctor" because would treat the poor without charge. He was the first doctor in Nicaragua to perform open-heart surgery, but he was also an expert on folk medicine. He wrote a number of books on the language and mythology of indigenous folks. The library here at the house reflects his breadth, and because he was so well read, the kids tend to be a well.

His wife is just as extraordinary. She's known as "La Mama," but she's a nurse and a pharmacist and a carpenter. She was also the first woman in Esteli to drive a car. See those handprints in plaster on the wall? The doctor had her make those because he thought her hands should be immortalized.

La Mama is the one who kept the family together during the war. The Guardia attacked the house four different times, damaging it severely. She literally redesigned the house and helped to rebuild it.

The history in this house is tremendous. Axel spent three years with the guerrillas, and three of his brothers and one of his sisters also fought. There are all kinds of military people coming through, so I get to overhear a lot of what's going on—no secrets, I assume, but lots of news.

It was chemistry between Axel and me. I trusted his character from the beginning. We were married in a civil ceremony exactly forty-six days after that first encounter at the finca. The justice of the peace read the ceremony, and at certain points we had to say "Si." Well, in the middle of all that, my two-year-old nephew thought he wasn't getting enough attention and started climbing up into my arms. I was so distracted I didn't know I was supposed to do anything, until about three people poked me in the ribs and whispered, "Say 'si' "—and there I was! Married!

I didn't write my parents until after this occurred. I was afraid to. My mother wrote back immediately and was supportive. But I didn't hear from my father for two months. Eventually, he sent me a letter saying, "Well, you do have a tendency to pull fast ones. I just hope that you have the same kind of joyous marriage your mother and I have."

I think their greatest disappointment is that I've kind of abandoned the ministry. They haven't always been able to understand the things I've done, but they understand parish ministry. When I was ordained, my mother made my robes and my sister did my stole and my father ordained me. They had been really proud. So it was quite an adjustment when I decided to stay here. On the other hand, a lot of the reason I'm so able to adjust to radical changes is that my parents have given me such a sense of security.

Different groups here feel very differently about the Sandinistas. The saddest thing, I think, is that there are a number of men who fought with the Sandinistas and spent years of their lives organizing—some from the time they were ten years old. They've killed people—and I'm convinced that when you kill somebody it changes you forever. They've fought for their families. They've seen their friends die. And now they feel betrayed; they feel that the Sandinistas have reneged on their promises. They've promised to provide a better economic base, to provide pluralism. Now, I've even heard some people say, "We used to have one dictator; now we have seven."

There's a widespread sense that there is a power vacuum, but everyone's afraid to try to fill it because they don't know how the Sandinistas would react. I was talking to a group of young men, all of whom had been in the underground against Somoza. We had all gone swimming and were sitting around by the water. Everybody had their AKA-47s, as usual, and they had fun doing target practice and talking about old times and good targets they had hit.

Then they started talking about the present situation, and they became bitter, bitter, bitter. They said, "Right now all we want is to do our work. We're producers. We're the people who work the hardest." They consider many of the rah-rah Sandinistas to be lazy types who let the rest of the cooperative do the work. As independent producers, they see themselves as working really hard. They're all paying people more than minimum wage and making sure the country gets some of the things it needs, but they're not getting the recognition because private owners and private workers are on the ideological fringes.

It's not that they're harassed, but they don't get the kind of aid they need. You cannot get loans to buy property. It's hard to get hold of the farm equipment you need, and the repair parts aren't available, whereas the cooperatives seem to get more of the parts and seeds and fertilizer. They kept saying, "We fought for the Sandinistas and look what we get."

Well, another American and I proceeded to push them. We said, "You're really angry. You say none of the political parties are any good. It looks like somebody like yourselves has to step in and organize a party that can provide really strong opposition—not the *La Prensa* opposition, not the old Somocistas, but a true opposition."

They all said, "Yes, yes. We need a new party and we need a charismatic leader." But there was all this hesitation. Part of it was that they had been through so much and just wanted to live their lives. But they were also uncertain as to how the Sandinistas would react.

At the same time, I asked these people if they supported the contras. They said, "Absolutely not! That's not the way to change what's going on here."

Besides the private producers, who feel betrayed, there are the campesinos, the peasants, who seem to be feeling more confused. In many ways, they have less than before. They heard all these promises, but not too much has materialized for them. Some have learned to organize, and that's good. There's lots more opportunity for education and to become professional. There was better health care at first, until the medicine shortages started. But, on the whole, they seem unsure about what's going on. They say, "I really don't want my kid being drafted, and it worries me that we can't get beans sometimes." Above all, it's a sense of "Here we go again." They're awfully tired.

It's real obvious that a lot of these problems have arisen because of the huge amounts of resources being poured into the war. There are far more people in the military this year, and they have to be fed and clothed and trained. The contras are making much more effective strikes, especially in attacking the producing cooperatives and large farms that would supply rice, tobacco, coffee. The U.S. veto of international monetary aid is very damaging to this economy.

On the other hand, I wouldn't be surprised if there's some mismanagement going on. There's a bureaucracy for every kind of program. Some people are really irritated that the government is building so many new offices when people are without housing.

When I started realizing the depth of the problems and discontent here, my initial response was to feel betrayed by the solidarity movement in the United States. I felt that they had not been giving me the truth. I went through a terrible struggle with my own ideological perspective.

What I've ended up saying is this. On one hand, the Sandinistas have made some really fierce mistakes. There are power struggles and ideological struggles in the directorate, both over how much to back down in dealing with the U.S. and over who is running Nicaragua. They're poorly organized. They don't distribute their goods very well. Sometimes all the frijoles for the region will end up in Esteli and all the cooking oil will be sent to Matagalpa. They're so ideological that they set themselves apart from the rest of the world.

On the other hand, they've played an incredibly significant role in alleviating the suffering of the people in this country. And certainly a lot of their problems can be acounted for by the fact that they've got one of the strongest powers on earth trying to obliterate them. If you want to make a rigid, ideological group of people more so, that's the way to do it.

Saturdays and Sundays tend to be drinking days around here. That's what Nicaragua's like. That's when the political discussions start coming up. Friends and even families will descend into name-calling: "You're a contra"—"You're a Sandinista fanatic." I've even seen political fist fights.

But whatever people may think of the Sandinistas, there's almost universal hatred and fear of the contras. I'm always afraid—especially at night and early in the morning, because dawn and dusk are the most dangerous times. I had to learn not to sit on the porch and read with a lantern at night up at the finca because that would set us up as a target. I've had lots of nightmares.

Axel and I were walking up near the finca once, and we came upon a contra camp that had just been vacated. We saw this little piece of paper on the ground in the middle of nowhere, and we just knew. My reaction was to hit the ground instantaneously. Then we turned our heads in the same direction and there were the ashes of a fire with three fresh cigarettes on top—and it had rained the night before. We snooped around a bit more and found a hammock and a tarp—and campesinos don't go sleeping out in the woods.

This was three kilometers from the finca. Then, on the path, we discovered that someone had been walking along, bleeding. The blood was maybe twenty-four hours old. We decided to get out of there, because you don't want to run into someone who is half dead and has a gun. We turned off the path—and came upon a house that had been just blown to smithereens. There were pieces of tile everywhere. It had been recent, because the tree branches around the house were damaged but the leaves and fruit on them hadn't wilted yet. Now we were really concerned with getting out of there. We headed up this cliff, passing the remains of an army camp on the way, and got back to the house as fast as we could. When we got back to Esteli, we read in the papers that there had been a major combat two days before. The Sandinistas had killed twenty-six contras.

We sleep with an AKA-47 by the bed. I'm really torn about whether I should learn to use it. I learned early how to disarm guns, because I don't like it when the kids get too close to the weapons.

Jesus, the caretaker at the finca, told me recently that she's more scared now than during the insurrection. The Somocistas were brutal, but the contras are worse: you get caught between them and the Sandinistas, and there's nothing you can do. She said that, the first time the contras ever come by and say, "We want that cow," she'll give it to them and she'll pack her family and move back into Esteli.

The contras are hated for their cruelty. They attack the civilian population and they don't just kill people. They maim and they torture. A friend of mine set out one night to help a victim of a contra attack. But he got to the hospital and discovered that the guy was two days dead. He had had battery acid rubbed into his eyes and hair and genitals. He had cigarette burns all over his body. His tongue was cut out. His genitals were cut out and stuffed into his mouth. My friend said, "How did he die?" and everyone laughed. But it was really hard to tell because the body had been so damaged. It's a psychological war. Everybody's terrified contras because they maim like that, they rape women. . . . They're not even human. They're more like machines.

Ironically, living here, I'm finding it harder to keep up on the real work of trying to help the Nicaraguan people. I write lots of letters home to legislators and to friends, and I hope those letters will be shared widely. I'm working on making contacts in the community to figure out some work I can do, like setting up a clinic or teaching. But at this point I'm still trying to absorb the language—and, what's harder, the culture, so I don't grate on people by being different. While everything is so new, one of the interesting lessons I have to learn is how to be dependent, which I am. I don't know the language. I don't know the culture. I'm not working. Fortunately, I have a husband who is not into machismo.

I think there will be ways to reestablish my ministry in some way down here. But it will be very different, and I can't say what form it will take until I've learned this culture and how I fit into this culture. I know that North American white administrative ideas don't fit in here—they're considered pushy and aggressive. I'm going to have to learn a whole new carriage for myself. But I don't think I've left the ministry behind.

Jim Feltz

Father Jim Feltz looks singularly out of place in the lobby of the Intercontinental Hotel in Managua. Even in the middle of war and economic chaos, the spirit of the place is of frivolity and pretension. An all-you-can-eat buffet pours out a cornucopia of salads, roasts and pates, cakes and tortes, all to the serenade of a piano that could have been imported from Rick's Place in Casablanca. Most of the loungers in the lobby are dressed for fun or at least for show: press crews in pressed khaki, vacationers and business people, and even an International Lions Club convention during our visit.

Jim is in Managua for a few days to have his jeep fixed. He is also taking a breather from his work as priest in the rural parish of Paiwas which is actually thirty-three villages, connected only by horse and mule trails. We picked the hotel lobby for our talk for its convenience, but the more we explored the reality of his life in the countryside, the more he seemed oppressed and even angered by our present surroundings.

In his plaid shirt and dark pants, Jim is conspicuous in his modesty. His build is slight and his hair balding. His voice is low and his manner is that of a man who does not enjoy public visibility—until he gets warmed up on the subject of Nicaragua and the values of liberation theology which brought him here. Jim is a priest whose identification with the poor is deep and permanent. He seems at a loss to discuss himself outside the framework of this commitment, but when he talks about his experiences and hopes in living it out, he suddenly becomes a charismatic figure.

A Chicago native who spent the early years of his priesthood in Peru, Jim has now sunk such deep roots in Nicaragua that he talks matter-of-factly about five-year plans for his parish. But the unknown factor here, and the subject of this interview, is the course of the counterrevolution which by early 1985 had claimed the lives of one hundred in his parish and had led him into several chilling encounters with the contras.

I think there's been an organic unity to my life. I wanted a religious vocation even when I was a kid, and that's what I did, first as a brother and then as a priest. There weren't a lot of exceptional or extremely difficult decisions to make.

I was born in 1937 in a small town called Boydville, Wisconsin, and I was raised in a working-class Catholic neighborhood on the north side of Milwaukee. My father worked in a car frame factory as a welder. My mother was the manager of a Fanny Farmer candy store. I was heavily into the Boy Scouts and school activities—a fairly typical childhood.

After eighth grade, I went to a suburb of St. Louis called Kirkwood, Missouri, to study in a preparatory seminary of the Marionist congregation. At the time, I wanted to be a working brother, which meant helping with masonry and manual labor. As it turned out, I became a teacher, first doing university studies in San Antonio, Texas. I taught fifth grade in St. Louis for two years and then high school in San Antonio for four. I got a master's degree in Latin and philosophy from St. Louis University.

I guess things started to change for me when I went over to Switzerland for four years to study theology in the mid-1960s. These were intense times in Europe. There was a lot of protesting in the student community against the U.S. involvement in Vietnam. My exposure to people who were critical of United States foreign policy helped me see things in a different light. I became more critical, too, having lived outside the country for so long.

Finally, I was ordained a priest in 1970. That's when I began my Latin American experience. I was invited to spend six months in Colombia and then went on to Peru for seven years. At first, I taught school in Lima. Then I went to the second largest city in Peru, Arequipa, and worked among the poor as well as teaching English at the university. After that, I moved way out into the countryside, a four-hour drive from Arequipa up and down tremendous mountains, to work full-time among poor campesinos.

I'd say my exposure to Latin America—and particularly to liberation theology—has changed my life more drastically than anything else. Liberation theology is a rereading of the Scriptures in their historical context. When you read all these stories about poor people and rich ones, displaced populations and kings, and struggles for freedom, you go on to analyze why some people are exploited and why some few people are very rich. You read the Bible with your feet on the ground in the world around you. That gives it a new energy that really is liberating. It kind of fills your life with a new insight as to what it means to be a Christian, to be prophetic.

In short, it means identifying with the poor. It says the message of Christ and the call to learn and share with your fellow men is an intense call. You have to try to change what is oppressing people. You can't just look at it. You can't just watch people suffer and tell them to pray. You have to pray with them, and then organize with them to change their oppression.

When I first went to South America, I taught in a wealthy upper-class high school and everything was very convenient. But, as I learned about liberation theology, I chose to move out of that school because the idea of giving the gospel to future lawyers and doctors and merchants who would continue to exploit their own people did not seem like a coherent identification with the poor.

I tried to help organize a union of housemaids and others. That was an education for me, just seeing these women commit themselves and struggle on behalf of their sisters who were being exploited so directly. With that also came a call to be authentic in my own commitment to working with the poor. I couldn't hang back. I had to be willing to commit myself.

When I moved up into the Andes mountains, those concerns continued. The idea there was to form a union among the campesinos, who were completely unorganized and who had a pretty tough struggle up there at four thousand meters above sea level.

In 1979, I went back to the States and worked among the Spanish-speaking Mexican population on the southwest side of Chicago. I enjoyed that quite a bit, but I never stopped being homesick for Latin America. Part of what drew me back to the States was an allergy; in Peru, I had asthma all the time. So I was kind of on the lookout for a place to work in Latin America with a friendlier climate. By then, I'd begun reading about Nicaragua and working with a solidarity committee in Chicago.

Let's see, what was it that impressed me about Nicaragua at first? Well, the land reform was one thing. The government took all the unused land of Somoza and his cronies and distributed it among the landless, while leaving the rest of the private farmers their land as long as they were producing. That seemed fair. I also remember a speech given by Jaime Wheelock, the minister of agriculture, to a group of international supporters. His point was about sovereignty. He said that Nicaraguans would be willing to go back to the living standards of the 1940s if necessary to preserve their sovereignty. This impressed me. Self-determination is such a basic value.

So I got interested. I had contacts through the church, so I was able to come down to Nicaragua with invitations to work from the bishops in Esteli and Bluefields. I came down in July of 1981, traveled around, and by the 10th of August I was pretty sure where I wanted to be—in Paiwas, up in Zelaya Central, right in the heart of the country. I stayed, even though it meant leaving the Marionist order because it doesn't maintain a community down here. Instead, I became a priest in the diocese of Bluefields.

Paiwas is a parish of forty-three thousand people spread out among thirty-three townships. It's two to four hours on horseback across a township, and two days' travel across the parish on muleback. We use the mules for long-distance travel because they're stronger and can put up with the mud better than the horses. The roads are few and far between, and are only passable about two months of the year. The poorer families live in bamboo houses with thatched roofs. As a family gets richer, it might get a tin roof and even wooden siding. The wealthiest people of all become cattle ranchers. The crops are corn and beans, raised by families for their own consumption. They also raise chickens and turkeys and cattle and pigs. Most of these areas are so remote that they have to be very selective about what they try to ship to market. Milk has to be made into cheese—this very salty cheese you find everywhere in Nicaragua—and corn can only be used to feed to pigs which can then be taken out.

Most of the people are mountain people who have moved into this "agricultural frontier" in the last generation. They've been chopping away at the rain forest from west to east, living with a machete and an ax, just as earlier generations did farther west. They're not a people with a lot of ingrained traditions, and I see that as an advantage. They've gotten accustomed easily to this new kind of church, where the lay leaders and the Delegates of the Word run the show while the priest only visits them once or twice a year. They're quite flexible as to new ideas.

There are a few comforts. In the small town where the parish has its office and I have my house, there is electricity. In fact, it arrived the week I came to town. My first contact with the people of Paiwas was to organize a workshop on electrical wiring—basically, how not to electrocute yourself—and that was very popular, so I felt welcome immediately.

When I first met these people, they were, in general, enthusiastic about the revolutionary process and real well organized in their local communities. They had gone through the literacy campaign of 1980, with many people learning to read and write at ripe old ages. It meant a lot to them that someone had taken the time to teach them, to bring them out of the shadows and into the light. I think it had made them much more self-confident. After the teachers went back to the cities, many of them kept on studying by themselves, reading the New Testament. They learned for the first time to stand up in church and read for other people, so many people were able to take an active role in the church for the first time.

The challenge there is still unfolding. I see new dimensions of it daily. It's simply a community of campesinos—peasants—living off in isolation. But they're a real community. They have well-developed lay participation in the church. Lay people preach the word and maintain the Christian rites among themselves. I wanted to work in a community with that kind of strong leadership.

Also, the people's interest in the Sandinista process was very encouraging. There was enthusiastic support for adult education. There was enthusiastic support for the health program, which meant people willing to take vaccines out into these very rural communities—going through the rocks and mud to pick up the vaccines, through the rocks and mud again to administer them, and again to return the containers to the health center. I can't tell you how impressed I was by that commitment of these poor people. The government was supplying them with the means to participate—the training in education and health, the means to form cooperatives—and they were making good use of it.

Don't get me wrong. The place isn't Utopia. It's an isolated area and it rains a lot. There's mud all over the place—I mean a lot of mud, all year around—and I don't like mud. It's hot and humid, and I don't like heat or humidity. So there are inconveniences.

When I arrived, my plan was to make two tours a year to all the remote missions in the parish, which would mean a total of four months on horseback. The last couple of years, though, I've only been able to make the rounds once a year because of the war situation. When I'm not out on a tour, I organize courses so that campesinos can come down from the mountains to study the sacraments, to have different kinds of educational forums and church activities.

Also, a lot of my energy has gone into promoting cooperatives—trying to get people to understand what it would be like to work in them. We had the idea of setting up these pig farms—twenty-four of them. I saw a need for the people to live closer together instead of on these isolated farms. In small hamlets, they could produce together as well as individually—just like in the Acts of the Apostles, when the Christians put their goods together and lived collectively. Living closer together, they could celebrate the Word on Sunday without having to walk two hours. And they could also defend themselves, which is important because, since 1981, the contras have been inflicting deaths and damage on the population. But with organized defense, the grade-school teacher could keep teaching, and the health volunteers could keep working. These things had been stymied since the contras began operating in our area. So joining together seemed a natural idea, and the people backed it. But the contras have even gotten in the way of that.

Country life can be demanding and hectic. Every now and then it really helps me to get out of there for a few days. Right now, I'm here in Managua not only to get my car fixed but also to get away from the daily demands, to think a little bit for myself. But there are lots of satisfying things about life in Paiwas, and lots to do. I have a little darkroom which I built to do amateur photography, which also provides a tool for the people to watch their history unfold. They can see where they've been and analyze their own history.

For entertainment, we get films from INCINE, the government film library. We make music—when we have enough guitar strings to go around. And we have a gardening project. The Nicaraguan people traditionally aren't very well informed about gardening, nor do they have the seeds for vegetables. They're pretty much locked into a diet of rice and beans and corn, and they don't get enough variety in vitamins. So I started this garden as a hobby, and it's now taken on a more serious dimension as part of a government program which is promoting vegetable gardens.

When I came, I came to stay. We've just organized another five-year plan for the parish, and I feel enthusiastic about trying to put it into practice. It took me three or four years just to get to know the situation more than superficially, and now I think I'm in a condition to work with the people concretely and organically. So the next five years I'll probably be in Paiwas. Maybe after that I'll try someplace else in the Bluefields diocese. I don't want to get too tired of the mud in one place.

Almost as soon as I arrived, I heard reports of violence by the counterrevolutionaries. In August of 1981, the news came in that four people had been killed out in the countryside. They had been members of a recently organized militia, but they were unarmed at the time. In fact, they were burying a companion who had drowned, and this band of contras put them under the gun. They were shot trying to escape. Of course, that incident didn't mean as much to me as it did to people who knew them.

The first tragedy to touch me personally was the death of Emiliano Perez, who was one of the best Delegates of the Word in our area. He was also a municipal judge and a promoter of local causes like the building of the health center. He was killed while on judicial business five minutes away from one of the chapters that I was visiting. What happened was this. About twenty of us were in a meeting in the chapel, going over the plans for a new mission. A band of contras came in and held us all under the gun. Two of them had war rifles and uniforms, and another five were in civilian dress with just pistols. They came on and intimidated everybody. They took people aside and asked them if they were in any way involved in the adult education, in health care, or the militia. They threatened that, if people continued to be organized, they would be killed or have their houses burned.

When they were leaving and tossing out their final threats, they said, "Oh, and we've just killed Emiliano Perez. He's lying not too far from here, but if anyone comes to his aid we will find out and that person will die—especially if the authorities are told." Well, this other American priest, Bob Stark, and I went out to pick up Emiliano, and we found him nearby. His body was still warm. His arms were broken and he had bullet wounds in his chest. We commandeered a pickup truck and tried to get him into Rio Blanco to a hospital, but it was a forty-five minute drive and he didn't make it. He died in my arms.

I'd known Emiliano pretty well. He had ten kids. All during the ride, I was thinking how I'd have to tell his wife and family. This was a really personal tragedy—you get to be close to someone fast when you live in such a small town.

This was the first real bloody encounter that brought home to me the kind of operations my own government is supporting. It's a big frustration to be from North America and to see that. The people of Nicaragua are intelligent and resourceful, but they've been marginalized for so long. Now they have hope, but that hope is being snuffed out by the contras, the economic aggression, all the policies of the U.S.

Over the last four years, more than a hundred of my parishioners have been killed and many more injured and left homeless by the contras. And in almost every case, the targets have been unarmed civilians who were prominent in the community. These victims are not warriors armed to the teeth and out to ambush the contras or something. They're people living on farms who are just trying to protect themselves. For example: In July of 1982 an adult education teacher was murdered and his body thrown into the river. The grade school in Paiwas bears his name because he was so well loved. In December, the coordinator of adult education from another township was killed. In that same township, in February of 1983, there was an attack at 5:00 A.M. against eight people who had recently formed a farming cooperative.

By this time, the attacking bands had begun to get larger—there were thirty in this one—and much better equipped, with new uniforms and weapons. These bands would sometimes identify themselves as members of the FDN, the main contra group from Honduras, or ARDE, from Costa Rica. But more often they would just come in shooting. They make no effort to win the people over ideologically. They might try to buy people by saying things like "Come along with us. Reagan is giving us money. Here's sixty thousand cordobas if you come along. We have good weapons and good clothes. And give me your Bible, because we want to show people down the line that we're Christians." Once they even stole the Bible from a Delegate of the Word after burning his house down and threatening him with death.

In August of 1983, they killed six people and burned down eight houses. As the people were burying their dead the next day, the parting salvo was to shoot a mortar across the river at them. Luckily they didn't aim it right, but this was the kind of impression they make on the people. In the next village, they killed three. One of the fellows had his throat cut and his eyes dug out. Another fellow was hanged from the ceiling of his own house. In another village, a woman was forced to kneel before them and they blew the top of her head off. It's terrorism.

This has been going on steadily since then, and the tactics are so barbaric they can't make sense except as a means of instilling terror. They kill people who are in any way sympathetic to the Sandinistas or organized in the militia or involved in food distribution. They raped a girl of fourteen and then cut her head off and put it on a post along the road to impress people who passed by. They made three or four women lie down in the mud and shot at them at point-blank range with their automatic rifles. Miraculously, only one was killed.

I still carry a picture of Cristina, a woman from my parish. A group of contras decided to use her for target practice—literally. In all, four bullets went through her. When I got there to visit two weeks later, she was just receiving home remedies. Her head was infected and her hand was swelling up, but miraculously her chest wound had healed. Eventually we got her down to Paiwas, which was no small feat because we had to send a boat up for her. From there, we got her to Matagalpa and then to Managua, where she had several operations. Now she's OK.

Of course, one of the most serious kinds of damage the contras have done is to scare away doctors who have come from around the world to help Nicaragua. There was a time when Paiwas was without a doctor for that reason. We had an excellent group of doctors and nurses from Italy, France, and Germany. They would go off for weeks at a time to attend people in the mountains. But the French doctor and the German doctor were killed, and then the Italian government said, "This is too dangerous for our people," so they pulled back their doctor and nurses.

Anyway, those months in the fall of '82, with all those attacks, were simply awful. But they had one good result. The people began to realize that they could defend themselves if the militia were better organized and better armed, and if they lived together in small hamlets instead of in isolation. So they decided to do that. And they got turned on to the idea of these pig farm cooperatives as well. They got funding from agencies in the U.S., Canada, and Germany. The plan was primitive, but adequate. They began to have preparatory workshops.

Then, on May 13, 1984, thirty-five people were killed in a morning attack by a band of three hundred counterrevolutionaries who came in shooting. Now, the contras could have come in with ten people with rifles and said, "Hands up," and it would have been all over, because the people had been celebrating the night before, drinking and dancing, and were all pretty zonked. But the contras came in with mortar shells and then hand grenades and machine guns, so there were thirty-five killed. That kind of put the cooperative project on hold.

In some of these communities, the contras do have a small local support base. Why? First, there is a long tradition of anticommunism in Central America, and people who have been fed this ideology all their lives are naturally suspicious of the Sandinista revolution. They don't understand it. Also, realistically, things are worse in some respects for the campesinos than they were under Somoza. You can't get rubber boots. You can't get this machete, or the file to sharpen the machete. Transportation to the nearest town costs five times as much. You don't get sugar because the people delivering it have been threatened by the contras, but the peasant doesn't understand that this is the reason. Some of the peasants blame the government, and the contras capitalize on that discontent.

So here you are, a campesino, having a harder and harder time making a living. Here comes a band of three hundred contras through your village. Their reputation has been established as to what they can do to you if you disagree with them. At the same time, you're impressed by their numbers and their nice new equipment. They have digital watches and a whole lot of rations. It's understandable that some people are seduced into joining them.

Since that big massacre in May of 1984, there have been some ambushes along the highways. The biggest one was at the end of January, 1985, when seven dump trucks were burned on the highway that's being built between Rio Blanco and Siuna. They killed two technicians who were preparing to become engineers.

You kind of become accustomed after a while to living with a war. But I'm amazed by the durability, the flexibility, and the vitality of these people. They just don't let themselves be overwhelmed. People have learned not to panic when they hear that the contras are near. They just ask, "How near?" But every time I take the highway from Paiwas to Rio Blanco, I'm sensitive to the fact that you can be shot, or the road can be mined. I once came upon the aftermath of an ambush of a military combat troop carrier half an hour after the attack, and saw the dead and dying and wounded and crippled.

I personally have been in the hands of the contras three times. The first was when Emiliano Perez was killed. The second time was in May of 1984, when I bumped into a group that eventually came to be about eight hundred strong. In fact, I saw them go off toward the area where some of them eventually killed the thirty-five people. I was out on a mission in the woods and found myself trapped behind their lines for about three days, so I saw their movements but wasn't able to get out to warn my people. When they finally found me, they tried to fan the flames of discontent among the people in my presence and also tried to impress upon me the justice of their cause. They made me talk with their jefe [leader] twice, about an hour each time. He wanted to know what I thought of their movement. He insisted that it was a groundswell of people toward democracy. I told him that what I knew of their movement was what they had done to Cristina and to Emiliano Perez and others. He said, "We've had some troublemakers infiltrate our ranks, but we've eliminated them now." Then they went off to kill thirty-five more.

A few days later, I was riding a public bus and they stopped it and made everyone get off. They interrogated me again, along the same lines, but this time they were much more belligerent. I felt much more threatened, but eventually they let me go.

That was pretty tense. I didn't know what they would do to me. Until now, I think I've been protected by the fact that I'm from the U.S. But I test it each time I go into the countryside. I just hope they're politically savvy enough to know how foolish it would be to kill an American priest.

As things have gotten worse, people in the really rural areas have simply found it impossible to stay in their homes. Many of them have gone to other areas to be with relatives, but hundreds of families are living as refugees in Paiwas and Rio Blanco. They're doing OK—the basics have been taken care of by the state and by charitable organizations. They have prefabricated houses in Paiwas, but they're always running short of this or that.

The main problem is still defense. The people are willing to defend themselves, but it's a matter of having the tranquillity to organize it. The contras would love to take a couple of our little towns and close off the highway that goes from Paiwas to Rio Blanco, which is our only supply route. Up until now, they haven't been able to take any place and hold it. They just don't have the ambition or the courage. And their campaigns have definitely been counterproductive in one respect. When they move in so savagely—I mean, they make Attila look like kindergarten—the main thing they do is convince the people to organize. Where the local militia had sixty or eighty people, suddenly it has five hundred.

In a sense, these local militias are the greatest evidence of the Sandinista government's popularity. I mean, they're handing out weapons right and left. What other government does that? Could you imagine the U.S. government arming the blacks in the inner cities and promoting their organization? If the people wanted to get rid of the Sandinistas, there are enough weapons around that they could do it tomorrow.

One thing that makes all this risk worthwhile is the phenomenal strength of these people. Every time we bury someone who has been killed by the contras, the people respond with a lot of pain and sorrow, but at the same time with more conviction than ever. And the youth are so involved, so mature—not a marijuana youth at all. They're working hard to get their degrees and do some useful work. They realize there's more to life than crawling into lockstep with the totalitarian capitalist system. They're keeping a lot of values alive.

When you get down to it, Nicaragua is a symbol for the people of the U.S. as well as for the Latin American continent. Brazil and Uruguay are definitely perking up their ears, and so are some people in the U.S. It's not a groundswell yet, but it could become one. Nicaragua is a sign of what can be done at the local level, with very humble means, to bring about reform. It's like an ember glowing in the dark, being blown on by people who have big spirits and are willing to sacrifice their own skin to keep this ember glowing.

To go back to the United States now is a real culture shock. It's very intimidating to see all the crass display of wealth. Reagan may talk about godless communists, but I think the practical atheism of the United States is a much greater danger—the worship of the golden calf. I just wish more people from the U.S. would travel outside the country, even as tourists, and open their eyes to what's going on.

People in the U.S. *have* to be aware, and have to sacrifice some of their excess wealth. The United States has taken so much wealth out of Nicaragua and caused so much damage. When North Americans offer some help, it's not charity; it's not virtue; it's restitution. You can't simply dream of a just world or preach the gospel of social justice. You have to make concrete moves at the local level and be willing to pay the consequences. That might mean red-baiting, or even being beaten up on the street.

As for me, I'm no longer just an American priest. I've become part of Nicaragua. Nicaragua's values have become my values, and I really feel part of building this new society here. It's definitely a motivation to get out of bed in the morning.

Nancy Donovan

San Juan de Limay reminds many visitors of a ghost-town set up in a U.S. western. But Sister Nancy Donovan went there to set up a Maryknoll mission house on the invitation of a priest who described it as "the Cinderella of the diocese." She has been in the middle of hard times there, but her words still reflect that same love for the place in all its primitiveness.

Located in the mountains of Esteli province, Limay is connected to the town of Esteli by road, but the forty-kilometer trip is hazardous because the road was ambushed literally dozens of times by contras in 1984. The town's main street is lined by telephone wires, but they have been useless since the main lines were cut by contras in the fall of 1984. And these material losses only rub salt into the deep suffering of Limay, the kidnappings and murders that have beset this rural population since the contras began pushing deeper into central Nicaragua.

Nancy Donovan became a public figure in the U.S. in early 1985—not, as she may have preferred, for the humanitarian work she has been doing in Limay for years, but for an encounter she herself had with contra troops. While trying to hitchhike into Esteli for a meeting of religious workers, Nancy was captured and held for several hours. Although she was released unharmed shortly before dark, she was behind contra lines long enough to observe their U.S.-made equipment and uniforms, hear them boast about supply runs from foreign countries, and hear the gunfire as kidnapped civilians were shot in a nearby ravine.

I met with Nancy Donovan in a very different setting. Shortly after her capture and release, she came to the United States to testify before Congress and to take a well-deserved break with her family. She told me the following story in the affluent town of Westbury, Connecticut, as green and peaceful as Limay is dusty and dangerous.

I was born in Waterbury, Connecticut, in 1932. My father sold motorcycles, so we grew up riding around on them all the time, and that's one of my fondest childhood memories.

Right after high school, I became a Maryknoll sister. (Maryknoll is the Catholic Foreign Mission Society of America.) I knew it was what I wanted—I had been brought up with a strong Catholic faith and with a deep desire to do something for the poor in less developed countries. But it was very hard to leave home when I was so young. We all cried when I finally went off to Maryknoll.

After my training, my first assignment was in Guatemala. The hardest thing for me, having just become a sister, was that we had to wear lay clothes there instead of our habits. That was a disappointment.

At first, I worked in a girls' school in Guatemala City. But that experience wasn't what I had in mind, because these were mostly the children of the wealthy. So, during my school vacations, I would go work in really needy communities. I guess the attraction there was that the people were so simple and sincere, so much in need but also with so much to offer. Being there helped me as much as it helped them.

After a few years in Guatemala City, I was able to transfer out into the countryside. We saw some very interesting changes. We helped the local people and especially the Indians organize cooperatives. We started a school for the poor Indians, and I was there long enough to see the kids who started kindergarten graduate from the sixth grade. As they started to study, they began to feel more like part of society. Before long, the town was changing quite a bit.

Altogether, I was in Guatemala sixteen years, in several different towns. Eventually, my turn came to come back to the States for a few years to give service at the Maryknoll Center so that everybody would have a chance to go to the missions. When I came back, I found it very, very difficult to talk to people about what I had seen and done. I couldn't find anybody who seemed to understand, and I kept asking myself what the problem was.

One time, I brought up some Indians from Guatemala who were working on a cooperative, and I took them around to various stores so they could get an idea of the possibilities for selling things. Well, I took them into a supermarket, and there were all these aisles of cat and dog food, and I knew that their children back in Guatemala didn't have any food. That's when I really became aware of how much we take for granted in this culture, and how much we waste.

In the early 1970s, I went to Mexico and worked with the Jesuits in some little towns in Chiapas. There, I made it a point to learn some of the native language—I got pretty fluent in fact—and found that I could get much closer to the people that way. Again, I was working at organizing cooperatives: a savings and loan cooperative, a consumer cooperative, an agricultural cooperative. The idea was to help the rural people get a fair price in selling their products and make it easier to buy the things they needed. There was a lot of enthusiasm: when people got together to talk about the problems of doing business, the organizing efforts just flowed from their talks. But eventually we realized we had gone as far as we could because of the whole capitalistic arrangement. Ultimately, the government stepped in and set up distribution centers and undermined our cooperative.

About this time, there was an earthquake in Guatemala. Even though they were poor and far away, the people in our cooperative decided they wanted to do something to help. So these poor Indians in Mexico took up a collection of corn, beans, coffee, and other things people would need, and they borrowed a pickup truck, and we took a truckload of supplies down to Guatemala. That was one of the most beautiful expressions of solidarity I've ever seen.

Not too long after that, we heard in Mexico that there was a struggle in Nicaragua, and we followed that avidly. Then Somoza was finally overthrown, and soon after that there was a call for volunteers to go down to Nicaragua. Well, I was interested, very interested. I talked it over with the Indian community where I was working in Mexico, asked them how they would feel if I went down. They thought for a long time and then said it would be OK as long as I came back to tell them about it. So I went to Nicaragua for four months. I figured it would be a nice change, and that maybe I'd learn something to help the people of Chiapas.

It was very beautiful, what I saw in those four months. But I also saw that the Nicaraguan experience was something you had to grow with. So I went back to tell the Indians of Chiapas about it. I asked them how things had gone without me. And then I asked them if I could leave them and stay in Nicaragua. They weren't so sure but they said yes.

At that time, the Maryknoll sisters were just opening up a house in Ocotal, just a few miles from the Honduran border. That's where I went. Even then, in 1980, there were a few contras coming over and people getting hurt. It was obvious that the contras were Somocistas. You see, the National Guard under Somoza had drawn heavily from that border population because they were so poor and couldn't do anything else to make a living. So the Guardia had families there, and they would come back and steal cattle and supplies from time to time. They had no power then, but they would keep coming back and occasionally they would harm somebody. It was definitely scary to have them around.

But coming to Nicaragua was exciting, and being there still is, because you can feel the hope and the excitement of the people. When the literacy campaign started, people in the countryside were afraid because they heard rumors warning them about the communists and the Cubans who were supposedly coming into their homes. They thought these people might hurt them. But then the young people arrived from the cities. They were high-school kids—some even from grammar school. They had been told to regard the families they would be living with as their own, to obey the parents and everything. They were not only there to teach reading. They were supposed to help around the house and just be part of the family.

Well, when the literacy campaign was over, everybody got to give an evaluation. And the almost universal response was, "When they came, we were afraid, but when they left, we cried." And it was mutual. The kids hated to leave.

I got to know the countryside pretty well living up there. We went out a lot, even walked in areas that were considered dangerous because of the contras. If you're going to work near the border, you have to know that's a risk. But the church people were very supportive and generally excited about the situation. I was amazed at the hope and the positive developments.

The religious people were especially beautiful. I remember going to visit one little old lady way out in the countryside. When I got there, she was reading the Bible. She said to me, "During the insurrection, when we were trying to get rid of Somoza, I used to get such consolation from reading the Book of the Maccabees." That really got to me—this little old lady out in a hut in the middle of nowhere, reading the Book of the Maccabees, which I had only read once. Well, I took it out again and, when you start reading it in a war zone, you really understand it a lot better.

This is the way we always read the Bible now, in the light of our own experience, and we get so much more out of it because of the situation we're living in. The people of Nicaragua are so skilled at doing that, even though they never studied it.

Well, it seemed to me that Nicaragua's plan from the beginning of the revolution was to help the poor, really to help them do things for themselves. All my time in Guatemala and Mexico, I had been trying to create services and set up institutions for the poor all by myself. Here, the government was ready to teach them reading and writing, to give them plots of land, to show them how to organize, to help them get good prices for their crops. I found that I could do a lot more church work in Nicaragua than in Guatemala or Mexico because the government was taking care of these other things.

After about a year and a half with the Maryknoll sisters in Ocotal, one of the Jesuit priests invited a couple of us to work in San Juan de Limay, which the bishop calls "the Cinderella of the diocese" because nobody wanted to go there. Nobody stayed there long. It's far from everything. It's very hot and dry. It doesn't have much going for it—no recreation, hardly anything but the bare essentials.

Well, two of us sisters decided to go there with this priest. At the beginning, I minded the heat a good bit. Nicaragua's hot, but Limay's hotter, and it doesn't even cool down much at night. There are very few trees, partly because people haven't been very careful about conservation and partly because at one time a lot of them were cut down to clear the land for cotton. There's water, but it's all gone underground and you have to dig wells to bring it up.

Now the government has a reforestation project—it has planted about seven hundred thousand trees to try to draw this water back up. And there's a tobacco project, with a good irrigation system. The people of Limay are very happy with the changes they've seen over the last five years: a high school, a preschool, a children's dining room, telephone lines, electric lights, all kinds of things. By now, I've grown to love the place. I think it's very beautiful.

The Sandinistas are not perfect in anything. They're just members of the bungling human race, and they make mistakes as we all do. From the beginning, they've said, "Part of our revolution includes a self-evaluation. We talk about what's wrong in order to improve it." They clearly like to sit down and listen to the people, but out in the remote areas there simply isn't enough access and then things get out of control.

In Limay, we've had serious transportation problems. After lots of asking, they finally gave us a bus. We needed a truck, too, but we haven't gotten that. Bureaucracy is a big problem. They don't have enough leadership training or enough human relations courses; they put unprepared people into positions of responsibility. Messages don't always get passed down from the top or up from the people.

These days, it's dangerous in Limay, and it's getting more so. There have been some contras coming in and out of Honduras ever since the triumph, but starting in early 1984 their activity got a whole lot worse. That was when they started attacking us, because they didn't like all those changes. They have a radio station that broadcasts from Honduras, and on it they broadcast the names of the people who are on their black list, who are marked for death. Naturally, people get a little nervous to hear their names read. We've gotten all kinds of messages that basically say they're out to get the town.

People are getting more and more concerned about the situation, now that the contras have started kidnapping. They kidnap and kidnap and kidnap. That's why, when I hear all these accounts of how the contra forces are growing—five hundred a month, according to Jeane Kirkpatrick—I understand why. I have seventeen names I can give you right now of people who were kidnapped and haven't gotten back. In all, thirty-five people I know have been kidnapped, including myself, but three of us have been released, fourteen escaped, and many, many more are still in custody. I haven't even had time to keep track of all the names.

To give you an idea of how they operate, suppose that a boy goes out to tether his horse and never comes back. The father goes looking for him and finds tracks of the contras. That's the end of the young boy. It's especially difficult because, if the father is involved in some way in defending the town, he's very hesitant to shoot because his son might be with the attackers. That's what the contras do when they kidnap people—put them in uniform so you can't tell who they are. We know all this because we hear stories from those who have escaped, and because campesinos have a way of finding out information.

And it's not just the kidnapping. People are being killed all the time. We spend much of our time in the cemetery and consoling families. The contras seem to like to go after civilians—anyone who's doing anything to help the town: road workers, telephone workers, teachers. They definitely do not look for direct combat with the army. If they kill army people, it's usually in ambushes.

One of the saddest things is the people who live in really remote places, who are completely helpless when the contras come by. They start out giving them a drink of water—which is a simple, Christian thing to do—and end up involved. Out in the campo, somebody will come by and ask for a glass of water, so you give it. Then, next week, they'll come back and ask to buy tortillas. The next time, they may want to buy a cow. Pretty soon, you figure out that they're contras. But you also figure out that your neighbors may be talking about you because you've already been helping them. And how do you protect yourself? You get into a very compromised position.

At the same time, some people may have relatives who are contras, and others may hear that the contras are fighting communism. The contras say that the Sandinistas are communist and that means they're against religion, and a certain portion of the population gets very worried about what this means. So some people do support them for a combination of those reasons.

Because the roads are so bad and everything's so dangerous, we don't travel much. Every couple of months I get down to Managua, and I try to see a movie and get some ice cream when that happens. But what really keeps me going is the meetings we have with other religious people who are trying to confront some of the problems we are confronting in the war zone. We get together quite often, and we share our fears and our joys and our preoccupations. When something happens in one town or another, we try to show our solidarity by going to visit.

We also feel the support of our friends, including many in the States. Lately, one of the greatest sources of support has been the Witness for Peace groups who come down to find out what's going on. That's very encouraging, because these people really come out of a concern and a desire to know. We never try to convert anybody. We just say, "If you want to know what's going on in the revolution, talk to the people. But talk to some who live in the war zone, not only in Managua." So many people think they've really seen what's going on in Nicaragua, but they've never come to the war zone. They've never been awakened in the night by shots, never felt that fear. They've never accompanied a grieving family at a wake and at a funeral. They've never traveled with Sandinista soldiers or with the militia or young people keeping "vigilancia"—neighborhood watch— at night. That's the way you find out what's going on.

Well, what happened to me was that I was on my way to a meeting called by our bishop in Esteli. We have a little jeep, but the tires are bad. So I hitched a ride with a pickup truck that was moving a family that had been displaced a few weeks before. Just a few kilometers outside of Limay, there was a tractor parked in the road. I wasn't paying any attention until everyone gasped and all these men in blue uniforms came from behind the tractor and stopped us. They got us out, and I looked down in the gully, and there were about twenty-five civilians held captive down there. They were mostly women and children.

After about ten minutes, those of us in the pickup truck were told we could get back in. I was very concerned about the people in the gully, and I was also afraid the same thing would happen as when they burned the bus: they had two ambushes along the same road. So I said, "There's probably another ambush ahead," and I got out to try to get back to town by a side path.

I hadn't gone far when some contras came out and stopped me. I could hear shooting, so I knew they must be killing people. They were amazed to see me there. They couldn't figure out what I was doing. They said, "Where are you coming from?" I said, "Limay." They said, "Where are you going?" I said, "Limay." I think it was obvious to them that I was going to try and go back to warn people in town, and so they wouldn't let me go. Actually, though, they didn't treat me badly. They were interested in finding out something about me, and I was interested in finding out something about them, so we were able to talk a little bit.

The hard part was that there was a lot of fighting somewhere around us. You could hear gunshots and mortar fire up on the hill. One of the contras, who had a walkie-talkie, turned it on loud and you could hear men shouting and giving orders and shooting. You could presume that people were being killed. I prayed for them, but couldn't do a thing about it. I felt very sad, but there was nothing I could do.

After a while, they said, "We're going now," and they put me in line, single file, with all these soldiers in uniform. There were some other civilians, but they were taken to another area. We started walking. At the very beginning, they had said they would let me go later on, so I kept reminding them of that, but they just said, "Keep walking."

I was OK, because I just felt the presence of God. I just felt that if this was the result of my trying to warn the people, then, whatever happened, I had chosen this road. I thought they might keep their promise to let me go, but then again they might not. I was OK, but I was mostly concerned about what was happening along the road to the rest of the civilians I had seen. So I kept asking them to let me go, but they kept taking me farther and farther in the wrong direction, through rivers and up and down, past thickets and all.

I saw other people, dressed in uniforms, who seemed to be there against their will. There was an old man carrying a very heavy knapsack. He kept sitting down and resting. They would say, "Come on, old man. Get up. Keep walking." He would say, "I can't. It's too heavy. The straps are cutting into my shoulders." And they'd say, "Come on, old man. You can do it." It was obvious that he didn't want to be there. I think he was one of the people who had been kidnapped a few weeks earlier.

Anyway, we kept going, meeting up with other groups until there were about sixty of us. We were sitting under a mango tree, and it was getting late. Finally I said, "Look, I've got to go back because it's late and I can't be out after dark."

Finally, I convinced them to call their chief, because they were obviously not the ones making the decisions. Out came these four men who were definitely leaders. They were quite brusque, quite abrupt. They grabbed my bag and started going through it and asked me questions, and I just felt that I was in the presence of evil. You know, I had never had much experience with evil before, but I felt that they were evil.

They asked me what I was doing out on the road, which was not a great problem, but then they started going through my things, including my address book, and I was concerned that they would do some harm to someone who happened to be in that book. So I said to them, "I'm really getting very annoyed at this." And one of them looked at me coldly and responded, "*You're* getting annoyed?" At that point, I figured the best thing I could do was keep my mouth shut and let them talk about me. I guess they decided this was not going to get them anywhere, so they abruptly said, "You can go now."

It took me several hours to walk home. I didn't know if I'd meet more of them on the road or be caught in a battle with troops or what would happen. At first, I let myself cry a little. But then I said, "This is no time for that," and I just prayed and concentrated on getting home as fast as possible.

When I got back to Limay, I found thirteen bodies. In the next couple of days, two more turned up. I knew a lot of these people and their families. The ones who had been killed up on the hill had been machine-gunned, but then their truck had been set on fire so that the bodies were all burned. The ones who had been killed down by the tractor had been all torn apart. You see, the contras don't just kill. They mutilate, I guess to make the people more upset and frightened. This was very hard for the people to deal with: not only were their children dead; they were mutilated so badly.

I went to the funerals a little bit that night, but eventually my friends came and found me and convinced me that I should go to bed. It was really quite hard to see all this. The next morning, we had to bury a lot of these people. The government came in with a helicopter to take out those who were from out of town—some had been road construction workers. Besides the ones who were killed, many were kidnapped, and they haven't come back.

Later in the spring, I came up to the U.S. and testified before Congress during the debate over continued funding of the contras. I made my statement, and they listened politely, but my impression was that they really didn't want to hear any more.

I was sure they would ask me all kinds of things about the statement during the question period, but they didn't seem to have heard it at all. One Congressman asked me about a mural he had heard about in a church in Managua which depicted Jesus as a soldier or something. Now, I'm not an art critic, and I honestly didn't think that was as important as the fact that these atrocities were being committed against a civilian population. But he apparently found the artwork disturbing.

What I found more disturbing was that Congress was ignoring the question of how these atrocities can be stopped. We were talking about murals on churches! I think the Jesus that we believe in is much more concerned about whether people are being hurt than about how he is depicted. He is a living God, living among the people, and when an atrocity is committed, it's done to a member of the Christian community, because we're all brothers and sisters in Christ. To me this is all very important.

Pat Hynds

Here is a story with no shortage of morals. Pat Hynds is another of these political individuals totally absorbed in her work and finding obvious nourishment in it. A long path took Pat from life as a Los Angeles homemaker to the demanding existence she now thrives on, juggling roles as a researcher and writer for the Central American Historical Institute in Managua and as an administrator of Maryknoll's lay mission program for Latin America. Tragedy and loss in young adulthood opened the way for personal redefinition and rediscovery of the interest in social justice that had been part of her upbringing. While raising a family after the death of her husband, Pat moved from survival jobs as a secretary into bilingual education and from there into a deep and abiding interest in the roots of the Chicano population with whom she worked. Getting hooked on Latin American issues and returning to school to learn more, were only short steps from there. Pat's personal story is interesting not only for her emergence as a strong, self-defined woman, but for her articulateness about the road she took to arrive there.

Pat's story is chosen to end this collection because her work makes her such a knowledgeable observer of both the Nicaraguan reality and the policy decisions of our own government which shape that reality. Speaking "as an American and a Christian," she vehemently criticizes the Reagan Administration's hostility toward Nicaragua, but expresses hope that increased people-to-people contact will create pressure for more humane, constructive relations between our two countries.

I'm forty-six. When Latin America began to pervade my consciousness, I was a mother and a student in Los Angeles. Let me backtrack a bit. I married very young. I had four children in four years. When they were roughly six through ten, my husband was killed in a car accident.

It was pretty rough. At that point, I went to work as a secretary, but it was obvious that I wouldn't be contented doing that for the rest of my life. I realized that my kids would be ready to leave home before long, so I decided to go back to school at Cal State Northridge. Since I was interested in working with Hispanic young people, the work I initially chose was teaching English as a second language.

I ended up getting a bachelor's degree in Spanish and Chicano studies, with a teaching credential, then ultimately going for a master's in Mexican-American studies with a specialist credential in bilingual education. Somewhere in there, I taught for three years, and then discovered Maryknoll.

In the process of going back to school, I learned, or relearned, some unexpected things: the whole idea of a Christianity that means a commitment of some kind, not just commitment to bingo and rummage sales, but to trying to make the world a better place in whatever way you can. The Chicano studies department was very activist, both with respect to Chicano issues in the U.S. and to Latin America. Its effect on me was a rekindling of my conscience—and my consciousness about the larger world—after all those years in which my primary identity had been as a housewife and mother.

This personal reawakening just happened to coincide with the Nicaraguan insurrection, so it was hard not to perk up my ears when so much was going on. Hearing about the new government's active interest in the needs of the poor, all the emphasis on making human welfare the number one priority, interested me very much as a Catholic. To me, it was an enactment of the principles the church had talked about in Vatican II, Medellín, and Puebla. I was really interested in seeing if a government could pull it off, making the needs of the poor its priority.

I guess the roots of my concern for social justice go even deeper. I was educated in Wyoming, in Dominican sisters' schools, where a lot of emphasis was put on social justice issues. It was during the 1950s, so we talked a lot about overcoming racial prejudice. I mean, in Wyoming nobody did much about it, but at least it was brought out as an issue to be discussed. But then I went to college for a year, married at nineteen, and spent my time immersed in babies and diapers and all.

Interestingly, Wyoming has a very large percentage of Hispanic Americans. So Chicano studies were really a throwback to the issues I'd been concerned with growing up, the kind of indignation I felt in high school when I'd see classmates discriminated against because they were Hispanic. Working as a secretary in a high school near my house, I couldn't help but notice that the Hispanic kids were going through the exact same thing, still getting shoved into shop classes and told they shouldn't aspire to go to college. That interested me in moving from being a secretary to working in bilingual education to help these kids. In the process, I got interested in Latin America as a means of understanding the roots the Hispanic kids came from.

I came to Nicaragua in March of 1981. But first, like all Maryknoll lay missionaries, I went through a full semester of orientation: academic classes and a lot of area studies about the country, plus learning to get along in groups.

I got here in the midst of preparations for the celebration of the second anniversary of the revolution, and right after Reagan took office. That turned out to be an especially interesting time to arrive, because I could just see the changes in policy and their effects. They were very visible. You could really see the decline in relations, the increase in diplomatic, political, military, and economic pressure against Nicaragua under Reagan.

From the start, I've felt safe under the Nicaraguan government. This is a point on which just about everybody agrees: people generally don't live in fear of the police or the army. It's really incredible how much that changed with the revolution. Oh, I imagine that, if you were planning the counterrevolution in your back room, you might be a little concerned if the police came to your door. Otherwise, no. When you're stopped on the street—and certainly we foreigners are often asked for ID—never do you have that icy panic that sets in if you're stopped in Salvador or Guatemala. They tend to fall over themselves apologizing for disturbing you.

In fact, let me illustrate that with the story of an encounter I had not too long ago with a Sandinista policeman. I was at home, working, pretty oblivious to my surroundings. Suddenly, a neighbor pounded on my door and started hollering. When I came out, there was a police officer in the process of removing the license plate from my car. I asked what the problem was, and he answered that I was illegally parked. Well, the "no parking" sign was pretty clearly pointing in the opposite direction from where my car sat, and I indicated as much. But he was adamant. My car could have blocked traffic turning the corner, in his opinion, and therefore was illegally parked, regardless of what the sign said. Still, he saw some wisdom in my point. So he let me move my car, after a lengthy argument. In Salvador or Guatemala, you just wouldn't get into that kind of discussion for any reason.

But there's more. During the argument, my door blew shut and, of course, the keys were inside. So this "totalitarian" police officer climbs up the trellis next to my house, and drops into the courtyard, landing in the sink with a scream! It was unbelievable! Out he came, letting me in the front door, and, with a warning to be more careful about where I parked, he was gone. This is typical of their attitude, their willingness to be helpful.

Maryknoll lay missioners can serve in a huge variety of ways: health care, teaching, helping refugees. When I came, I guess I expected to work in education, since that had been my background in Los Angeles. But I began to hear all this concern about misinformation, lack of information about Nicaragua in the U.S. The Central American Historical Institute, which has been around for many years, was talking about expanding its program to include creating an alternative source of information about Nicaragua for people in the U.S. and other countries. When I came, that was in the talking stage, and it was easy to get enthusiastic. So I joined another American woman and a Jesuit to put together what is now *Envio*, a monthly publication in English and Spanish. In just a few years, it has gone from a three-person operation—with our little shoestring staff doing everything including licking stamps and finding volunteers to carry the mail—to being a full-fledged, professional project.

A second part of my job is speaking with visiting delegations and tours, all different kinds of groups who come down to Nicaragua to look things over. The institute is one of the resources that people rely on in trying to get a perspective on what's happening in Nicaragua, especially if they want something not connected with the government and in English. It's exhausting work, but it really is one of the few hopes—that the American people will come down and see what's happening and go home and tell their friends.

As if that weren't enough, I took on a third responsibility in the fall of 1984. I am now involved in helping to develop and coordinate the Maryknoll lay mission program all over Latin America. So I spend a little more than half the year in Nicaragua working with the Historical Institute and the rest of my time traveling. As I've traveled around Latin America and seen the repression and chaos in other countries, I've gained even more confidence in Nicaragua and respect for what they're trying to do here.

For me, the constant change of routine helps prevent burnout. I enjoy going to the weekly vigils our U.S. Citizens Committee has in front of the embassy—they turn into a social event to catch up with people you don't have time to see in between. And there are times when just sitting down to a meal with some special person who understands what you're going through is a real treat.

There's not a lot of time for recreation. Many of us down here tend to feel that this is a very serious moment in history. Although rationally you say to yourself, "I am not going to solve this problem by myself or even with everybody else down here," there still is the tendency to want to put a lot of energy into this work.

My life here is very intense and extremely busy, mainly because of the number of U.S. people who come down and want information. Adding to the intensity is the fact that Nicaragua is such a small country, and political decisions, changes in policy, church decisions, whatever, tend to be felt immediately. There's a tremendous feeling of living at a very historic moment and of being really privileged to participate in it. It's that same thing people said about living in Chile during Allende's term. I hope it doesn't come to the same disastrous end, but the excitement is similar.

A major part of my job has been keeping on top of what's going on down here. Now, during a good part of the time that I've been down here, there has been a state of emergency which has involved press censorship. But, in addition to the formal news sources—and in any country you have to wonder how ample they are—there's a whole unofficial network. We get valuable information from members of the U.S. Citizens Committee, some of whom live in outlying areas. We're also in frequent communication with religious workers in other parts of the country. We tend to believe church people because their information has consistently proved accurate and because most of them don't have a particular political ax to grind. They aren't flaming Sandinistas and they aren't contras. Some of them have been here for twenty years and are very interested in seeing that the people get what's due to them. In terms of an overall picture, we have a better feel for what's going on than the reporters who come in for twenty-four or forty-eight hours and are off again, giving the impression that they've seen the whole of Nicaragua.

I have two criteria for deciding whether I endorse the basic thrust of the Sandinistas' policies. First, I ask myself if Nicaragua is going forward or backward compared to the situation under Somoza. And I think the answer is that there's clear, obvious improvement. And, secondly, I evaluate human rights progress by looking at Nicaragua in the context of the rest of Central America. Horrendous abuses—disappearances and torture, political assassination—are the way of life in Salvador, Guatemala, and increasingly Honduras.

I'm not an expert on various styles of Marxism. But I think it's safe to say that the most extreme range of what's even considered here is nothing like what you'd see in the Soviet Union and maybe even Cuba. The Sandinistas are pragmatic, even those who are most enthusiastic about Marxism. They recognize the cultural and material factors they have to deal with here.

Economically, they seem to have learned from the difficulties of other socialist countries. There are differences among them, but I think most Sandinista leaders genuinely believe in a mixed economy. And all of them know—they can't help knowing—that they simply don't have the wherewithal to turn everything into state operations. They don't have the technicians, they don't have the skilled hands. And so you've got an economy that's still, according to the latest figures I've seen, fifty-five percent privately operated.

Another example: a few in the government might think that religion is the opiate of the masses and be personally not too hot on it, but they're not going to try some sweeping thing like eliminating religion, as some commentators in the States seem to think.

So, overall, the country doesn't seem to be moving terribly rapidly toward further socialism. But one exception is a move to nationalize distribution in areas that weren't nationalized before, and I think this is a move against speculation, hoarding, price gouging, which are really screwing up the food distribution system here. These problems, and the success or failure of attempted solutions, are bound to have repercussions at the base level of the population. For example, there's a fantastic shortage of spare parts, so you've got a lot of distribution vehicles that aren't running. And public transportation has gone way downhill. People in outlying areas like Masaya who used to take the bus into Managua every day to work are finding the same number of people crammed into half as many buses, because the rest of the fleet is off the road for lack of parts. That has really made people's lives harder.

Support for the Sandinistas has eroded to some degree since the euphoric days right after the revolution. The social costs of the war have been enormous, and I mean the economic war Nicaragua faces as well as the military one. People get very tired. So they'll say, "At least under Somoza, there was plenty in the stores. At least there weren't lines. Maybe it's better to give in." But that's still a minority of the people. Counterbalancing that, there's also a strong sense that Nicaragua is standing on its own feet for the first time, and I think people are determined not to let that go.

I think the Sandinistas have bent over backwards to make things palatable to small business, property owners, and so on. They're offering one hundred percent financing in agriculture to big and small farmers, as well as a guaranteed market and guaranteed prices when the crops come through. What rubs some in the private sector the wrong way is that there are limitations on how much profit can be made. There are measures to see that people aren't stashing all their profits in Miami or in a Swiss bank account when the country is in such desperate need, that people aren't just letting their land lie fallow when so much depends on production. Now, some people see things like that as infringements on their rights, and others see them as efforts to make people act somewhat responsibly.

I mean, the poor also have rights: the right to survive and to live in some dignity. I really believe that God created this world with enough material things that nobody has to starve to death. If people are starving, it doesn't mean that God willed two-thirds of the earth's population to be poor; it's because human beings have set up structures that have that effect. There has to be some give and take, but the poor can't give any more.

The whole picture of Nicaragua in the U.S. media is based on misinformation. When I came down here, it was fashionable for the press back home to refer to the "leftist" government of Nicaragua. Then it was the Marxist-Leninist-totalitarian-police-state government of Nicaragua. Now it's the communist government of Nicaragua.

It's funny, but even when things are written accurately enough in the media, a headline or the context of the piece can create a completely false impression. I'll give you two examples. *Time* magazine's coverage of the third anniversary celebration is a little dated, but the point is still valid. They showed the Sandinistas and the whole Council of State in their tropical shirts and straw hats, just as it happened, but with a caption that said, "Sandinistas celebrate their third anniversary in Moscow." Now that seems beyond your basic typo error, as far as I'm concerned. They don't wear tropical shirts and straw hats in Moscow.

I was stuck in an airport, waiting for a plane that seemed never to come, and I picked up a paper that had an article about Americans in Nicaragua. The article itself was a UPI story, and not bad. They quoted me and an American nun who's been here for twenty years and several other people, all fairly accurately from what I could make out. But the headline said, "Sandinista groupies and others flock to Nicaragua." Well, with a title like that, who's going to give any credibility to anything that those people in that story say?

Recently, the hysteria has escalated. It seems to be reaching some sort of fever pitch, with Reagan's talk about a moral obligation to support the contras. Take Reagan's image of this place as the "dungeon of totalitarianism.'' Absurd! Vice President Bush has been quoted as saying that fifty churches had been burned here. I cannot imagine what he could be referring to unless he's going clear back to the movement of the Miskitos off the river in December of '81 and January of '82 in which some villages were burned after the people were moved out. As usual, he didn't bother providing documentation. The administration has basically been turning reality upside down, calling the contras freedom fighters and the Sandinistas terrorists.

If you have some doubts as to whether these contras are freedom fighters, here are a few samples of the kinds of stories we hear all the time. In the summer of 1984, a band of them came in and took over a village above Bluefields. What they did was single out people in front of everyone else. One was a Creole—the term they use here for black—teacher who had been very supportive of people's involvement in the revolutionary process. They singled him out and, in the plaza, in front of all the people standing there watching, literally cut the man into pieces. This is the kind of thing we hear over and over: people cut up in pieces in front of spouses, children; babies beheaded; just absolutely unbelievable actions—and they're against civilians, mind you, not against anybody bearing a gun or in uniform.

Some of these attacks are random, like when a band of contras is traveling along a road and your path crosses theirs and, wham, you get it. But there is also extensive evidence that they go into areas looking for people who could be considered community leaders. That would include adult education teachers, anyone who works for the department of health or the agrarian reform or any government program. It would include Delegates of the Word, Catholic lay leaders, anyone who might encourage people to get involved in community activities.

And always, the baffling question is why, except to terrorize the people, terrorize sectors of the country that would otherwise be doing something productive. The message is always very clear: you participate in anything that has anything to do with revolutionary change in the country and you will be on the death list. It does have its effect. It causes people to be afraid to be organized, afraid to be involved. That message was very clear in Matagalpa in the summer of 1984 when they killed a well-to-do, non-Sandinista coffee producer, Noel Rivera. He was not political, period. The message seemed to be to the private sector, to the medium-well-off or well-off agricultural producers who are continuing to participate in the economy: ''You'd better watch out because we're after you.''

When you've got people being killed all over the country, that polarizes the situation in other respects. It creates a tendency to look at people who are strongly critical of the revolution and equate them with contras, or at least wonder about their loyalty, and that's not necessarily fair. The space for legitimate criticism narrows when you've got this large contra force and so much killing. For all Reagan's talk about wanting to reinforce the democratic forces in Nicaragua, he's doing the exact opposite.

His policies in support of the contras are radicalizing people on one side or the other because, in a war, it's very difficult to maintain that no-person's-land there in the middle.

I'd think the Reagan administration would be moved to rethink its premises by now. The U.S. admits that, without its contributions of money and arms and training, the counterrevolutionaries in Nicaragua wouldn't have a chance. Don't you think that might send a message to somebody that maybe, just maybe, we're supporting unpopular positions?

But even if the administration's charges were true—and, if four years of living here have convinced me of anything, they've convinced me that the charges are not true—they still wouldn't justify the illegal, immoral, and counterproductive policies our government is carrying out. There's been a lot of comparison to Vietnam over the years. To me, one of the strongest points of comparison is that the American people are once more being lied to about what we're really doing there.

For three years the Reagan administration said, "Our only intention is to pressure the Sandinistas to stop the arms flow to El Salvador," arms flow they still haven't managed to document. During that time, the only arms flow that was evident to the whole world was the arms flow from the United States into Honduras, Salvador, and to the contras.

Then, in January of 1985, the facade was finally dropped and Reagan said, "We want to make the Sandinistas says 'Uncle.'" Sounds like a rather immature foreign policy, doesn't it?

He said, "We want to change the structure of the Nicaraguan government." By what right? If the United States were going to destabilize governments whose policies were repressive toward their citizens, there is a long line of governments ahead of Nicaragua to be destabilized—Chile, Guatemala, Paraguay, on and on and on.

Then we talk abut our need to defend the Western Hemisphere from outside interference—but the one blatant case of outside interference or military action in the hemisphere was the Falklands war in which the United States took Britain's part against Argentina. So even there we're not doing what we say we're doing.

T.D. Allman has written an interesting book which I just finished reading called *Unmanifest Destiny*. In it he says that the United States has the military power and might to destroy countries and to destroy people, but it can't seem to learn that it can't militarily impose democracy on other countries. Every place we've tried, it's been a total failure: Guatemala, Chile, the Dominican Republic, South Korea.

The United States, for well over a hundred years, seems to have had this notion that Latin America is its possession. We say "sphere of influence," but it seems to be much more. Really, we seem to be viewing the Latin American countries as our colonies. We determine what governments stand and what governments fall, and the criterion is "Do they support our interests of not?" If anybody wants anything that goes out of those bounds, then they stand to be overthrown with the excuse that this is really communist aggression.

When you get down to it, I think the idea of the Russians really taking over a country in this hemisphere is about as likely as us taking over Afghanistan. It's not going to happen. Everyone understands the rules of the game too well. The Soviets are probably going to take advantage of opportunities that come their way, usually caused by our aggressive action, just as we will take advantage of opportunities on the peripheries of the Soviet domain. But to call Nicaragua a Soviet beachhead in this hemisphere borders on the absurd. Nicaragua is one one-hundredth the size of the United States. It's like a bug that you could step on at any moment if it ever seriously threatened you. But it's hard to figure out just how it would threaten us. It has no navy. It has no air force. Our fantasies of Nicaraguan expansionism are totally beyond reality.

Living here through all this, the most heartbreaking thing is to see the mothers following the coffins down the street. They'll say, "We thought this was over. We thought when we won the war, when we overthrew Somoza, that the killing, the torture, the brutality had ended, and here we're going through it one more time." They look at you and say, "Will you just ask your government to please leave us alone and let us get on with the job of putting our country back together?"

To me that's the tragedy: to see the United States verging on moral bankruptcy in our policy toward this country and lying about what we're doing. Reagan's a great champion against terrorism. But what do you call mining the harbors of another sovereign country with whom we have diplomatic relations, if not terrorism? What do you call arming an army to overthrow another country if not terrorism?

The rhetoric that goes on and on, building Nicaragua into some sort of monster that it isn't, does nothing but make us appear to have no values or principles in the eyes of the world. Our actions in front of the World Court were an example. Nicaragua came up with a proposal to send back Cuban military advisers, to stop unilaterally all new arms imports, and to invite a congressional delegation down, with free access to all their military bases to prove that their military capability was strictly defensive. The Reagan administration's response was that this was a Soviet-style propaganda show. I mean, what more can they do?

As an American and a Christian, what I'm seeing is America not following the principles it says are its basis for action, and certainly not following the Gospel. It's not whether the Sandinistas are angels or devils, but what we as Americans are doing that should be the focus of our debate. When I see my country, which I love very much, doing these kinds of things, I have not only a right but an obligation to say, "Hey, this isn't right."

It's interesting now to go back to the U.S. Some of my friends, while they aren't super-political, are interested in what's going on down here. They're supportive. But, with other people, sadly, I find that I don't have much to talk about. Some of the people I used to work with in the aerospace industry don't even want to have lunch with me because they're concerned about their security clearances. It saddens me to think that the U.S. has become a place that's so shaped by the whole national security mentality.

As for my kids, they probably think I'm a little bit crazy. I do make an interesting conversation piece. People ask, "Where's your mother?" And they say, "She's in Nicaragua working with the revolution." They might prefer to have me closer to home, but they also recognize that I'm doing something I enjoy, that's satisfying.

I will also admit that this is a far cry from being a housewife in Reseda, California. I have to wash my jeans in cold water on a cement scrub board, which is less than fun. I've cut back my material possessions quite a bit. In Los Angeles, although I wasn't rich, I had a seven- or eight-room house with stuff spread all around. Now, everything I own is in one room. And I still have more than a majority of Nicaraguans by a long shot. You learn not only to live simply, but to appreciate the simplicity.

My commitment to Maryknoll was originally for three years. I signed my second three year contract in 1984, and I hope that it will continue to be in Nicaragua. Of course, a lot will depend on what Reagan decides to do. I don't have a martyr complex. I really would like to be around a while longer. The fact that I have four kids in the States probably enters into that. Still, I'd like to keep on doing what I'm doing as long as possible.

That's not to say there haven't been any scary moments already. When the airport, near my house, was bombed, for example. And one time, traveling on the Atlantic coast, we gave a ride to some people who turned out to be contras, and that was certainly scary.

It's a weird feeling to recognize that what frightens me is brought on by my own government. But this is also a very strong incentive to get the word out back home that this craziness isn't what the United States is all about. Being here, I guess I've also experienced an even greater growth in faith, or in understanding of what faith means. It's come to me that, if faith has any value at all, it's in how you live it out. You have to work toward a more just system here on earth and that means getting involved.

Afterword

There Is No Choice

The struggle of the people of Nicaragua does not have to be legitimized by any external force, by the presence or non-presence of North Americans, by the visits or non-visit of people from the U.S. From the first U.S. military incursion in 1898 to the present, the Nicaraguan people have endured attacks on their lives, their bodies, their spirit. The government of the U.S. has continually violated Nicaragua's efforts to shape its own history, to be recognized as a sovereign nation, to create its own process.

Yet the Nicaraguan people still try to build bridges, still beg for peace, still invite North Americans to come and see. The bridge we build is fragile, they say. Our reality is different from yours. For us the weeping of the people is all of our pain. It is the collective wound of thousands of our poor, who understand that revolution is not a single event but rather a life process. It is not neat, not ordered, not quick, not easy. In Nicaragua the bridges are bespattered with the blood of the people—women, children, elderly, young soldiers, refugees fleeing from the contra attacks. Theirs is a struggle for human survival, human dignity, and a nation's claim to self-determination.

For many North Americans who live in Nicaragua, the struggle of the people has become their struggle. They have not accepted an escape hatch. They have stayed; seventeen have told their stories in this book. Theirs is a message of faith and hope, of service and advocacy. As builders of bridges, their lives have earned them the right of passage across the bridge. Their testimony helps to gather in the rest of us. For it is never easy for a North American to cross a bridge, particularly a bridge that has been designed by those who are different, who speak another language, who image another color, who birth new social systems, who nurture new unities, who build new myths.

Bridges coax us to listen to the cry of the people, even though governments and ideologies, mined harbors and enforced embargoes block out the sound. As people of faith, we are challenged to act in solidarity with the revolutionary process of Nicaragua. This demands a willingness to enter into the world of the other and suffer it. The experience of wholeness is overwhelming as the connection between faith and politics is concretized. Clearly, the process is centered in their Sandino history, in the Exodus call to freedom, and then discovered in the symbols, the chants, and the eyes of the people who are the builders. Revolutionary hope springs from the energy of this collective and thus becomes the conscience of the world.

There is in Nicaragua for those who stay and those who visit, no matter how briefly, a deep conviction that what is being born, even though it is threatened by death, is an expression of hope for a life that is better and a goodness that is self-evident.

Solidarity with the people of Nicaragua, therefore, cannot be a routine and empty formula. It is grounded in co-responsibility and finds strength in public witness. It lives from the faith of people and a readiness to cross the bridge—to be involved in the struggle for justice.

Sister Marjorie Tuite, O.P.
Director for Ecumenical Citizen Action, Church Women United
National Coordinator, National Assembly of Religious Women

Appendix

To See With Our Own Eyes

Nicaragua is closer to Miami than are many of the vacation paradises we consider it perfectly reasonable to visit. Yet many of us in North America who genuinely want to understand the situation better haven't yet realized the simplest way to do that: to see for ourselves. Nicaragua might as well be Tierra del Fuego for all the direct contact many of us have had with its people, its culture, and the day-to-day realities of its struggle to survive. As our government continues its efforts to isolate Nicaragua economically and politically, each of us suffers a dangerous isolation as a result.

We are ripe for manipulation by the many different sides of the conflict as long as we remain uninformed. Is Nicaragua an aggressor against democracy in the hemisphere, or is it a victim of aggression? Either way, it is not in our best interest to remain neutral.

For all the mystique and controversy that surrounds Nicaragua, it is an easy country to visit in many respects. Except in combat zones, where permits are required, travel is unconstrained and visitors are encouraged to talk with Nicaraguans and to hear their stories firsthand. Food, lodging, and transportation are inexpensive, with hostels or "hospidajes" easy to find in cities. For the traveler with some competence in Spanish, it is perfectly reasonable to visit Nicaragua independently, as this writer did—although the adventurer should heed several warnings. Post-earthquake Managua is an easy place in which to get hopelessly lost. And austerity prevails in public transportation and consumer goods.

Interest in Nicaragua here in the U.S. has already led to the creation of several mechanisms to support North Americans who want to learn about the situation or even to help out. There are tours, schools, work brigades and peace actions geared to a variety of schedules and special interests. While some reflect the political perspective of the sponsoring organization, all of them offer enough unstructured access to the country and its people to let the visitor figure things out independently.

Tours

The National Network in Solidarity with the Nicaraguan People (NNSNP), 2025 Eye Street, NW, Suite 1117, Washington, DC 20006. (202) 223-2328.

NNSNP is an umbrella group, founded in 1979, which coordinates local committees acting to stop U.S. military intervention in Nicaragua and to enhance people-to-people understanding. Study tours are frequently organized by local affiliates or the national office.

Tropical Tours, 141 E. 44th Street, #409, New York, NY 10017. (212) 599-1441.

This commercial travel agency is experienced in organizing special interest tours (e.g., labor unions, church, agriculture, education, culture) for groups of seven or more and for individuals. Packages can be tailored to the needs of particular groups, but typically include air and land travel, hotel accommodations, a bilingual guide, and arrangements for social and political functions while in Nicaragua.

Oxfam America, 115 Broadway, Boston, MA 02116. (617) 482-1211.

Oxfam is an international, nonprofit agency which supports self-help projects in development and disaster relief in poor countries. Its educational program includes two to three week tours to study the systemic causes of poverty and underdevelopment. Some are sector-specific, but others include a wide range of people.

North American Congress on Latin America (NACLA), 151 W. 19th Street, New York, NY 10011. (212) 989-8890.

This research center publishes the respected journal, *Report on the Americas*, on the political economy of the region. It sponsors infrequent but high-quality study tours.

The Guardian Tours, 33 W. 17th Street, New York, NY 10011. (212) 691-0404.

The Guardian, an independent, radical newsweekly established in 1948, sponsors tours to Nicaragua and other countries experiencing significant social change.

Center for Global Service and Education, Augsburg College, 731 21st Avenue South, Minneapolis, MN 55454. (612) 330-1159.

Founded in 1983, the center is committed to education which "expands our world view and deepens our understanding of issues related to global justice and human liberation," including travel seminars to Latin America for church and community groups.

Marazul Tours, 250 W. 57th Street, Suite 1312, New York, NY 10107. (212) 582-9570 or (toll free) (800) 223-5334.

Marazul is the largest U.S. operator of tours to Nicaragua, making all arrangements for individuals and groups of seven or more.

Nicaragua-Honduras Education Project, 1322 18th Street NW, Washington, DC 20009. (202) 822-8357.

An organization founded to promote an informed foreign policy by sponsoring fact-finding delegations among prominent citizens, NHEP seeks to serve community leaders with access to media and willingness to take an active part in the policy debate on their return.

Schools

Nuevo Instituto de Centro America (NICA), PO Box 1409, Cambridge, MA 02238. (617) 497-7142.

Participants in this 5-week program study Spanish half the day with Nicaraguan teachers, work on aid and development projects in the community, and stay with Nicaraguan families. Located ninety miles north of Managua in Esteli, a city of forty thousand surrounded by farm country, NICA brings North Americans in close contact with the people and problems of Nicaragua through a packed program of field trips, seminars, and cultural events.

Casa Nicaraguense de Espanol, 141 E. 44th Street, Room 409, New York, NY 10017. (212) 949-4126

A Spanish language center in Managua which offers programs two to eight weeks long, CNE also offers broad opportunities to share the Nicaraguan experience by living with families in a working-class barrio, hearing speakers from both government and antigovernment circles, and participating in varied field trips. These have included excursions to a model prison for ex-Somocistas; seminars with representatives of labor unions and mass organizations; a visit to *La Prensa,* the opposition newspaper; and a trip to the northern border to hear firsthand accounts of the impact of the war.

Work Brigades

Many North Americans have found that a powerful way to understand the experience of Nicaraguans is by sharing in the hard work of these people to rebuild their economy. Work brigades are open both to people with special talents (medicine, agriculture, construction, arts) and to those who are willing to work hard and learn new skills. As Nicaraguan students and workers more often find their lives interrupted by the demands of the contra war, the support of "internacionalistas" from Europe as well as the U.S. will make more and more difference in projects such as:

harvesting coffee and cotton, on which Nicaragua's foreign exchange depends;

reforestation to overcome the impact of years of indiscriminate logging by multinational companies during the Somoza era;

public health programs to continue the country's progress against malaria, measles, polio, and poor sanitation and to aid the victims of the war;

construction of housing and public buildings to compensate for the destruction of the 1972 earthquake;

"cultural workers" brigades, periodically organized by the Nicaraguan Ministry of Culture to bring musicians, visual artists, poets, and others down to teach skills and to enhance the morale of troops, students, and others.

Information about work brigades can be obtained from several sources:

National Network in Solidarity with the Nicaraguan People (NNSNP), 2025 Eye Street, NW #1117, Washington, DC 20006. (202) 223-2328 (construction, community development).

Nicaragua Exchange, 239 Centre Street, New York, NY 10013. (212) 219-8620 (harvesting, reforestation, and more).

Central America Health Rights Network (CAHRN), c/o 217 Haven Avenue, Apartment 5F, New York, NY 10033. (212) 694-3944 (medical brigades of skilled health care professionals).

Committee for Health Rights in Central America (CHRICA), 1827 Haight Street, Box 5, San Francisco, CA 94117. (415) 821-6471.

Witness for Peace, PO Box 29241, Washington, DC 20017. (202) 636-3642.
    A brigade with a very special character, this ecumenical project offers a chance to spend time in the zones of conflict along the northern border. Witnesses participate in community development projects and aid victims of the fighting. Witness for Peace has been maintaining a continuous, nonviolent presence in the most vulnerable areas of Nicaragua in the hope that North Americans there might awaken a sense of some accountability in our government.

Peace Brigades International, 4722 Baltimore Avenue, Philadelphia, PA 19143. (215) 724-1464.
    PBI is in the process of developing a project similar to Witness for Peace on Nicaragua's southern border.

These trips are strenuous and sometimes risky, but they offer the irreplaceable opportunity to know the situation in Central America firsthand. Sleeping accommodations in the countryside are sometimes just a lean-to. Brigadista work is hard and grubby, and gringo agricultural workers often bring back stories of embarrassment at their clumsiness at the tasks Nicaraguans have been doing since childhood. Schools and cultural programs that let a traveler share the Nicaraguan experience also let you share crowded accommodations, plain food, and an atmosphere of tension that sharpens every time a Blackbird spy plane breaks the sound barrier above Managua. Yet Nicaragua continues to draw visitors from the

U.S. who are dissatisfied with the picture painted by the six o'clock news and want to see for themselves.

The Next Best Thing To Being There

Clearly, not everyone who is concerned about the Central American situation has the time, money, or freedom from commitment to pack up and check it out, even for a limited period. For those who don't quite feel ready for this step, some suggestions:

Get involved in one of the many projects of humanitarian aid being organized in this country. Collecting medical supplies, school books, used office equipment, tools, and industrial hardware can help the Nicaraguan people survive and help you make direct contacts that can enhance your understanding.

Many "citizens reparations" projects—from the people of the U.S. to the people of Nicaragua—are being coordinated by **HAND (Humanitarian Aid for Nicaraguan Democracy**, c/o NNSNP, 2025 Eye Street NW, Washington, DC 20006; 202-232-2328.

Medical supplies and support for hospitals and clinics are being provided through **National Central America Health Rights Network**, PO Box 04464, Milwaukee, WI 53204.

Scientific and technical aid, especially computer-related projects, is being organized by **Tech-nica**, c/o 1227 Fourth Street, Santa Monica, CA 90401; 213-394-1183.

A people-to-people aid project open to all is the creation of Sister City connections such as those between New Haven and Leon or Boulder and Jalapa. This allows local hospitals, schools, industries, and community groups to raise specific materials needed by their "sister" institutions in Nicaragua. Find out more through the **U.S.-Nicaragua Friendship City Association**, PO Box 7452, Boulder, CO 08306; 303-442-0460.

Humanitarian aid is being raised for the two hundred thousand displaced persons within Nicaragua by the *Let Nicaragua Live Campaign*, c/o HAND, 2025 Eye Street NW, Suite 1117, Washington, DC 20006; 202-223-2328.

Tools and industrial equipment are being gathered and shipped by **Tools for Peace**, c/o Oxfam America, 115 Broadway, Boston, MA 02116; 617-482-1211.

Sponsor a brigadista or help with fundraising in your church, school, or company.

Help organize a house meeting or community event at which returning brigadistas can show slides and share stories about their experiences in Nicaragua.

More Resources From
New Society Publishers

To order, send check or money order to **New Society Publishers**, 4722 Baltimore Avenue, Philadelphia, PA 19143. For postage and handling, add $1.50 for he first book and 40¢ for each additional book.

HEART POLITICS
by Fran Peavey, with Myra Levy and Charles Varon
Foreword by Frances Moore Lappé

"A lively journey from innocence into the world where people suffer oppression, contempt, disease and war, it's really an investigation into a minute-by-minute determination to change the world in neighborhoods and nations. Here is great happiness in the struggle, original humor, and the example of joy!"

—Grace Paley

Heart Politics takes us on our own journey toward a fresh way of seeing ourselves, and shows us that we can respond to the critical issues of our time with humanity and humor. *Heart Politics* is politics as if people really mattered!

Illustrated. 208 pages. 1986.
Hardcover $29.95
Paperback:

$9.95

WE ARE ALL PART OF ONE ANOTHER: A BARBARA DEMING READER

"I have had the dream that women should at last be the ones to truly experiment with nonviolent struggle, discover its full force."

Essays, speeches, letters, stories, poems by America's foremost writer on issues of women and peace, feminism and nonviolence, spanning four decades. Lovingly edited by activist-writer Jane Meyerding; Black feminist writer Barbara Smith, founder of Kitchen Table Press, has graciously contributed a foreword. A book no activist of the '80s will want to be without!

"Barbara Deming is the voice of conscience for her generation and all those to follow, measured in reason, compassionate, clear, requiring: the voice of a friend."
—Jane Rule

"Wisdom, modesty, responsiveness, love: all of these qualities live in her writings, a treasured gift to the world."
—Leah Fritz

320 pages. 1984.
Hardcover: $24.95
Paperback: $10.95

REWEAVING THE WEB OF LIFE: FEMINISM AND NONVIOLENCE

edited by Pam McAllister

". . . happens to be one of the most important books you'll ever read."
—*The Village Voice*

"Stressing the connection between patriarcy and war, sex and violence, this book makes it clear that nonviolence can be an assertive, positive force. It's provocative reading for anyone interested in surviving and changing the nuclear age." —*Ms. Magazine*

More than 50 Contributors — Women's History — Women and the Struggle Against Militarism — Violence and Its Origins — Nonviolence and Women's Self-Defense — Interviews — Songs — Poems — Stories — Provocative Proposals — Photographs — Annotated Bibliography — Index

Voted "Best New Book—1983"
—*WIN Magazine Annual Book Poll*

448 pages.
Hardcover: $19.95
Paperback: $10.95

DESPAIR AND PERSONAL POWER IN THE NUCLEAR AGE
by Joanna Rogers Macy

Despair and Personal Power in the Nuclear Age is the first major book to examine our psychological responses to planetary perils and to lay the theoretical foundations for an empowering, personally-centered approach to social change. Included are sections on awakening in the nuclear age, relating to children and young people, guided mediatations, empowered rituals, and a special section on "Spiritual Exercises for a Time of Apocalypse."

This book was described and excerpted in *New Age Journal* and *Fellowship Magazine*, recommended for public libraries by *Library Journal*, and selected for inclusion in the 1984 Women's Reading Program, General Board for Global Ministries, United Methodist Church.

200 pages. Appendices, resource lists, exercises. 1983.
Hardcover: $19.95
Paperback: $8.95

WATERMELONS NOT WAR! A SUPPORT BOOK FOR PARENTING IN THE NUCLEAR AGE
by Kate Cloud, Ellie Deegan, Alice Evans, Hayat Imam, and Barbara Signer
Afterword by Dr. Helen Caldicott

Five mothers in the Boston area have been meeting regularly for four years to give each other support, to demystify nuclear technology into terms parents *and children* can understand, and to find ways of acting which will give their children a future. The result is *Watermelons Not War! A Support Book for Parenting in the Nuclear Age.*

Articles describing this project appeared in *Ms. Magazine*, *Whole Life Times*, and *Sojourner*.

Large Format. Beautifully Illustrated. Annotated Bibliography.
160 pages. 1984.
Hardcover: $19.95
Paperback: $9.95

OUR FUTURE AT STAKE: A TEENAGERS GUIDE TO STOPPING THE NUCLEAR ARMS RACE
by Melinda Moore & Laurie Olsen, Citizens Policy Center

"The problem with getting my friends involved with the nuclear issue is that they don't know enough about it or even where to get information. i am a teacher now. i give them plenty of information whether they like it or not."

—Lena Flores, 17

Informative, beautifully illustrated and photographed resource for education and action. Includes personal statements by teenagers themselves. Handy glossary and chronology for teenagers seeking to understand the nuclear arms madness. Ideal for school, church, and community groups.

Illustrated. 68 pages. Large format. 1984.
Hardcover: $19.95
Paperback: $7.95

¡BASTA! NO MANDATE FOR WAR: A PLEDGE OF RESISTANCE HANDBOOK
by Emergency Response Network

More than 50,000 Americans nationwide have now pledged to protest any escalation in U.S foreign and/or military intervention in Central America. This handbook offers a brief guide to the situation in Nicaragua and El Salvador, information about the "Pledge of Resistance" campaign, reflections on nonviolence and the ongoing struggle in Central America, and preparation and training materials for nonviolent action. Includes agendas, resources, checklists for planning and working in any local area.

Heavily ilustrated. Large format. 96 pages. 1986.
Hardcover: $24.95
Paperback:　$6.50

THE DEADLY CONNECTION: NUCLEAR WAR & U.S. INTERVENTION
by the New England Regional Office of the American Friends Service Committee, Joseph Gerson, editor
Foreword by Bishop Thomas J. Gumbleton

The Deadly Connection explores in depth the relationship between U.S. nuclear policy and past, present, and future U.S. military intervention around the globe. it argues that current military weapons policies are not an aberration but part of a "seamless web" of foreign policy and military strategies created and maintained by both political parties over the past forty years.

Sections include "The Meaning of the Deadly Connection," "First Strike Policy and U.S. Intervention," "Intervention for U.S. Bases and Installations," "Third World Nuclear Triggers," and "Strategies for Survival." The more than twenty authors include Randall Forsberg, Daniel Ellsberg, Michael Klare, Noam Chomsky, Kassahun Checole, Melinda Fine, Charito Planas, Ngo Vinh Long, and Maude Easter.

266 pages. 1986.
Hardcover: $28.95
Paperback:　$8.95